WISDOM
ESSENTIALS

WISDOM ESSENTIALS

THE
PENTALOGY

THAT WHICH IS DIFFICULT IF NOT IMPOSSIBLE
TO FIND ANYWHERE ELSE—ALL IN ONE PLACE

J. BARTHOLOMEW WALKER

Quadrakoff Publications Group, LLC
Wilmington, Delaware
USA

Copyright ©2020, 2017 Quadrakoff Publications Group, LLC All rights reserved.

Except as noted, All Scripture passages taken from The Holy Bible, King James Version.

All NASB scriptures taken from The New American Standard Bible® Copyright © 1960, 1962, 1963, 1968, 1971, 1972, 1973, 1975, 1977, 1995 by the Lockman Foundation, LaHabra, CA.

Special thanks to the Lockman Foundation for the finest Bible version available; as well as for their permission to use the same. All Scripture passages taken from The Holy Bible, King James Version, are as noted.

ISBN: 978-1948219-02-0

All rights reserved. No part of this publication may be reproduced, stored in a retrieval system or transmitted, in any form, or by any means, electronic, mechanical, recorded, photocopied, or otherwise, without the prior written permission of both the copyright owner and the above publisher of this book, except by a reviewer who may quote brief passages in a review.

The scanning, uploading, and distribution of this book via the Internet or via any other means without the permission of the publisher is illegal and punishable by law. Please purchase only authorized electronic editions and do not participate in or encourage electronic piracy of copyrightable materials. Your support of the author's rights is appreciated.

Any and all characters appearing that are not in any of the versions of the Bible are fictional. Any resemblance to any living person is strictly coincidental.

Printed in the United States of America.

"The absence of the knowledge of a clearly identifiable *cause*,
for a clearly known *effect*; never provides license for a
causeless effect; but in fact provides the impetus to discover it.

Unless of course one is the *Primum Movens*—
the first mover,
or that one *effect* with no *cause*."

Emma B. Quadrakoff

Contents

Foreword -- i

Donald Trump Candidacy
According to Matthew? --- 1

It's Not Just A Theory -- 39

SHÂMAR TO SHARIA --- 93

Calvary's Hidden Truths -- 119

Inevitable Balance -- 159

Glossary -- 217

Bibliographies -- 231

About The MeekRaker
Series Title --- 251

Bibliography -- 257

FOREWORD

It is commonplace that trees and plants are known by their respective fruits. This is merely another way to describe *cause* and *effect*. The *effect* of that *cause* which is commonly known as an apple tree, is apples. Thus if one desires the effect known as apples, one obtains the cause; i.e.; plant an apple tree. From the cause-effect perspective, it matters little if this is done directly, or indirectly by obtaining apples from someone else who obtained the cause—the principle is the same.

When effects are perceived for which no clearly identifiable cause can be found, this generally leads to speculation. This is best seen with that which we call *life*. Life is that condition of union or intersection of the material with something else. When that union or intersection with that "something else" is gone, the condition of life as we understand it no longer exists. When this condition of "life" ceases; the material portion which "remains," is subject to and obeys natural law. But while the condition of life exists, the material portion consistently disobeys natural law, albeit within certain limitations. But since little is actually known about that *cause* for which the *effect* is what is known as life, all manner of speculation thrives.

But there are many other effects for which no material cause can be found. In *"Donald Trump Candidacy According to Matthew?,"*

i

his meteoric rise and seeming inability to fail are explained according to Biblical principles. Since this is a non-political work, his success was not actually prophesied, but no other conclusion could possibly have been drawn—*and this was published long before he was even nominated.* In *"SHÂMAR TO SHARIA,* the process of radical indoctrination is analyzed, and is shown to be a perversion of that very same thing God instructed man to do with the Commandments, and how this is not in any way limited to terrorists. *"It's Not Just A Theory"* examines the relationship between behavior and longevity according to both science and the Scriptures; and "according to both" also includes major consistencies. *"Calvary's Hidden Truths"* reveals many unknown facts about what actually occurred at that time. *"Inevitable Balance"* scientifically and Biblically explains that which is often observed but rarely understood: Why "What Goes Around Comes Around;" AKA *karma*, or the "law of compensation."

Originally published as individual monographs, a need was demonstrated to provide all of this information in one volume. So here is the response to that need. It is titled *"Wisdom Essentials The Pentalogy;"* and it seems fair to say that it would be extremely difficult, if not *impossible* to find this information anywhere else.— *QPG, LLC, Wilmington DE*

Dunamis or supernatural power, and dynamikós or natural power, are separate and distinct entities. When any power disobeys natural law; by definition this has to be dunamis—if it is in fact the case that natural law is violated. Whether this power is to one's liking or not changes nothing with respect to what it is. But dunamis or supernatural power rarely, if ever, occurs as a single unit.

Donald Trump Candidacy According to Matthew?

Back in June of 2015, Emma and I were watching the news, and analyzing the announcement of Donald Trump seeking the presidency of the United States.

It took a while to observe all of the factors, but we were quite aware of what Yogi Berra is reputed to have said: "You can observe a lot by watching." So we watched, and watched, and still watched.

We especially watched the "experts," hearing the word "apoplectic" so many times, that I was forced to look it up to make sure it was being utilized correctly—and it seems that most of the time it was.

Finally I looked at Emma and said: "I think he (Donald Trump) might have a talantŏn." Emma kind of looked at me for a while and then said: "I think you may be correct. There really is no other possible explanation."

April 2016,
Wilmington, DE

Now precisely what is a talantŏn? It cannot be looked up in an English dictionary, as it is not a word in English. The best one generally can do is to find an explanation related to the Bible that is often quite misleading, and quite incorrect.

Talantŏn is often considered to be the root of the word *talent*. Talent as used in the Biblical sense is generally considered to be a Hebrew unit of weight; with there often being differences between a *common* talent and a *royal* talent. However the root of talent is the Greek word *talantŏn*, and is not a Hebrew word. Thus this relationship to a unit of *physical* weight was inserted later, with *talent* proffered as a Hebrew word; which it is not, and never was.

But it cannot be overemphasized that a talent or talantŏn is not a mere unit of weight such as an ounce, a pound, a ton or a kilogram. These are mere *objective* units of measure for the "*quantity* of a thing." A talent or talantŏn is much less objective and much less quantifiable than this. A talent or talantŏn is a *subjective* weight that is a balancing weight, or a weight to be carried.

A talent or talantŏn is thus a balancing weight for something else; but whether or not it is ultimately actually *carried* is a matter of one's choice. That "something else" or *balance* for a talantŏn is known as *dunamis*; and in the New Testament dunamis is used to indicate and is properly translated as "*supernatural* power." This is in comparison to the Greek word *dynamikós*, which is *natural* power.

There is a Hebrew word which indicates the presence of *both* this supernatural power (Greek *dunamis*), *and* this weight (Greek *talantŏn*); and this Hebrew word is *massâ'*. It is for this reason that *massâ'* is sometimes translated with words such as "oracle;" and is sometimes translated as some type of "weight" in the Old Testament.

Having recently reviewed a Chapter about this very same subject for an upcoming new book, (currently in post production); we thought it appropriate to release some excerpts from that Chapter at this time. These excerpts have been abridged so as to only include details we believe provide the necessary background which is pertinent to understanding the subject of this monograph.

To be clear, this is not in any way any type of political *endorsement* of anyone; but rather to merely provide a Biblical explanation for a phenomenon that up to this point has been inexplicable. It must also be noted that because of time constraints, this is the "beta" version.

In the interest of accuracy, the diacritics for these words were included in this introduction, and are necessarily maintained in the following chapter excerpts:

Beginning of excerpt:

[. . . In Matthew 25:14-30 we are told the famous parable of the talents. We know that this is a parable and not an actual story, because generally when Jesus told parables, no proper names were used. When it is a recollection of actual events, usually proper names were used.

It must be noted that in Luke 19:12-27 there exists a similar story. These two parables can easily be conflated, but there are very significant differences between them. Because of these differences, it seems unlikely that Matthew and Luke are merely have differing accounts of the same event; but rather that only one account is correct—that of course being the one that makes the most sense.

In order to maintain intellectual honesty, this parable is first presented here in its entirety

Following is Matthew 25:14-30, with the verse numbers removed for ease of reading:

*"For it is just like a man about to go on a journey,
who called his own slaves
and entrusted his possessions to them.
To one he gave five talents,
to another, two, and to another,
one, each according to his own ability;
and he went on his journey.*

*Immediately the one who had received the five
talents went and traded with them,
and gained five more talents.
In the same manner the one who had
received the two talents gained two more.
But he who received the one talent went away,
and dug a hole in the ground
and hid his master's money.*

*Now after a long time the master of those slaves
came and settled accounts with them.*

*The one who had received the five talents
came up and brought five more talents,
saying, 'Master, you entrusted five talents to me.
See, I have gained five more talents.'
His master said to him, 'Well done,
good and faithful slave.
You were faithful with a few things,
I will put you in charge of many things;
enter into the joy of your master.'*

*Also the one who had received the
two talents came up and said,
'Master, you entrusted two talents to me.
See, I have gained two more talents.'
His master said to him, 'Well done,
good and faithful slave.
You were faithful with a few things,
I will put you in charge of many things;
enter into the joy of your master.'*

Donald Trump Candidacy According to Matthew?

*And the one also who had received the
one talent came up and said,
'Master, I knew you to be a hard man,
reaping where you did not sow and
gathering where you scattered no seed.
'And I was afraid, and went away and
hid your talent in the ground.
See, you have what is yours.'*

*But his master answered and said to him,
'You wicked, lazy slave, you knew
that I reap where I did not sow and
gather where I scattered no seed.
'Then you ought to have put my money
in the bank, and on my arrival
I would have received my money back
with interest. Therefore take away the talent
from him, and give it to the one
who has the ten talents.'*

*For to everyone who has,
more shall be given,
and he will have an abundance;
but from the one who does not have,
even what he does have shall be taken away.
Throw out the worthless slave into the
outer darkness; in that place there will
be weeping and gnashing of teeth.'"*[1]

The way it reads, this slave master decides to go on a journey. So before he leaves, he calls his three slaves in for a meeting, and distributes all of his possessions to these three. It doesn't actually say all, but that is a fair read. He gives them these talents according to their ability. Likely the *head* slave got five, the *middle* slave two, and the *apprentice* slave one.

He then gives no instructions whatsoever as to what should be done with these possessions. Neither does he indicate if or when he will be returning; nor is there any indication as to *if* or *when* what he *"gave"* the "slaves;" it does state "gave;" is to be returned to him.

He finally comes back. In his absence, two of the slaves traded the talents and resulting in 100% profit. One slave hid the talent by burying it in the ground. It is not actually stated whether any or all of these slaves individually had the title of "the apprentice."

So what does the slave master then do? He congratulates the two who risked his money by trading, and allows them both to keep not only all of the original money, but also lets them keep their profits as well. But to the one who hid the money; a rather conservative investment guaranteeing principal; he rebukes him, takes the money back and gives it to the one who now has ten, making it eleven for one servant, and zero for the other.

What principle are we to learn from this parable? *"For to everyone who has, more shall be given, and he will have an abundance; but from the one who does not have, even what he does have shall be taken away."*

So then by this reasoning; in life, the appropriate *Christian* thing to do would then be to find the "least of these" and take away some of what they already have. Since this clearly would contradict many of Jesus' other teachings, this simply cannot be the point of this story.

In order to understand the wisdom contained in this parable, the logical very first question to be asked is precisely what was it that Jesus was actually speaking *about*? Part of this answer is contained in the very first sentence, wherein it states: "For *it* is just like..." (emphasis added) The question then becomes: "Precisely what is it that "it" represents; that is *"just like"* that which follows?"

"It" is a third person pronoun, referring to something else. "It" represents a rather large category of actualities. In fact, anything not being masculine or feminine in nature would qualify to be included in this "it" category.

To find the meaning of this particular "it," going all the way back to the beginning of the chapter where this story later appears; Matthew 25:1; provides some insight.

Matthew Chapter 25 begins with 25:1, where Jesus is speaking and tells us:

Donald Trump Candidacy According to Matthew?

"Then the kingdom of heaven will be comparable to..."[2]

Thus it seems likely that Jesus is also speaking about this very same "kingdom of heaven," in this parable which is also contained in Chapter 25, but in later verses 14-30—in some way or manner.

However, it must be noted that here in verse 1, Jesus is speaking about what *"will be;"* whereas later in verse 14, (where this "Talent Man" story begins), He is speaking about what currently *"is:" "For it is just like a man..."*

Jesus indicated in verse 1 what the Kingdom of Heaven *"will be;"* and will be *"then,"* or at some *future* time, as the verse begins with *"then."* Therefore this *"will be"* cannot be now, or at least was not yet at the time Jesus said this. This is an important distinction, because what the *"kingdom of heaven"* currently *"is"*, is something which affects our lives *now*; as opposed to what it *"will be,"* at whatever time the *"then"* represents; which *will not* affect us, at least not directly, until the *"then."*

Precisely what is this "kingdom of heaven?" Generally, there are two definitions of "heaven," depending on whether the singular or the plural is used; and whether or not preceded by the definite article: "the."

Heaven in the singular is generally understood to be where God resides, and a place where our immortal "pneuma," or *soul*, begins its journey; and with salvation, the place to where it will ultimately return. It is never, (except by Petrovsky), referred to as "the heaven."

"*The heavens*" however, generally refers to the sky and outward. "Heavens" is generally referred to in the plural and rarely without the "the." The "s" in the phrase: "For heaven's sake," is possessive and not plural.

It is interesting to again inquire as to precisely where God was when he created the heavens and the earth. Clearly he was not yet residing in a place that had yet to be created. Thus, as previously addressed, clearly there must be two different meanings for this word "heaven."

The actual Greek word in Matthew 25:1 which is translated as "heaven" is:

> "3772 ŏuranŏs; perh.from the same as 3735 (through the idea of *elevation*); the *sky*; by extens. *heaven* (as the abode of God); by impl. *happiness, power, eternity*; spec. the *Gospel, (Christianity)*: - air, heaven ([-ly]), sky."[3]

> "3735 ŏrŏs; prob. from an obsol. ŏrō (to *rise* or "*rear*"; perh. akin to *142*; comp. *3733*); a *mountain* (as *lifting* itself above the plain): - hill, mount (-ain)."[4]

In Luke 11:2; where the "Lord's prayer" appears; (≈Our Father who art in heaven. . .); "heaven" is also 3772 ŏuranŏs.[5]

If a fair analysis of this word "heaven" or ŏuranŏs is undertaken, it would initially seem that the meaning has much more to do with physical elevation, air, to rise or to rear, lifting, a hill, or a mountain, rather than the abode of God; which according to Strong's, is derived only by extension of ŏuranŏs.

However; from Jesus Himself using an Aramaic word which translates to the Greek word ŏuranŏs; both in Luke when providing the "Lord's Prayer;" and here in Matthew, at the beginning of Chapter 25; it seems clear that He is speaking of "Heaven" where the Father is, and not "the heavens," where celestial bodies revolve. Furthermore; this parable in no way resembles any type of Astronomy lecture. One might try to argue that the "Master" represents the Sun, and the three servants the three innermost planets or some such; but this would likely be highly unsuccessful—unless some type of hallucinogens were also involved.

The actual word translated as "kingdom" is:

> "932 basilĕia; from *935*; prop. *royalty*, i.e. (abstr.) *rule*, or (concr.) a *realm* (lit. or fig.): - kingdom + reign."[6]

So it would seem reasonable to conclude that the "it" to which Jesus is referring with respect to the parable, is the "kingdom of heaven." And this likely refers not only to the "place" in which God resides; but rather, refers to the entire *immaterial* realm, and the rules associated therein.

"In verse 1 of Matthew 25, Jesus referred to what the kingdom of heaven *"will be"* at the *"then."* Here in this parable, in verse 14 of Matthew 25, He is speaking of what heaven *is*, and *is now*.

The parable was spoken by Jesus in Aramaic, and written in Greek. Thus there are only inexact synonyms for terminology between Greek and the Old Testament Hebrew equivalents; and that is only part of the problem.

Jesus told us: *"For it is just like a man about to go on a journey, who called his own slaves and entrusted his possessions to them. To one he gave five talents, to another, two, and to another, one, each according to his own ability; and he went on his journey."*

According to Strong's, the word *slave* (singular) actually appears only once in the entire Bible; in Jeremiah 2:14, where a distinction is being made between a slave and a servant.[7]

And the word *slaves* (plural), only appears once in the entire Bible, and is in Revelation 18:13. And in Revelation, the actual word translated as "slaves" is *soma*, generally meaning body.[8]

The actual Greek word translated as "slaves" here in Matthew is:

> "*1401* dŏulŏs; from *1210*; a slave (lit. or fig., invol or vol.; frequently therefore in a qualified sense of subjection or subserviency): - bond (-man), servant."[9]

This may seem a bit crazy; in that Strong's does not list *slave* (singular) as appearing anywhere in the entire Bible, except in Jeremiah; and yet the very first word in the definition of dŏulŏs is slave. It gets a bit worse, as Strong provides *nothing* for the actual word in Jeremiah that is translated as slave (singular).[10]

Thus it is a fair conclusion, at least according to Strong, that there is no original word known in the entire Bible that corresponds to slave in the singular; and only a word meaning *body* that is translates as slaves in the plural; the first word in the definition of dŏulŏs notwithstanding. In fact, Strongest Strong's classifies the word "slave" as "NIH" meaning "Not in Hebrew," citing Jeremiah as the example of an *added* word.[11]

Based upon the word dŏulŏs appearing elsewhere in the Bible, and always being translated as *servant* every other time; it seems likely that *slave* would be an incorrect translation. (This of course relates to the New Testament Greek.) Furthermore; according to Strong, dŏulŏs can be voluntary or involuntary, and thus could be either. Dŏulŏs appears to have to do with the *condition* of subservience or submission, rather than any specific type of *relationship* that produced this condition.

It is unclear precisely what it is that constitutes "voluntary slavery." Thus, *servant* seems to be the better definition for dŏulŏs—particularly in the context of the parable. In this parable, Jesus is explaining a mechanism by which God's servants (H. Sapiens) voluntarily; i.e.; free will choosing; to serve him.

The mistranslated word "talent" has several definitions. It is sometimes a unit of weight which can range from 75 pounds for a *common* talent, to 150 pounds for a *royal* talent.[12]

In the entire Old Testament, the Hebrew word *translated* as "talent," except once, is:

> "3603 kikkâr; from 3769; a *circle*, i.e. (by impl.) a circumjacent *tract* or region, espec. the *Ghôr* or valley of the Jordan; also a (round) *loaf*; also a *talent* (or large [round] coin): - loaf, morsel, piece, plain, talent."[13]

This only other actual word translated as "talent' is:

> "3604 kikkêr (Chald.); corresp. to 3603; a *talent*; - talent."[14]

Thus the idea that "talent" is any type of Hebrew unit of measure; whether common or royal; is in no way supported factually. For whatever reason(s), translators elected to insert the word "talent" for *kikkâr* and *kikkêr* in the *Old Testament* translations.

The actual *Greek* word appearing in Matthew 25 translated as talent is:

> "5007 talantŏn; neut. Of a presumed der. of the orig. form of tiaō (to *bear*; equiv. to 5342); a *balance* (as *supporting* weights), i.e. (by impl.) a certain *weight* (and thence a *coin* or rather *sum* of money) or "*talent*": - talent."[15]

Here the concept of talent representing a certain weight is only by *implication*. This "implication" explanation is likely the "tail wagging the dog;" as Strong did his work in the late 19th century, long after many of the mistranslations by the "experts" had taken place.

The above stated "equivalent" word for talantŏn is:

> "5342 phěrō; a prim. verb...to "*bear*" or *carry*"[16]

And of course, there is the common definition of talent; which refers to capabilities, generally considered to be innate; allowing someone to be able to, or have the capability to perform certain things in a manner which far exceeds the norm. *Talent* refers to this capability, *talented* refers to the individual who has the talent, and *gifted* is a term often used to describe the process whereby, or the reason the talented individual received or has said talent; and and as will be seen, this; (gifted); is more than arguably a misnomer.

There is a distinct difference between the meanings of the Old Testament Hebrew *kikkâr* or *kikkêr*; irrespective of its incorrect translation as talent; and the New Testament Greek *talantŏn*. The Hebrew essentially means circle, the meaning related to money likely only from the shape of a coin. [*There exists a derogatory word for Jewish people which will not be repeated here. Many believe that the root of this word is kikkâr. The reason likely has to do with illiterate Jewish immigrants to the United States having to sign their name and refusing to sign with an "X," because of the similarities to the Christian cross; thus instead signing their name with a circle.*]

The Greek word *talantŏn* has nothing whatsoever to do with any shape; including the circle. Rather, it represents bearing, balance and perhaps; but only by implication; a specified and accurate weight. A twenty dollar US gold coin is just shy of one ounce troy pure gold. It is circular, but also represents a specific certain weight of gold. *Kikkâr* could be used to describe this as a coin, or its value as a coin, and some small fraction of the weight of the Hebrew "phantom" talent could *incorrectly* be used to describe its weight in gold. The confusion between the meanings of the terms may have arisen from this relationship.

However, the original Greek word used in the parable is *talantŏn*. Thus it would be prudent to assume that the *actual* definition of the *actual* word *actually* used, is what Jesus *actually* meant. Therefore, it would be fair to say that each of the servants was given a weight to bear, a weight or something as a balance to something else, and from the *immaterial* perspective a "certain" weight. The use of "certain weight" can be interpreted two ways. It can refer to the *amount* of the weight as certain, such as one ounce troy; or it can refer to the *existence* of some *balancing* weight as a certainty; irrespective of the amount.

Since the definitions of *talantŏn* primarily have to do with the act of bearing, carrying, balancing etc., irrespective of the *amount* of any weight, this appears to be the correct meaning; rather than a sum of money or weight of precious metals equivalent to some agreed upon value. The use of *talantŏn* as money, is never literal, but only by implication. How much *talantŏn* was each given and why? They were each given different amounts based upon their abilities. It must be noted that they were not each given *talantŏn* according to their *accomplishments*, but rather according to their *abilities*—not according to what they had *done*, but rather according to what they were *capable* of doing.

The actual Greek word translated here as "ability" is the aforementioned:

> "*1411* dunamis; from *1410*; *force* (lit. or fig.); spec. miraculous *power* (usually by impl. a *miracle* itself): - ability, abundance, meaning, might (-ily, -y, -y deed), worker of) miracle (-s), power, strength, violence, mighty (wonderful) work."[17]

This word *dunamis*; must clearly be distinguished from the English word "dynamic;" which is derived from the Greek word *dynamikós*, which means "powerful; dýnamis, which means power; and dýnasthai, which means be able or have power."[18]

The abilities referenced in this parable were their *supernatural* or *miraculous* abilities (dunamis); and not any type of *natural* abilities (dynamikós). This is not to say that they did not have any natural abilities; but rather that their natural abilities are not referenced, and thus have nothing to do with the parable.

In physics, the derived word *dyne* represents a measurement or unit of *natural* force existing in the *material* realm; which when applied to a *mass*, results in *work* or the movement of the mass.

There seems to yet be no equivalent word derived from *dunamis*; which would represent a measurement or unit of *supernatural* force in the *immaterial* realm; which when applied, results in work or the movement of possibly immaterial phenomenon, or more relevant to this parable; capable of ultimately making resultant changes in *material* phenomenon; but here from *dunamic* (supernatural) and not *dynamic* (natural) factors.

This being the case: the word *duna* is hereby coined, and is defined as the unit of measure of immaterial force, capable of making material changes *via* the *immaterial* realm. It must be pointed out that although the force acts in the *immaterial* realm, the ultimate purpose is to affect changes in the *material* realm; and thus does not exclusively result in changes solely in the immaterial realm.

Although an exact accepted value, quantity or magnitude of a *duna* cannot actually be numerically calculated at this time, it can nevertheless be used to measure *relative* amounts of supernatural power. If this seems idiotic, absurd or useless; it must be remembered that in mathematics, "*i*" represents a quantity equaling the value of the square root of negative one. With respect to "*i*," this represents an *imaginary* number; as there is no known number when multiplied by itself will yield a negative product; hence the choice of that particular letter for the variable. The square root of a negative number simply does not exist; or at least has no actuality in our material world. But with respect to *duna*, immaterial power does exist.

Thus unlike in mathematics; where a term was selected to quantify a non-existent entity; here it is a bit different, in that it is the *quantification* of the something which *does* exist into a unit, albeit that only the *relative* value, and not the *actual* value is known.

Again, the key to this definition of *dunamis* is that it is *supernatural* or "miraculous," or a "miracle," or "wonderful," (full of wonder), force or power. This is not merely *natural* or *dynamikós* power or ability, but rather a *supernatural* or *miraculous* type of power.

Thus, each "servant" was given a *talantŏn* or weight to bear or balance or support; arguably of denoted measurable value, according to the amount of *dunamis* or supernatural power each had. There is a relationship between the terms. Because of the amount of *dunamis* or supernatural power given or possessed, there is a corresponding balancing weight or *responsibility* or *talantŏn*.

In order to avoid confusion, it would be prudent at this juncture to assign a term to describe and relatively quantify this amount of weight to bear or responsibility (*talantŏn*). This is necessary as said *talantŏn*, in this usage does not refer to *objective* physical weight as could be measured on a physical scale, but rather the *subjective* weight to the host.

This being the case: the word *tala* is hereby coined, and is defined as a unit of measure of immaterial, subjective, psychological, or emotional weight, capable of causing the host to exercise; and arguably is required to balance; his or her level of *dunamis*. The term *tala* must be used to avoid confusion with the *erroneous* translation as *talent* as a unit of *physical* weight, (pound, ounce, etc); or talent as innate *skill* which is completely free; i.e.; "gifted."

One could hypothetically assign a value of one *duna* per *tala*. Thus the servant who received five *tala*, was given this "weight" of five *tala*, because he had five *duna* of supernatural power. Likewise, the same could be said for the two, and one "talent" servants.

The failure to realize this, would likely result in a classic example of the failure to perceive sufficient actuality; or perhaps better phrased; a failure to sufficiently perceive *the* actuality. Given that this may seem somewhat tautological or oxymoronic; this includes: to fail to perceive even in a somewhat limited sense; the; or an; actuality *in-toto*.

The presence of *dunamis* or supernatural power is often incorrectly perceived and is generally considered to be a stand alone entity—meaning that the *dunamis* alone represents the entire actuality. But in fact, it is *both* the *dunamis* or supernatural power; *and* the *talantŏn* or the balancing weight or responsibility; that comprises the true one actuality. They each individually represent only a part of the actuality. This is why using the term "gifted" would be inaccurate; as "gifted" recognizes only the *dunamis*; and not the associated and inextricably linked *talantŏn*.

Proverbs 30:1 begins with the following:

> "The words of Agur the son
> of Jakeh, the oracle."[19]

The King James translation is: "even the prophesy," in place of "the oracle."[20]

And Malachi 1:1 begins with the following:

> "*The oracle of the word of the LORD to Israel through Malachi.*"[21]

In both of these verses, the word "oracle" appears. A fair interpretation of an oracle; is one who is able to provide revelation. Whether providing prophesy or retrophesy, oracles clearly exercise *dunamis*; at least when acting in the capacity of an oracle.

However; the *King James* translation of this very same Malachi 1:1, provides "burden" as the translation, rather than "oracle:"

The KJV of Malachi 1:1 is:

> "*The burden of the word of the LORD to Israel by Malachi.*"[22]

The actual word translated as "oracle" in both verses is:

> "4853 massâ'; from 5375; a *burden*; spec. *tribute*, or (abstr.) *porterage*; fig. an *utterance*,..." chiefly a *doom*, espec. *singing*; mental, *desire*: - burden, carry away, prophesy, x they set, song, tribute."[23]

> "5375 nâsâ' or nâcâh; a prim. root; to *lift* in a great variety of applications."[24]

"Porterage" generally refers to carrying a weight or burden; e.g.; a porter.

Thus there are several seemingly unrelated meanings to massâ' et seq. They can be translated as an *utterance*, likely prophetic or retrophesitic in nature; as well as a *burden* or *lifting*; as well as *desire* and *ability*.

As a result, it seems clear that massâ' represents the understanding or comprehension of a given actuality in Hebrew; for which the use of both *dunamis* as well as *talantŏn*, and comprehending their relationship; is required for understanding or comprehending of the very same actuality in Greek—[(Hebrew) *massâ'* = (Greek) *dunamis* + (Greek) *talantŏn*].

Dunamis may *appear* to exist alone; but cannot exist without the corresponding talantŏn. However; the mere *existence* of the talantŏn, does not necessarily mean it will be carried.

Luke 12:48 confirms this spiritual or immaterial rule of balance by telling us:

> "...From everyone who has been given much,
> much will be required;
> and to whom they entrusted much,
> of him they will ask all the more."[25]

Here in Luke, the aforementioned concept of the Hebrew word massâ'; or the requirement that among other things; the quantity of both "*dunamis* + *talantŏn*" necessarily be considered in order to ascertain an actuality, is confirmed.

And Jesus goes on with the parable: "*Immediately the one who had received the five talents went and traded with them, and gained five more talents. In the same manner the one who had received the two talents gained two more. But he who received the one talent went away, and dug a hole in the ground and hid his master's money.*"

A cursory reading seems pretty simple. Two of the men took the money and traded with it, resulting in a profit of 100%—except for two minor problems. The same being: that it (*talantŏn*) was not money, but that burden which is necessarily associated with supernatural power; and it is not precisely known what is actually meant by "traded."

The original Greek word translated as "traded" is:

"*2038* ĕrgazŏmai; mid. from *2041*; to *toil* (as a task,

occupation, etc.)..."²⁶

"*2041* ĕrgŏn; from a prim. (but obsol.) ĕrgō (to work); *toil* (as an effort or occupation); by impl. and act: - deed, doing, labour, work."²⁷

Ěrgazŏmai is the root of the term ergs, energy, and ergonomics.

The term "traded" can be misleading, as it can refer to a situation where possession of items can be exchanged or swapped, without any corresponding increase in total wealth. "Trading" may result in increase in wealth for the parties involved in the exchange, but there is no increase in *total* societal wealth. There is no actual work being done in the literal sense, so there is no increase in total wealth.

Clearly the definition of ĕrgazŏmai requires actual "work," "toil," effort, etc., and thus can refer to "trades" such as the construction *trade*; which *can* increase total wealth, because the value or amount of wealth in the final product exceeds the value or wealth of the components.

Precisely what type of work or *ĕrgazŏmai* was it in which these servants engaged? It appears from the definition of *dunamis*, that it likely was miraculous work; "spec.(ifically) miraculous power (usually by impl. a miracle itself)."

Here they worked their *dunamis*; or supernatural power, and not any *dynamikós*; or natural power.

Proverbs 14:23 tells us:

"*In all labor there is profit,
But mere talk leads only to poverty.*"²⁸

The parable continues:
"*Now after a long time the master of those slaves came and settled accounts with them.*

"*The one who had received the five talents came up and brought five more talents, saying, 'Master, you entrusted five talents to me.*

Donald Trump Candidacy According to Matthew?

See, I have gained five more talents.' "His master said to him, 'Well done, good and faithful slave. You were faithful with a few things, I will put you in charge of many things; enter into the joy of your master.'

"Also the one who had received the two talents came up and said, 'Master, you entrusted two talents to me. See, I have gained two more talents.' "His master said to him, 'Well done, good and faithful slave. You were faithful with a few things, I will put you in charge of many things; enter into the joy of your master."

What seems to be happening here; is that these two servants went out and "worked" their supernatural or miraculous abilities, far beyond what was required by the magnitude of their responsibilities. They began by being given a quantity of *tala* or weight to bear, according to the number of *duna* they each had possessed; as that is essentially what is stated. If the hypothetical relationship holds; one was given 5 tala, because he had 5 duna. The other was given 2 tala, because he had 2 duna. But they fulfilled their responsibilities so well, that they were ultimately given more tala. But the *actuality* includes both tala and duna. Meaning; that one cannot have one without the other.

And the "master's" response was consistent with this. They were put *"in charge of many things."*

The *"in charge of"* is actually:

> "2525 kathistēmi; from 2596 and 2476; to *place down* (permanently), i.e. (fig.) to *designate, constitute, convoy*:
> - appoint, be, conduct, make ordain, set."[29]

The word "things" does not appear in the original Greek. There exists no word which could be translated as "things" in this passage. The word "things" appears to have been added at some point in time, for whatever purported reason(s). This later addition of "things" results not in clarity, but confusion and obfuscation; by opening up tremendous and arguably unlimited possibilities as to what these "things" actually were. This is not quite as bad as the tendency today to call anything and everything immaterial "spirit," but nevertheless results in substantial confusion. The few and the many are correct; but no other word or words appear in this section regarding to what the few and many refer.

Thus, there is no explanation whatsoever provided as to the nature of the additional "things" they were put in charge of. Neither is there any detailed explanation of the original "few" with which they were "faithful;" except as stated in the beginning of the parable.

This being that the *few* and *many* were related to either these supernatural or miraculous powers, or *dunamis*; or they were related to the *talantŏn*; or to "bear or balance as supporting weights." Since they had already received the additional talantŏn or units of talas as a result of their work or "ergs; then by Hobson's choice, both the "few" and the "many" must refer to the units of duna.

It being the case that the few things with which they were faithful represented these miraculous powers; and it being the case that no additional description is provided about the additional "many" over which they were given *kathistēmi*, but only that there is some relationship between what was done with the "few" as a causative factor resulting in the statement about the "many."

Had there been a difference between the types of things that the few represented, and the subsequent many things, then likely this would have been stated. Thus, unlike it being possible by the later addition of "things;" it is not the character, characteristics or nature of the additional things over which they were given charge that is being stated, but rather solely concerning the *number* or *amount* of something.

This of course makes perfect sense, as the additional units of tala, or balancing weight taken on by them, had to be counterbalanced by obtaining additional units of duna.

The alternative explanation being; that the "few" and the "many" simply refer to the amount of *money* originally given to each of them; this arguably being like being given charge over few and many dollars. Aside from the previously mentioned problems associated with this position, there are more:

Firstly, if the position is taken that the above is all gibberish, and talent is merely a unit of *normal* weight; then likely between 375 and 750 pounds of weight was originally given to the *five* talent man; as it does not state whether these "talents" were *common* or *royal*.

Thus, when he returned, he would have been carrying between 750 and 1,500 pounds of weight. Along with this, is the problem that unless it is known what *material* it was of which the five talent man was originally carrying 375-750 pounds, there is no way to determine the value, if any; of either the original five, or subsequent five.

Second, is the use of the word "few." This term *few* is usually reserved for a quantity of more than two; as two is generally referred to as a *couple*; yet he stated the very same thing to the two talent man. Thus, it seems more than just speculation to suggest that he would have said the same thing to the one talent man, had he been "faithful" with that one talent.

Third, there is the "faithful" issue. There is no mention of what it was these servants were either instructed or expected to do with these talents. Yet upon their return, there actions are described as faithful. This implies prior knowledge on the part of the servants with respect to this.

Fourthly, would or does the amount of money, rather than "money" itself qualify numerically for these statements about few and many? If so then the five talent man was given a *large* few, the two talent a *medium* few, and the one talent man arguably a *small* few. Or does it make more sense that the few and the many refer to either the numbers of dunas or to the number of sub-types of *dunamis* or supernatural/miraculous power?

If this part of the parable were told in English today, it would begin as: "The rule of the immaterial realm is like a man who called his persons of subservience and entrusted his possessions to him. To one he gave five tala of balancing weight, to another two tala and another one tala. This was done to each according to said servant's supernatural power, or ability to do miraculous things."

The following rules provide some keys to the understanding the interplay of natural and supernatural forces:

I. "Nature will not permit the continued existence of an unbalanced actuality."

II. "The universe will obey your will to the extent that it is not inconsistent with; nor contradictory to; the will of God."

III. "When perceiving an *actuality*, one must exercise caution as to perceive as much of the actuality as possible, as this will determine one's *reality*; and it is our reality upon which we base our thoughts and actions. Likewise, caution must be exercised in order to not perceive as one actuality, that which is or are aspects of two separate actualities; or the reverse."

And the parable is concluded in two distinct parts:

First part:

"And the one also who had received the one talent came up and said, 'Master, I knew you to be a hard man, reaping where you did not sow and gathering where you scattered no seed. 'And I was afraid, and went away and hid your talent in the ground. See, you have what is yours.'"

Here in the first part, the servant is making three distinct statements:

1. He is calling the master a hard (not meek) hearted thief; as what other word better describes one who *reaps* where he did not sow and *gathering* where he had scattered no seed?
2. Secondly, he is stating that he was afraid of something, and because of this fear hid the talent in the ground.

3. Thirdly, the servant then seems to be trying to placate the master; by telling him that he now has something that belongs to the master; after just accusing him of whatever was his, (the master's); wasn't legitimately his, (the master's); in the first place.

Second part:

"But his master answered and said to him, 'you wicked, lazy slave, you knew that I reap where I did not sow and gather where I scattered no seed. Then you ought to have put my money in the bank, and on my arrival I would have received my money back with interest. Therefore take away the talent from him, and give it to the one who has the ten talents." For to everyone who has, more shall be given, and he will have an abundance; but from the one who does not have, even what he does have shall be taken away."

There are cause-effect relationships implied in this portion. This is so because of the appearance of the words "then" and "therefore"

What is actually being said by the master is: *"if"* what you (servant) are saying is true, *"then"* you ought to have. . ." Or more contemporarily phrased: "You knew that I was a thief huh? Then you should have. . ."

The talent being referred to as *money* in the story only happens two times: previously in Matthew 25:18, (appearing once: *"hid his master's money"*); when this servant's actions were described as if by a "third party" narration. And then again (appearing twice here: *"Then you ought to have put my money in the bank, and on my arrival I would have received my money back with interest."*) by the *master* in this passage.

The servant never refers to the talent as *money*; but rather maintains that it is *talent*.

And the master only refers to the talent as money, *after* the *"then"* or conditionally, and this is only pertinent *if* the servant's characterizations, ("*you knew that I reap where I did not sow and gather where I scattered no seed*"), of the master were in fact true.

But when the master then speaks to someone else regarding the servant; and is no longer speaking with the condition of the "if" hypothetically having been met; he *then* refers to it as *talent*, ("*take away the talent from him*"); and not money.

It is as though the usage of the term "money" is strictly reserved for use by others only, and used only by what the speaker, (the "master"), believes would be suitable from the servant's perspective—even though that term is never once used by the servant.

The actual word translated here and also in Matthew 25:18 translated as "money" is:

> "694 arguriŏn; neut. Of a presumed der. of 696; *silvery*, i.e. (by impl.) *cash*; spec. a *silverling* (i.e. *drachma* or *shekel*): - money, (piece of) silver (piece)."[30]

And with respect to *arguriŏn* being derived from 696, the same is:

> "696 argurŏs; from argŏs (*shining*); *silver* (the metal, in the articles or coin): - silver."[31]

This sounds somewhat reasonable, in that *money* would be a fair translation of *arguriŏn* meaning silvery, from *argurŏs*, which is from *argŏs*; given what was purportedly in use back in "those days."

However; note the qualification by Strong that the derivation of *arguriŏn* from 696 is merely "*presumed*."

There is also another problem developing here. This citation contains these two things: Firstly that 696 *argurŏs* is derived from *argŏs*; and then the definition is provided.

However it is the definition of *argurŏs* and not argŏs which is provided as: "*silver* (the metal, in the articles or coin): - silver."

When comparing *arguriŏn*, *argurŏs*, and *argŏs*; there seems to be either additional or missing letters, (ur), depending upon one's perspective; which seems to be a source of confusion.

Donald Trump Candidacy According to Matthew?

According to Strong, the word from which *argurŏs* is derived (*argŏs*), is:

> "692 argŏs; from *1* (as a neg. particle) [*1* is A as used in negation whatever follows and *2041*; *inactive*, i.e. *unemployed*; (by impl.) *lazy, useless*: - barren, idle, slow."[32]

And the above referenced 2041 is:

> "*2041* ĕrgŏn; from a prim. (but obsol.) ĕrgō (to work); toil (as an effort or occupation....."[33]

If this word *ĕrgŏn* sounds familiar, it is because *ĕrgŏn* was the word from which *ĕrgazŏmai*; previously *erroneously* translated as "traded," was derived; but that actually means *work*. Here however, with the addition of the negation; *argŏs* represents its opposite: "'inactive,' or no-work, or the opposite of work."

Thus it seems most reasonable that the original word used in the text, *argŏs*; is a combination of "a" as a prefix, providing "the negation of" whatever follows this prefix; which in this case is that same root of 2041 *ĕrgŏn*, which is *ĕrgō*.

Thus it seems quite likely that originally the word *argŏs* was aĕrgō, (the negation of "a" with ĕrgō, as the root of ĕrgŏn); and then over time *aĕrgō* became *argŏs*.

Based upon this; then describing the talent of the servant with one talent as "*money*," is quite erroneous. *Laziness* would be the best definition. This is further supported by the fact that the master did in fact refer to this servant as both "wicked" and "lazy," prior to the second appearance of the word translated as "money."

This is merely speculation, but since Argentum, (symbol Ag), is the correct term for the metal commonly known as silver, the roots of this term may in fact be related to a term based upon the concept of a "lazy man's" metal, as silver historically has been about one twentieth the value of gold.

Proverbs 14:23 did tell us that *"in all labor there is profit."* Thus if there is labor, there must be profit, and a relationship is established between labor and profit. So if there is any labor, then there must be some profit as "all," is "all" inclusive.

But this is a one way street, in that it does not *preclude* profit without labor. But according to the second half of 14:24, if one assumes that "*mere talk*" is equal to no labor, then poverty and only poverty is where this leads..."] (End of Excerpt)

[The remainder of the analysis of the "Talent Man" parable will be available upon publication of the upcoming new book.]

The following is provided from the most non-political standpoint possible. No endorsement (or non-endorsement) of any candidate or political ideology is either expressed or implied.

It seems that Donald J. Trump has been considering; (some would say threatening); to run for president of the United States for some time. It seems that this desire had been building in him for years, and he finally decided to do something about it.

This is often how a talantŏn will work—assuming of course that it is a talantŏn. The great science fiction writer Robert A. Heinlein was once asked about why he enjoyed writing. Although his exact response is unavailable, he essentially answered: "Good God, what ever gave you the idea I enjoyed writing?" He was then asked why he did it, if he didn't enjoy it. His answer was that he did it because it: "Hurts less to write than to not write."

Later in the chapter containing the above excerpt, the subject of the "a-talantŏn" is addressed. An a-talantŏn is not of God, but rather is a device of the enemy. The purpose of both the talantŏn and the a-talantŏn is not to get the *tsâbâ'* or H. Sapiens to act, but rather to *choose* to act. An a-talantŏn is a *counterfeit* version of the talantŏn.

However; unlike the a-talantŏn; with the talantŏn, there can be no violations of God's rules. No violations of any of the Commandments are required. This is not to say that one who is "working" a talantŏn will not in the process violate said rules or Commandments; but rather that this is not *required*. Any such violations are *errors* committed by the active party. These in fact represent *deviations* from what actions it is that are required by the talantŏn for success and balance.

With the a-talantŏn, the reverse is true. This is a key in making the determination as to which type of "weight;" (talantŏn vs. a-talantŏn); it is that one is experiencing. If any action inconsistent with the word of God is required in order to satisfy that which seems to be "heavy on one's heart;" then whatever it might otherwise be; is not a talantŏn.

The other main difference is the presence of dunamis, or supernatural power. With an a-talantŏn, the possibility of any significant levels of dunamis is essentially zero.

As previously stated, dunamis is supernatural power, and not natural power. This can manifest in many different forms, and often is not recognized as such until much later.

There are two keys to recognizing dunamis, as opposed to mere natural power:

> *Firstly*; there must be violations of what is considered to be natural law. The "considered to be" part of course is crucial. Dunamis is not always as immediately obvious as feeding all the people at a picnic with one loaf of bread and a fish. When any cause definitively produces an effect other than that which is definitively "natural," dunamis is likely present. This can manifest in the physical, such as turning water into wine; or can also take place in the non-physical.

Secondly; dunamis or dunamic "acts" generally tend to happen quickly. The miracle that is considered to be the longest in duration; is the provision of manna—which roughly translates as "what is it?" But in actuality this was an act of dunamis provided each day, and not one act lasting years; as manna would not keep. "Happen quickly" can also mean seeming to "come out of nowhere." Perhaps "suddenly" is a better description; i.e. quickly and not expected. However a "dunamisless" a-talantŏn can also seem to happen quickly. The seemingly instant rise of Elvis Presley representing the former; with the rise of ISIS representing the latter.

When a talantŏn is present, this talantŏn is the source of that "heavy on my heart" feeling that tends to prompt one into action. Depending on the nature of the recipient, they: "aint gonna have no peace," until they begin acting or introducing "ergs" into the system.

When natural force is applied, (ergs), in an attempt to balance or remove the weight, the result is that dunamis or supernatural force begins to manifest. Once this begins, seemingly impossible events begin to be observed. Again, this assumes it is in fact a talantŏn that is being "worked." The use of "true talantŏn" is purposely avoided here, as it is arguably tautological. This would be similar to: "his own autobiography;" as to who else could possibly be expected to write his autobiography.

In the "Talent Man" story, the servants had supernatural power (dunamis). They were given weight (talantŏn) according to the amount of dunamis. Two of the servants "worked" this weight by putting energy into the system.

The result of their efforts (*"You were faithful with a few things"*); was additional weight or talantŏns being given to them; and they were put *"in charge of many things; enter into the joy of your master."* This was done by first giving them additional weight, (talantŏns); and then given, (put in charge of), additional dunamis.

The *"enter into the joy of your master"* part should not be overlooked.

This parable provides an explanation of mechanisms and rules of, (for it is just like); the immaterial realm or the "kingdom of heaven." The *"joy of your master"* part refers to God as the master: *"Well done, good and faithful slave."*—remembering here that the correct translation is *servant*.

This talantŏn/dunamis/talantŏn process is just that. It is a process, and not designed to be a "one shot deal." However; assuming the process is understood, (which is and was the true purpose of the parable); it nevertheless remains the choice of the recipient as to how far the process proceeds—hence the inclusion of the "one talent man."

It seems fair to say that Donald Trump's entire professional career consisted of a series of processes that were at least *similar* to the above process. He began by borrowing one million dollars from his father; which is and was a lot of money; but not as much as it may seem given the real estate values in Manhattan, even at that time.

Why did he borrow it? In order to "work" a "desire" to build. He put ergs into this desire and began building an empire.

For "some reason" he elected to invest in Manhattan, despite his father's belief that Donald should invest in Brooklyn, as he himself had done. And as of this writing, Donald has grown his assets to somewhere in the ten billion dollar range.

Whether this was completely, partially, or not in any way due to dunamic forces cannot be stated at this juncture.

Whether this was merely a talantŏn/*dynamikós*/talantŏn (natural power) process, or an actual talantŏn/*dunamis*/talantŏn (supernatural power) process requires a bit of study.

What *can* be stated however; is that the level of his personal business success was a highly unusual outcome. This is not to say that it is or was a unique outcome, but clearly a highly unusual outcome. However; assuming that it in fact was this talantŏn/*dunamis* process, and not mere *dynamikós*; it must remembered that the same is available to all. Like many things, it is not the *presence* of the talantŏn that determines success, but rather one's *reaction* to it—once again, as per the generally misunderstood Talent Men parable.

Nevertheless, his personal businesses processes are quite similar to the processes described in the parable. Initially, he was in charge of the "few." He was "good and faithful" with what he was given, and was put in charge of the "many." This being an ongoing lifelong process and not a one time event, as the concepts of "few" and "many" are in fact relative terms. Last year's "many" can become this year's "few."

Does this mean that he never made mistakes? Of course not, because as the old saying goes: "Different levels, different devils." Only "One" was ever able to completely resist the actions of the enemy, and that "One" is not Donald Trump. And the "return" for the enemy is much greater with someone who is successful and well known—hence it is worth the expenditure of much more effort on the part of the enemy.

It is interesting to compare the common understanding of the characteristics of Donald Trump, with the actualities:

Most would consider the name Donald Trump to be synonymous with champagne and "pheasant under glass;" or perhaps "black tie" galas with priceless cognac. The fact is that he has never consumed an alcoholic beverage in his entire life. He prefers cheeseburgers, and often sends his butler out for one. Why does he send his butler out instead of getting the cheeseburger himself? Likely this is merely an issue of the value of his time, and his personal safety. One might also consider that the gold plated fixtures in his home and airplane could be merely because of the image he believes *should* project, given the nature of his businesses. On the other hand, gold will not rust.

Two things should be asked:

Firstly; How many people have shown more lifelong successes with the talantŏn/*dunamis*/talantŏn process than Donald Trump; even if one is unsure as to whether it is dunamis or dynamikós that was involved? Or more broadly; how many have shown a better understanding of the *process* revealed in the "Talent Man" parable—irrespective of whether the parable was understood, or even known?

And secondly; how many things on the earth represent a greater "many" than the presidency of the United States?

Many would say that Donald Trump actually began his presidential bid back in 1987. As years went on, he became more and more interested in "running," which culminated in his formal decision to do so in June of 2015. This is a rather long term talantŏn; but a talantŏn can sometimes be like that. It must also again be noted, the US Presidency is also a rather large "many"

No matter which aspect of his candidacy is examined; he seems to have broken, and continues to break essentially all of the known rules of politics.

When Trump announced his intentions to run for president, many of the "experts" simply laughed. As the result of being so certain that this "carnival barker" (the words of others), was merely seeking yet more publicity, his "intentions" were simply and summarily dismissed by the "experts."

Early on, Karl Rove was asked about the Trump candidacy and Rove's response was "Ignore him." Ed Rollins commented early on that Trump was "not a viable candidate."

There was; (and still is by many); all of the talk about Trump "having a high floor and a low ceiling." Then as time went on, like an elevator in one of his high rise buildings; both the floor and the ceiling kept rising. Then he became the frontrunner.

Initially, and as the campaign progressed, Trump began making statements that the "experts" were certain would completely sink his campaign; but instead his popularity increased. Often these "controversial" statements were subsequently expropriated by his competitors.

These "experts'" opinions should be analyzed from a cause-effect perspective. Whatever it was that Trump was saying at any given time; which made these experts certain that Trump would be harmed; represented a cause-effect relationship in their minds. The "rules" of politics dictate that the *effect* of these statements should be a *decrease* in popularity. This rule is based upon many years of experience, hence the term "experts; and thus in a sense represents "natural law." But with Trump, the effect of these statements was exactly the opposite of what would be expected to happen. Thus these many actions of Trump clearly and consistently violated "natural law;" at least in the mind of these "experts."

It must be noted that God will; up to a point; often overlook many of our faults, in order to get something accomplished. He knows that if He required perfection from any of His hosts before utilization by Him; nothing will ever happen. He thus utilizes "what is" rather than what "should be." Although we were created in His "image and likeness," none; (except One); remained or remains so.

In this sense and for good reason, the public is like God. Unlike the "experts;" the public will overlook certain faults in order to get behind someone who seems to be able to get things done.

The experts had the actuality; (that which *is*); and subsequent reality; (that which is *perceived*) completely wrong. The experts perceived; (their reality), only that part of the Trump actuality that consisted of what they considered to be errors on Trump's part. Thus in their minds that was all that mattered, and in their view Trump should have sunk. Thus; based upon their experience, whatever else represented the actuality of Donald Trump was largely irrelevant.

But the public saw it differently. The public perceived the actuality of Trump as that which the experts (the builders) rejected; and largely rejected that which the experts accepted. To them, any misstatements; (if they in fact were misstatements); on Trumps part, represented only a small part of the Trump actuality.

Trump is perceived by many as a "regular" guy, despite the billions he has amassed. The personal *reality* of the *actuality* of money can vary greatly. Money can be a source of pride, or merely a means of assessing the level of success. If the latter, then all of the usual "trappings" associated with such wealth simply do not matter. It must me remembered that the Bible tell us that it is the

Donald Trump Candidacy According to Matthew?

love of money, and not the money itself that is the root of evil. The Bible does not tell us that the love of *success* is the root of any type of evil. Thus if one's reality of the actuality of money is a measure of success, and it is success that is loved, then there would not be any associated evil.

It is interesting to watch the various players outside the Trump campaign. The so called "establishment" wing of his own party appears to largely hate him. Even those previously considered as outside the "establishment" appear to hate him. Whether or not these are the equivalent to modern day Pharisees or Sadducees, would be a matter of opinion.

There is an Emmanic Principle which states:

> "If you really want to know what a thing actually is;
> push on it and see what breaks."

This principle is highly applicable to the so called "establishment" wing of Trump's own political party. In fact; as of this writing, one of the other candidates; (the "establishment" candidate), is continuing to run; even though all admit he has absolutely no mathematical chance of winning the nomination *conventionally*. Yet at the same time he can *only* win the nomination "conventionally." This requires a bit of an explanation.

This other candidate's sole reasons for continuing to run is; to either try and stop Trump from gaining sufficient delegates to win the nomination fairly; and/or to have himself or someone; *anyone*; other than Trump be "anointed" by the party. He is thereby attempting to deliberately thwart the will of the primary voters, by attempting to have the *party* pick the nominee instead—*at the convention*. Said actions are the antithesis of the very democratic process itself. It seems that when the stress of the campaign was placed upon this particular individual; i.e.; via the aforementioned "push;" then his true nature was revealed.

Another candidate is engaging in the proliferation of an "a truth" campaign. Stating "a truth" instead of "the truth" can be one of the three ways of lying: (1) Telling an outright lie; (2) Stating the truth but only part of it; (3) Telling the complete truth, but in such a disbelieving manner that the listener believes the opposite. Claiming to be a devout "Christian," he nevertheless seems to find it necessary to do these things in order to stop Trump. Once again; "push" on it and see what breaks.

This same fellow also has almost no chance winning *conventionally*, (first definition); so in order to be the nominee, he must win it *conventionally*, (second definition). Without commenting on the *quality* of his political views; it can be stated that his views deviate far from the "establishment's" political views. Thus; any belief that he would or even could be chosen by the "establishment," seems to be quite delusional.

One reason for this; is that once the "mere superfluities" of the "purportation" of things such as democracy and the Constitution are stripped away; the "establishment" wings of the Democratic and Republican parties are quite similar. When pushed, it is either the acquisition or the retention of power that is the main driving force for both parties.

Principles such as the public *choosing* their own leader; instead of the same being *appointed* by those who are "anointed," and thus "much wiser" than the public; simply become obstacles to power. These "obstacles" must then be overcome in any way possible that does not include a term in prison.

It matters little that the "establishment" wing of one party openly espouses views which are less antithetical to personal freedom than the other party. The fact is that when either thing or any thing is "pushed;" the truth is revealed.

The present "establishment" Republican's view, is that the people are simply too incompetent to choose their own candidate; and in their view, Donald Trump being the consistent frontrunner represents conclusive evidence of this fact. Therefore the "establishment" must step in and thwart the will of the voters. This is: "forgive them for they know not what they do," without the "forgive them for" part.

This is all mentioned here; because it is important to understand that once action is taken (ergs) upon a talantŏn, the enemy

Donald Trump Candidacy According to Matthew?

immediately takes notice. In fact, the amount of ergs by those who are opposing a person who is "working" a talantŏn, can often be a good "barometer" of the amount of success the person working the talantŏn is actually achieving.

This is particularly interesting to watch; when those who are reputed to be of high moral character engage in actions antithetical to said reputation. Or; when those whose previous views of personal freedom and personal choice (live free or die), suddenly disappear when it comes to the public choosing the party nominee.

Going against one who is "working" a talantŏn, generally requires a large amount of force from the enemy; which he/it would not need to bother with had the talantŏn instead been buried. The amount of force the enemy exerts, is what he/it believes is necessary to counteract the ergs being applied to the talantŏn; and thus can be used to indicate the likelihood of success by the "working" of the talantŏn—at least in the mind of the enemy. But the enemy is incapable of victory against the dunamis created by the application of ergs to a talantŏn. In order to be victorious, the enemy can only be *given* victory; and only by the person with the talantŏn.

Can someone "working" a talantŏn fail? Most certainly; which is precisely how victory is *given* to an enemy who has insufficient power to *claim* it.

These actions of others who are the targets or recipients of these indirect (indirect with respect to Trump) attacks of the enemy are especially noteworthy, with the "reporting" of "what Trump said." This can easily be verified by watching the unedited clips.

For example:

> When Trump is speaking about the Mexican government sending; "They're sending;" criminals into the United States; (just as Fidel Castro once did); with the subject of his comments being the Mexican government; it is reported that Trump hates Hispanics and calls them all criminals. There is also a constant conflating of *legal* and *illegal* immigrants, to make it appear that Trump "hates" all immigrants.

When Trump comments (appropriately or otherwise) about an individual who just happens to not have a "y chromosome;" (i.e.; a female); it is reported that Trump hates women; as though he is attacking all women, simply because the person he "attacked" happened to be female. Yet the same argument is never raised when he "attacks" men. He is never accused of being "anti-male" because he "attacks" a person who just happens to have said "y chromosome." And then it is always Trump, and never the "reporter" who is called the sexist. If this "logic" were applied by the reporter on a *non-sexist* basis, the only possible conclusion would be that Trump must then in fact simply hate everyone.

When Trump states that "all lives matter," he is then called a "racist" because he will not make any differentiation as to whether or not a life matters based upon skin color.

These are not mentioned in order to advocate for Trump. Rather; because all of this is merely the result of various levels of weakness on the part of those individuals who are doing much worse than "failing to improve upon the silence." These *deceitful* actions are the direct result of the exploitation of their weaknesses by the one opposing the working of the talantŏn. It must be remembered that *"If it aint truth, it aint God."*

It should be asked for what possible reason(s) would Donald Trump want the Presidency of the United States?

Some might say money. However; that seems to be a bit short sighted, as there exists somewhere in the neighborhood of ten billion reasons why this is not likely to be so. In addition, he would have to detach himself from his personal interests; and instead settle for the salary provided for the presidency—a salary which he has already said he will not accept. Furthermore; he likely has already lost more money from giving up "The Apprentice," alone, than he could ever recoup legally as a "politician."

Donald Trump Candidacy According to Matthew?

Some might say power. Again, it is unclear whether Donald Trump would have more or less power as president, than he currently has. Clearly he has had substantial power over many politicians of both parties, for many years; as a result of his donations to them—something which his opponents dishonestly try to proffer as Trump's support for Democratic *political* positions.

Donald Trump himself stated why it is he wants to be President, but it seems many simply do not believe him.

He said that he loves his country, and indicated that he wants to use whatever he has that made his company great, for the benefit of the country. He further indicated that he simply wants to do for his country, what it is that he did for his company.

Given the enormous amount of time and effort (ergs) by him; and given the fact that Donald Trump has paid for his campaign without taxpayer dollars, or donations from special interests; he should be given the courtesy of being believed with regard to his motivations. Furthermore; we all; even those who may disagree with him; owe him thanks and due respect for what he has thus far undertaken.

Whether or not Donald Trump is "working" a talantŏn, and what the significance of this might be; is for each of us to determine.

Logically, the requirements for well being of the physical body should be such as to be consistent with both the nature and the requirements of that which it is designed to contain. It has been the reliance on opinion on material requirements, while ignoring immaterial requirements, that has caused the Biblical human ages to simply be non-believable.

It's Not Just A Theory

Is it true?
Romans 6:22-23 (KJV) tells us:

> *"But now being made free from sin,
> and become servants to God,
> ye have your fruit unto holiness,
> and the end everlasting life.
> For the wages of sin is death;
> but the gift of God is eternal life
> through Jesus Christ our Lord."*[1]

Here Paul is speaking of what is gained through Jesus (the) Christ.

The real question is whether or not he is lying. The fact of the matter, is that each and every person who was alive when Paul stated, (and likely actually wrote) this; including Paul; is in fact physically quite dead.

There is no possibility of prevarication here. Paul makes it quite clear that eternal life is obtained through Jesus Christ—yet there is no record of anyone at any time living eternally. The only possible known exception of course would be Jesus, (and possibly Elijah and/or Enoch); but Jesus did in fact "die" before He lived eternally. Great care is taken here to not state "ever lived eternally," for obvious reasons.

The actual Greek word translated as "life" is:

"2222: zōē; from *2198*; *life* (lit or fig.): - life (time). Comp. *5590*."[2]

The actual Greek word translated as "death" is:

"2288 thanatŏs; from *2348*; (prop. an adj. used as a noun) *death* (lit. or fig.): - x deadly, (be...) death."[3]

Assuming that Paul was telling the truth; clearly Paul was not speaking of *physical* life. The idea of *justification* resulting in salvation; refers not to physical life, but what many refer to as "spiritual" life. Paul is speaking of his belief of something which was made possible by He Who is: "The Anointed One," or "The Christ," or "The Messiah."

In accord with this belief, it was He, (Jesus), who provided a means by which that, or at least part of that, which is or was "breathed" into the *physical* body when *physical* life began; could return to its "spiritual" source, despite being soiled by sin. This "life" to which Paul refers, is this eternal connection to God. This represents an *immaterial* ("soul") to *immaterial* (God) connection.

But "physical life" is also a connection. That which is *"breathed"* into the physical body at birth is "connected" to the physical body as long as it, (the physical body), has this "life." When the connection begins; this is "physical birth." When the connection is severed; this is "physical death." Here this represents an *immaterial* to *material* connection. And although it seems that no one has ever maintained this connection longer than Methuselah; compared to "eternal," even Methuselah did not maintain this, (immaterial to material), connection for very long.

But what about this immaterial, ("soul"), connection to the material (physical) body?

Genesis 2:7 (KJV) tells us:

> *"And the LORD God formed man*
> *of the dust of the ground,*
> *and breathed into his nostrils*
> *the breath of life;*
> *and man became a living soul."*[4]

Here God "breathed," or in the original Hebrew:

> "5301 nâphach; a prim. root; to *puff*, in various applications..."[5]

This is the *action*, or the *means*, by which something was introduced into what would later be called "Adam's" nostrils.

What it was that God breathed or *nâphach*(ed) into what would later be called "Adam's" nostrils, was *breath*, or:

> "5397 n^eshâmâh; fr. 5395; a *puff*, i.e. *wind*, angry or vital *breath*...;"[6]

And the particular type of "puff" or "wind" that was "breathed" was:

> "2416 chay; from 2421; *alive*; hence raw (flesh); fresh (plant, water, year), strong; also (as noun, espec. in the

fem. sing. and masc. plur.) life (or living thing), whether lit. or fig..." [The very next word in Strong's (2417), is likewise: "chay (Chald.)" also means "*alive*" or "*life*," but here the original *Chaldean*.][7]

Here is seen a twofold process:
First, God formed the vessel utilizing matter. Then he breathed into this vessel, the n^{e}shâmâh, or breath of *chay*, or life.
As a result of this "Adam" became a "*living soul*," or:

"5315 nephesh; from 5314; prop. a *breathing* creature..."[8]

[Note: Adam was *formed* from *something*. This is in contradistinction to the events in Genesis 1:27 where God *created* man. The use of the term creation means to bring into existence from *nothing*; and is a translation of the Hebrew word *bârâ'*. Here in Genesis 2:7, God is not creating from nothing; but rather is *forming* from *something*. "Formed" as opposed to "created" is a translation of an entirely different word: *yâtsar*. These are two entirely separate and distinct events, with the creation of man likely occurring many hundreds of thousands of years ago; and the formation of adam or Adam occurring less than ten thousand yeas ago. It is because of the conflation and confusion of these two events that the actual Scriptural age of the earth is in dispute with science, and believed to be less than ten thousand years old. It is beyond the scope of this monograph to litigate this, but an exhaustive explanation can be found in the first four chapters of "Meekraker Beginnings..."]

Here it is God Himself Who is bringing into existence a man in a fashion similar to the method used in "normal" human gestation and birth. With H. Sapiens, first the vessel is formed, and when completed, exits the womb. *Then and only then*, breath is drawn in by the completed vessel, and it becomes a *living* or breathing physical entity. H. Sapiens even have an anatomical "insurance policy" in effect with regard to this, as the cardiac *foramen ovale*, (after birth becoming the *fossa ovale*); prevents the *premature* entrance of this breath.

One key point of this event is that here God did it Himself, without recourse, or any aid from man; i.e.; with no assistance from any of the offspring of the original *created* hosts.

The question must be asked as to what it is that is contained in this *breath*, (n^{e}shâmâh); of *life*, (chay)?

It is fair to say that at least two things are contained in this "breath of life."

Firstly; would be that which is often described as *soul*. Soul is often described; erroneously, incompletely, or otherwise; as "will, intellect, and emotions." "*I am*," or a sense or knowledge of existence or "*being*," is also another way to describe soul. Soul is the immaterial and immortal portion that requires justification for reconnection to God. This "I am," is the only thing that true solipsists actually "know." It is this "soul," for which the body or vessel is designed to contain.

The *second* thing contained in this "breath of life" is the means by which the vessel sustains and maintains itself. Known as the VLF or *vital life force* by some; *Innate Intelligence* by others, or *chi* by yet others; it is this VLF that is responsible for maintaining the vessel. It is this VLF that regulates growth and healing; and can transform a ham sandwich into skin, fingernails or whatever else it; within certain limitations; deems necessary.

Since this VLF comes from God, it must then necessarily be perfect when it is "transmitted."

A quick recap of Paul's words:

"But now being made free from sin,

> *and become servants to God,*
> *ye have your fruit unto holiness,*
> *and the end everlasting life.*
> *For the wages of sin is death;*
> *but the gift of God is eternal life*
> *through Jesus Christ our Lord."*

The question becomes whether or not what Paul stated could in any way apply to *physical* life.

With regard to the second verse, often; the word "penalty" is erroneously attributed to Paul, and not the word "wages;" thus making this "penalty of sin." Any such erroneous attribution, would of course change the meaning entirely.

The actual Greek word translated as "wages" is:

> "3800 ŏpsōniŏn; neut. of a presumed der. of the same as 3795; *rations* for a soldier, i.e. (by extens.) his *stipend* or *pay*: - wages."[9] (It must be noted that no *reasonable* relationship between 3800 and 3795 could be found.)

Clearly there is an implication of the giving of what is due here, without regard to any type of penalty or reward; but rather *balance*. Wages or *ŏpsōniŏn* are paid as a matter of entitlement, and are required for that which has been performed. Wages usually represent something positive that benefits the worker, for his or her *previous* efforts that benefitted the person paying the wages.

However; in a sense, most criminal "penalties" also represent wages; but here in the *negative* sense. These "criminal" "wages" or *ŏpsōniŏn*, usually represent something negative that harms the "worker," for his or her previous act or acts of omission or commission, which resulted in injury to some party or parties. These are required in order to *balance* said act or acts of omission or commission, that resulted in injury to some party or parties.

Clearly when Paul uses ŏpsōniŏn with regard to *"sin,"* he is not referring to the former positive ŏpsōniŏn; but rather the latter negative ŏpsōniŏn as contextually, said ŏpsōniŏn is "death."

It is also interesting that Paul chose ŏpsōniŏn; "no reasonable relationship," notwithstanding; that nevertheless according to Strong, refers to soldiers. This may be because according to the Father; (see Genesis 2:1 and elsewhere); all H. Sapiens are "hosts," (English), or "tsâbâ'," (Hebrew);"[10] and thus were created and designed to engage in warfare; arguably for redemption of that beyond themselves.

There is no question that engaging in certain types of "sinful" *physical* actions can result in early death. Here there is an observable relationship between these actions, and the effects of these actions on the biological vessel—suicide being a prime example. The wages or *ŏpsōniŏn* of attempted suicide; if successful; is physical death.

There is also no question that engaging in certain "*non-physical*" "actions" can have an effect on "longevity;"—either way.

Some of this can be explained in physical terms, and yet some cannot. "Stress;" as commonly understood; is considered to be a causative factor in certain types of physical ailments. Although the "stress" may be the result of physical causes; and thus the "stress" itself thus represents an *effect* of this cause; this "stress" in itself becomes a non-physical or *immaterial cause*, often with a subsequent physical or *material* result.

It matters little that the *cause* of the stress may originate in the physical, and thus be an actuality. The fact is that the "stress" itself is a *reality* and not an actuality, and thus is *subjective* in nature. The *effect* of the actual *cause* of the stress is the stress itself. But this immaterial reality of stress is now a *cause* and can have significant physical *effects* or results. And the actual cause of "stress" for one, may be a source of its opposite for another. Some cultures even celebrate physical death.

Positive experiences can work in a similar manner; but unlike stress, these can result in increased longevity and quality of life.

Today there are established "norms" as to what the "upper end" of longevity could possibly be; with few claiming these can be exceeded by any significant percentage. If it is so stipulated that the average person in the United States lives to about eighty years of age; then even a 30% change in this either way is extremely unusual—as most people live way beyond fifty six; and very few genuinely exceed one hundred and four years of age.

Methuselah lived 969 years;[11] and if a bit of math is done, it can be determined that Adam lived a minimum of 930 years. These represent increases over today's average longevity of 1211% and 1162% respectively; and thus are significant percentages of increases in longevity.

"But everyone 'knows' that this is 'mathematical hyperbole.'" Very few people today actually believe those "Bible" longevity numbers. This of course is part of the problem. There is one person who lived quite some time ago, who actually *believed* these numbers. This is a certainty, as it was he (Moses) himself, who is believed to have actually been the author initially involved in recording them.

However; in Psalms 90:8-10 (KJV), (Psalm 90 is considered to be of Mosaic authorship); where Moses is speaking to God, we are told:

> "*Thou hast set our iniquities before thee,*
> *our secret sins in the light of thy countenance.*
> *For all our days are passed away in thy wrath: we*
> *spend our years as a tale that is told.*
> *The days of our years are threescore years and ten;*
> *and if by reason of strength they be fourscore years,*
> *yet is their strength labour and sorrow;*
> *for it is soon cut off, and we fly away.*"[12]

Although this may read like Shakespeare; it is not. Here Moses is noting the relationship between sin; and what he is presenting as either what he considers premature physical death, or "man's" physical death itself. And it is curious that the number of years people physically lived at the time this was written (lifespan); was between seventy and eighty—roughly about the same as today, or perhaps just a few decades ago. According to Moses, this was because: "*Thou hast set our iniquities before thee, our secret sins in the light of thy countenance. For (because) all our days are passed away in thy wrath: we spend our years as a tale that is told."*

Moses further states how longevity is or can be increased from "threescore years and ten" (70 years); to "fourscore" (80 years); and that means is: *"by reason of strength."*

The actual Hebrew word translated here as "strength" is:

> 1369 gᵉbûwrâh; fem. pass. part. from the same as 1368; *force* (lit. or fig.);..."¹³

Thus the actual stated reason for said increased longevity is in fact not *strength*, but rather *force*.

In the *incorrect* translation of *gᵉbûwrâh* as "strength;" contextually, there is a clear implication that it is the magnitude of the capability to *resist* sin that increases longevity.

Presumably, said "strength" then results in less sinful behavior. Here the active party is the "sinner." Depending simply upon both upon the magnitude of the capability to resist sin, and presumably its utilization by the otherwise sinner; here according to "The Big M," longevity can be enhanced by about 14%.

However with the *correct* translation of gᵉbûwrâh as *force*, this changes things a bit. Here the active entity *at the time* is not the sinner, but rather is a *force*. It is actually written that "by reason of *force*" that longevity is enhanced.

Thus although the "sinner" may have had much say in being the *active* party in the creation of the *original* forces by his or her behavior; here the reason for the longevity *increase*, the sinner is now the *passive* party; as he is acted upon by this gᵉbûwrâh as the recipient of a *force*. This is another example of "equal and opposite reactions;" or what is often referred to as *karma*; but here in the specific as relates to behavior (cause), and to increased longevity (effect).

This is an important distinction. The strength; (*incorrect* translation of gᵉbûwrâh); to *behave* in a proper or sinless manner is always a current or "real time" phenomenon. One cannot *currently*, (real time), sin in the past; neither can one *currently* sin in the future. Each "real time" event is when decisions are actually made. Certainly one can regret past bad decisions, or pledge to do right in the future; but ultimately the specific decisions must be made "real time;" and thus are subject to a variety of factors, including the influence of the enemy, either directly or indirectly through others. ("I know I swore never to do it again, but I really needed the money.")

But a *force*; (*correct* translation of gᵉbûwrâh); is another matter. As is always the case with "equal and opposite reactions;" i.e.; *karma*; the return force is both inevitable and unavoidable. Thus in a sense, to the extent that one's *behavior* is such that it would create forces that tend to increase longevity as Moses stated (as a *cause*); the *result* of increased longevity, (as an *effect*), is a certainty; as this increase is directly precipitated by a *force*.

But where is this "force?" In the situation cited by Moses, it seems that the force is not generally needed until 70 (seventy) years of age. So precisely where resides this particular force for the preceding "*threescore years and ten*?"

Newton's laws of inertia, F=MA and equal and opposite reactions; are usually concerned strictly with the physical. However whenever any consciousness or any "I am" is exerting free will, there is also an *immaterial* component, which is in addition to the *material* components as addressed by Newton.

Thus the actual force created is a combination of that which is produced in the material, (the action); as well as that which is produced in the immaterial, (reason for the action). [The "*Second Intermission*" of "*MeekRaker Beginnings. . .*" provides a specific and highly detailed description of this process.]

Once any action is undertaken by a conscious being, *two* actual imbalances are created. One imbalance is in the material, with another simultaneously created in the immaterial. Thus the *true*, *complete*, or *total* force, (true actuality); is a combination of both material *and* immaterial forces.

The *material* part of the force is generally balanced quickly. It takes little time for a baseball or a golf ball to move once a force is imparted to it. Irrespective of the amount of time allocated to scheming; the actual *telling* of the words of a lie; or the actual *stealing* of something; happens relatively quickly. This is the balancing of the *physical* imbalance created by the action.

However the *immaterial* component of the action behaves a bit differently. Just as F=MA applies to the material, it also applies in the immaterial; but there is substantial leeway involved in the balancing of the *immaterial* portion of the force. Whatever the magnitude of the immaterial portion of the original force, there are essentially infinite combinations for the "return" of this force. The *immaterial* "MA," or that which balances the original *immaterial* force, actually consists of two factors:

First there is the magnitude of what is returned, or the M. Then there is the timing, (how rapidly), is this return, or the A. The product of these must always equal the magnitude of the original force or "F." Thus if the immaterial force is to be balanced quickly, this represents a large value for A, or the *acceleration* of the return to the original source. However with a "quick return," the *magnitude* of what is returned must be small in order to balance the original force. Similarly; if the magnitude or "M" is to be large; then the return must be slower; (less acceleration or "A" to return to the source); in order to balance the original force. This acceleration can be extremely slow (years), if a large return is to be provided. It is God alone Who determines both the magnitude and the acceleration of these (karmic) forces directed *to the source* of the original force.

These immaterial forces reside in the immaterial as an imbalance until they intersect the material at the appropriate time, as determined by God. And God is certainly smart enough to not provide the return of forces which will increase longevity until they are necessary.

The second appearance of *"strength,"* contained in: *"yet is their strength labour and sorrow; for it is soon cut off, and we fly away;"* is an entirely different word.

Here the actual Hebrew word translated as "strength" is in fact:

"7296 rôhab; from 7292; *pride. . .*"[14]

Although *"labour* (sic.)" seems to be a fair translation here, the actual Hebrew word translated as "*sorrow*" is:

> "205 'âven; from an unused root perh. mean. prop. to *pant* (hence to *exert* oneself, usually in vain; to *come* to *naught*) strictly *nothingness*; also *trouble, vanity, wickedness*; spec. an *idol*. . ."[5]

Thus a better translation would be: "Nevertheless in their *pride, labor,* and *nothingness;* because it is soon cut off, and we fly away;"

Moses himself lived to only one hundred and twenty years of age; but was in excellent physical condition when he died.[16]

Assuming Moses wrote Psalms 90 while he was still alive, and this represents a 50% increase over the "fourscore" stated here in Psalms 90; it is far from some the life spans of others that Moses had written about.

Was Moses a sinner? It is reasonably clear that it was not because the land that God had promised Abraham, Isaac, and Jacob was not *good* enough for Moses; that he was permitted only to see it.

But back to Paul's statement in Romans 6:22-23: "*But now being made free from sin, and become servants to God, ye have your fruit unto holiness, and the end everlasting life. For the wages of sin is death; but the gift of God is eternal life through Jesus Christ our Lord.*"

The actual Greek word translated as "free" is:

> "1659 ĕlĕuthĕrŏō; from 1658; to *liberate*, i.e. (fig.) to *exempt* (from mor., cer. or mortal liability): - deliver, make free."[7]

Thus this "*free from*" or *ĕlĕuthĕrŏō*, refers to some type of liberation or exemption from sin. This refers to a *binary* with respect to *immaterial* or *spiritual* life or "connection;" as it is the presence of *any* sin and not the quantity or magnitude of sin that precludes eternal connection to God.

Being "*free from sin*" refers to justification; rendering man "just as though he never sinned." This is why the characteristics of man's sin can become irrelevant *immaterially*, with respect to that eternal connection. This justification by Jesus prevents "spiritual" death or disconnection, as the result of or from any and all sin.

But being free from or *ĕlĕuthĕrŏō* from sin, is not the same as being "sin free."

Although man is ĕlĕuthĕrŏō from the contamination of sin *immaterially* with respect to justification with regard to *future* immaterial life; there has not been any type of justification provided for the *material* effects of sin. Materially, the "here and now" *material* wages of sin are still "physical death."

It cannot be overemphasized that *materially* here means not only the relatively quick *direct* material results of sin; but also the *indirect* material effect of sin, by the ultimate *material* return of manifestations (karma), as the result of the imbalances created in the *immaterial*.

This is likely why Jesus "gave up His Spirit" on the cross—He had no alternative. Being sin free, likely He simply could not die any other way. No sin—then no wages of sin or physical death. Death by crucifixion generally took 2-3 days, but Jesus gave up his life the same day the crucifixion began. This is why Pilate was surprised that Jesus was "dead already." Thus; contrary to the common belief of some, Jesus was not *killed*. This act, (killing), requires a third party to *"take"* Jesus' life; as opposed to how the Scriptures read in that He *gave* His life.

If this is so stipulated, then it seems that there is a relationship between sin and physical death; in that without sin there can be no physical death; and with sin physical death at some point in time is a certainty.

Proverbs 9:10-11 tells us:

"The fear of the LORD is the beginning of wisdom: and the knowledge of the holy is understanding. For by me thy days shall be multiplied, and the years of thy life shall be increased."[18]

As is generally the case, the word *"fear"* here in this context, should have been translated as "reverence."

The actual Hebrew word is:

> "3374 yir'âh; fem. of 3373; *fear* (also used as infin.); mor. *reverence*: - x dreadful, x exceedingly, fear (-fulness)."[19]

Here we are told that it is possible to increase the years of one's life by beginning *wisdom*, and obtaining *understanding*. This will happen by Him, (*"Me"*).

How does this happen? This happens by altering behavior from that which is *not* known or understood—perceiving some short term gain as a singular entity; to that which *is* understood. Once the long term results, (even outside of longevity), of upright behavior are known and understood; the result is less sin. This "by Him" will necessarily multiply days and increased years. It is not a matter of *"strength,"* but simply a matter of *forces*.

Exodus 20:12 tells us:

> "Honour thy father and thy mother:
> that thy days may be long upon the land
> which the LORD thy God giveth thee."[20]

Here again we are told of the relationship between behavior and longevity. The inclusion of *"upon the land which the Lord thy God giveth thee;"* is provided to be certain that it is understood that this refers to *physical* life.

It could be fair to consider old age and death as a sub-clinical disease. It would be more accurate to say that it is a pandemic sub-clinical disease which is always fatal; (except for one, or possibly as many as three: Jesus, and possibly Elijah and/or Enoch). Of course the concept that a "sub-clinical disease" that "everyone has which is always fatal;" seems absurd.

It would be *"fair-er;"* to consider old age and/or death, as a *clinical* disease, which remains unrecognized as such because of its ubiquitous nature. Since everyone ultimately acquires this disease; it is not considered as a disease, except in rare instances such as *progeria*.

Although *immaterially*, as little as even one sin guarantees *spiritual* death that can only be remedied by justification; the *amount* of sin is irrelevant with respect to justification.

With *physical* death, it seems that although even one sin results in the onset of the disease; the "prognosis" can vary greatly—*if longevity and health are the prime considerations*. These variations in longevity and health are the result of the *amount* of sin.

Sin is much more like a slow acting poison, administered over a long period of time; which accumulates in the system, and ultimately results in "physical death." The less sin administered; the greater amount of time before the onset of death. However; even with only one administration, *physical death becomes a certainty*. It would just take much longer to manifest.

But the onset and duration of "normal" old age and subsequent physical death is rather peculiar. There are various opinions regarding when this transition occurs; many believing that thirty three years of age is the average point of transition. Some may believe that this point is where catabolism, (breaking down), begins to overtake anabolism, (building up). There are also large variations in the outward physical manifestations of this disease.

So the actual cause of this unrecognized disease remains unknown. Since the morbidity and mortality is 100%, it is believed that the causative factor of this unrecognized disease must simply be the presence of life—that being both a prerequisite and a common factor. If one is alive; then barring any trauma, there must necessarily still be physical death at some point; this merely being a "fact of life."

But while it is most certainly true and cannot be argued, that all who are living are in fact living; there is also another *activity* that currently all commonly engage in; and that other activity is *sin*. Being physically alive is a binary, but sinning; although another ultimate certainty; is much more varied. Since all men sin, and the wages of sin is death; ultimately all "H. Sapiens" soldiers obtain their *ŏpsōniŏn* or "rations, stipend, or pay."

If a *recognized* clinical disease is diagnosed; then this disease state is recognized, and appropriate treatment can be instituted.

But if an *unrecognized* pandemic disease is in progress, along with the belief that the signs and symptoms are not because of any *disease*, but rather are because of *design*; then nothing *will* be done, because it is believed that there is nothing that *needs* to be done, or *can* be done.

In the "miracles" of the Bible, where diseased persons were healed by Jesus and others; this generally represented the "casting out" of the entity that was responsible for the malady. (To be accurate; usually this was actually a matter of authority, and not supernatural power; except in those cases where gross visible physical changes were immediate.) In each of these cases, these were recognizable, (physical or mental), diseases.

According to the testimony; the demonic infiltration had reached the level where it (or they), was or were, capable of causing sufficient disruption, as to produce the signs and symptoms of disease. Leprosy, blood disorders, withered hands and the like, were not considered a normal "part of life." These had passed the threshold for clinical disease.

However; merely because interfering entities have not succeeded in sufficient disruptions as to produce clinical signs and symptoms indicative of *recognized* or *recognizable* disease; this does not mean that there are no disruptions that are taking place.

"Everyone dies from something." This "one" is unfortunately true. If the position is taken that old age and subsequent physical death is by design; barring clinical disease, trauma, etc.; then all die by design. But if the position is taken that physical death is not by design; then all "natural" death, (barring trauma); is in fact by some type of *disease*; irrespective of how long "old age" takes to be fatal.

If the *"wages of sin is death;"* whether "spiritual" death or "physical" death; then there is a clear implication that without sin, there would be no death. Surely this is so in the sense of "spiritual" death. Of what use would justification be for one who never sinned? The problem is that this only happened once. There is only that one man who never sinned; yet he still died. It is true that He died; but again it is also true that neither anyone nor anything killed Him. He *chose* to give up the immaterial/material connection, and the record is clear on this. Attempts were made to kill Him and each failed. He told His disciples that no man could kill him; and again, the account of this willful severing of the immaterial/material connection by Him is recorded.

This leads to an interesting dilemma: Had Jesus *not chosen* to sever that immaterial/material connection; then it is arguable that He would have lived forever. Since He had never sinned, there were no wages, and physical death would not have been possible.

However; had He chosen to not sever that immaterial/material connection; this itself would have been a sinful act, as this was one of the main reasons for His physical existence. Attacks about this decision, (to go through with it); formed the basis for what happened at Gethsemane.

"The years have been kind to him;" is an expression which in a sense is antithetical to Paul's wisdom. Here there is an unusual condition under observation; with attribution to this anomaly being an unspecified, but relatively long duration of time. The truth is likely that "he had been kind to the years;" in the sense of working a "low paying" job in the sin department. Here at least there is a reasonable cause for the observed effect.

The facts are that aging is a disease which violates biological law; and biological law violates non-biological law. What could this mean, and does this make any degree of sense?

Non-biological law generally *decreases* the level of organization as a function of time. Diffusion, osmosis, radioactive decay; all result in lower levels of organization and higher levels of entropy. Geographical changes over time; result in lower levels of organization. The proper maintenance of a home; is a means to minimize and reverse these disorganizing forces. Fences must be painted; as a painted fence represents a much higher level of organization, which natural forces will over time disorganize. The list goes on.

But biological laws result in *higher* levels of organization. The changes that occur in a developing embryo seem miraculous. The human body can transform relatively low levels of matter such as oxygen, water and simple organic compounds into levels of organization so complex, that even today they are barely understood. The structure of the nervous system; as well as the chemicals used in its functioning; can "automatically" be made or modified from much less organized forms of matter such as fruits, vegetables, and hunks of animal muscle. The same can be said of the remainder of the human structure.

To suggest that this biological process, (maintaining the vessel or body), by design and thus on its own, somehow begins to fail at some point in time; *without* any interfering factors; represents an "explanation" which is based upon observation only. In order for this to be true, then this Vital Life Force, Innate Intelligence, or chi, must change, (begin to fail), as a matter of *intentional* and *deliberate* design; i.e.; "God's will." [It should be asked which specific *subsets* of that *set* known as "God," contain imperfection?]

The alternative explanation being; that it is caused by an *interfering* factor, to which no one currently alive has 100% immunity; and thus *all* eventually will contract this disease.

Any empirically based assumption(s) that it is the *organizing* force (VLF) which fails by design; does not in any way mean that this assumption is correct. Neither does it mean that another causative factor does not exist.

In the physical science of electricity, one of the most fundamental laws is Ohm's Law; expressed as $E = IR$.

Here **E** is **E**lectromotive force or voltage; **I** is the current, flow of electrons or **I**ntensity; and **R** is the **R**esistance to that flow.

This law describes the relationship of the simple circuit. In order for current to flow, there must be: a current or movement of electrons; a force driving that current; and a load through which to drive it.

As stated in this law, the larger the driving force (E), the greater the amount of electron flow (I), through a given resistance or load (R); and the greater this resistance (R), the lesser amount of electron flow (I) for a given force (E). [Step on a garden hose and less water flows, unless the pressure is increased.]

Ohm's law is a *material* law; and like all material laws, there is a corresponding law in the *immaterial* from which it came. One example of this law in the immaterial; relates to the intentions and actions of the enemy to supplant that which is in, or is of the image and likeness of God; with that which is of him—that is; that which is not of God but is of the *enemy*.

That which is of him, (the enemy), and not of Him; is analogous to the current. The enemy needs to get his current to flow into the hosts (H. Sapiens). As in an electrical circuit, once the current gets into the hosts; then changes begin.

The enemy does this in two very basic ways with respect to this same E = IR law; with each method attempting to use forces, but with different tactical; (but the same strategic); intentions.

Firstly; he does this by the utilization of forces against the hosts that are analogous to voltage. He "cranks up" this voltage in order to get current to flow from him to the hosts. Much "actionable intelligence" can be gained by carefully observing the nature of these "voltage increases." This is because unlike voltage, there is a *subjective* component. What would be low voltage to one host, can be the same as high voltage to another; and vice versa. (This can often be the reason for what seems to be pettiness.) These forces are custom designed to produce the maximum voltage, (and ultimately maximum current flow); *for that particular host*; and thus there is much intelligence that can be obtained by the design and timing of the attack—but it also must be remembered that the enemy is not always correct.

However; just as in Ohm's law, in order for this to work; there must be the load, and that load of course is the host. But being made in the image and likeness of God; that load (host) is not a particularly good *conductor* for the enemy's "current." This necessarily means that the host *is* a particularly good *resistor*. In order to maximize the current flow for a given voltage, the enemy will also attempt to lower the host's *resistance*. Here also much "actionable intelligence" can be gained by carefully observing the nature of these attempts at lowering resistance; as the enemy will attack those areas he or it perceives as weak. But again, it must be remembered that the enemy is not always correct.

Job 1:10 tells us:

> *"Hast not thou made an hedge about him,*
> *and about his house,*
> *and about all that he hath on every side?*
> *thou hast blessed the work of his hands,*
> *and his substance is increased in the land."*[21]

Here Satan is complaining to God that He has *"made an* (sic.) *hedge"* around Job. This "hedge" results in increased resistance. And according to Ohm's law, increased resistance means less current flow, for a given voltage. Satan is essentially complaining here that the resistance is way too high, and he cannot get significant current to flow into Job. But he admits here that God is the one who "made" this hedge.

This "hedge" is actually:

> "7753 sûwk a prim. root; to *entwine*, i.e. *shut* in (for formation, protection or restraint):- fence, (make an) hedge (up)."[22]

This may seem unrelated at first, but is in fact quite relevant:

When God refers to "keeping" His commandments in Exodus 20, most believe that this "keep" or "keeping" means *obey*.

Here in Exodus the actual Hebrew word is:

> "8104: shâmar; A prim. root; prop. to *hedge* about (as with thorns), i.e. *guard*; gen. to *protect, attend to,* etc.: - beware, be circumspect, take heed (to self), keep (-er, self), mark, look narrowly, observe, preserve, regard,

reserve, save (self), sure, (that lay) wait (for), watch (-man)."²³ [See MeekRaker Monograph #601 "Shâmar to Sharia"]

Thus God is not talking about *obedience*; but *protecting* His commandments with an (allegorical) "hedge." To the extent that this "hedge" is built; this also increases the host's resistance, thus making the enemy's current flow to the host difficult. This is similar to the hedge around Job; but here this "hedge" or the act of *shâmar* must be *chosen* to be made by *man*.

A fair argument can be made that in a sense, this "God made" "hedge" or *sûwk* in the case of Job, is or was primarily for the *material*; and the "man made" "hedge" or *shâmar* is for the *immaterial*. It could further be argued that this "God made" hedge varies with *action*; and the "man made" hedge varies with *thoughts*.

As this "hedgeogenic" resistance increases, either less current will flow; or the enemy must somehow "crank up" the voltage. And there are limits; albeit sometimes changeable; to the "voltages" available to him.

What about the hosts not merely maximizing the *resistance*, but also affecting the *voltage* applied by the enemy?

Paul told us how to do the former, in Ephesians 6:10-17. However unbeknownst to many, he also told us how to do the latter; but since it is a short phrase which appears at the end of a lengthy passage concerning numerous *defensive* measures, it generally goes unnoticed. What is important is that when this offensive measure is utilized; and this *cannot* be overemphasized; *it should never be combined with anything that is of the enemy*.

Ephesians 6:17 tells us:

> "And take the helmet of salvation,
> and the sword of the Spirit,
> which is the word of God:"²⁴

Tucked in here at the very end of a long list of defensive,

(increasing resistance), measures in all of the verses preceding verse 17, and beginning here in verse 17 after the second "and;" something rather interesting appears. In fact; therein lies a "bomb." And it is a rather interesting and quite powerful "bomb;"—the same representing the provision of a key instruction:

> *"(take) the sword of the Spirit,*
> *which is the word of God."*

This instruction is the only *offensive,* (voltage lowering), instruction given in these famous, (Ephesians 6:10-17), verses.

What does "(take) *the sword of the Spirit, which is the word of God*" actually mean?

The actual Greek word translated as "sword" is:

> "*3162* machaira; prob. fem. of a presumed der. of *3163*; a *knife,* i.e. *dirk;* fig. *war,* judicial *punishment:* - sword."[25]

As can be seen, the translation as "sword" is misleading. A dirk is not a sword. "Knife" or "Dagger" would be a better translation. These are designed for "up close and personal" combat. This is important because this, (close up and tailor made), is precisely how the enemy attacks.

The "figurative" meaning should also be noted—that of "judicial punishment." There is an old saying: "Don't stick your head in the boxing ring if you don't want to get punched." It is the enemy who chooses to institute an attack. If the result is encountering a counterattack with a dirk, and he/it leaves a bit "bloodied;" then he or it deserved it. But again, this should never be combined with anything that is of the enemy such as anger, hatred, etc. It is *justice,* ("judicial punishment"); and not *vengeance,* that should be sought. If that which is of the enemy is *at any time* utilized, this can then easily be utilized by the enemy as a foothold.

The actual Greek word translated as "spirit" is:

> "*4151* pněuma; from *4154*; a *current* of air, i.e. *breath* (*blast*) or a *breeze;* by anal. or fig. a *spirit,* i.e. (human)

the rational *soul*, (by impl.) *vital principle*, mental *disposition* etc..."[26]

Thus; "the knife of the soul" is a better translation. And precisely what is this "knife of the soul?"

It is the *"word of God."* What is this "word," and why is it a machaira or "knife?"

The actual Greek "word" translated here in Ephesians as "word" is:

"4487 rhēma; from 4483; an *utterance* (individ., collect. or spec.); by impl. a *matter* or *topic* (espec. of narration, command or dispute); with a neg. *naught* whatever..."[27]

John 1:1 tells us:

"*In the beginning was the Word,
and the Word was with God,
and the Word was God.*"[28]

However the actual Greek word translated three times here in John as "word," is not *rhēma*, but rather:

"3056 lŏgŏs; from 3004; something *said* (including the *thought*); by impl. a *topic* (subject of discourse), also *reasoning* (the mental faculty) or *motive*; by extens. a *computation*; spec. (with the art. In John) the Divine Expression (i.e. Christ)..."[29]

So it must be asked what the difference is between these two Greek words, each translated as "word?" The same being *rhēma* and *lŏgŏs*; and furthermore, why it was *rhēma* that was used in *Ephesians*; but it was *lŏgŏs* that was used in *John*?

Paul was giving us instructions for *future* behavior; and John was recollecting *past* events. Thus *rhēma*; meaning an *utterance*, refers to what God *is* or *will be* saying "real time." *Lŏgŏs* refers to what God has or had already "said."

Assuming Moses actually wrote early Genesis, what he recorded was the *rhēma* he was receiving "real time" from God; as he was not physically alive when those events in early Genesis transpired. In fact it seems no one was. (This process is what is referred to as *retrophesy* in "*MeekRaker Beginnings...*") Once it was recorded, however, and not being received "real time;" it then became *lŏgŏs*. The *means* of said recording; e.g.; oral memorization, long continuous scrolls, or today's Bible format; changes nothing with regard to this.

Thus this *rhēma* in "*word of God*," refers primarily to what God *will be* uttering "real time;" and represents the "knife" portion of this "knife of the soul." But this is not to say that in the absence of the reception of any rhēma, that lŏgŏs cannot be utilized just as Jesus did when the enemy attacked Him. It must be remembered that the enemy "ran away" after this particular event.[30]

Paul's use of *rhēma*, and not *lŏgŏs*, indicates a *preference*, but does not necessarily represent an absolute. Again, Jesus seems to have done pretty well with the: "It is written. . ." It is not clear that any *Greek* word exists, that includes both *rhēma* and *lŏgŏs*.

Thus when attacking the enemy with the "knife of the soul," *rhēma* is preferred; but *lŏgŏs* is also an option. It must be noted that both contain that which is of God; and that neither *original* verbiage contains anything which is of the enemy. ["*Original*" cannot be overstressed here, because as can be seen; translating both *rhēma* and *lŏgŏs* merely as "word," is at best inadequate.]

It should not be overlooked that the definition of *lŏgŏs* also includes "something *said* (including the *thought*)...; "*reasoning* (the mental faculty) or *motive*...;" and "the Divine *Expression* (i.e. Christ)..."

Thus contained in the definition of lŏgŏs are the various aspects; both *material* and *immaterial*; to what may seem to be mere speech or merely "saying something." This seems to confirm the immaterial component of *any* action—here speech. The *action*; the *thought*, the *reason*, and the *motive*; are all components of the actuality. And as there are equal and opposite reactions for the material part; the same will necessarily occur for the immaterial components.

It must also again be noted that according to Strong, the use of "lŏgŏs" can also refer to: "the Divine *Expression* (i.e. *Christ*)." Strong did not say Jesus; but rather: "i.e.," (Latin: *id est*), or "in other words:" "Christ." This "Divine Expression" (caps noted), thus does not likely refer to Jesus; who is *The* Christ (*the* Anointed One); but rather to *the* Christ or the Anointing itself; which of course refers to The *Holy Ghost* or Third part of the Trinity, and not to the Son, or Second part.

Thus this last part of the definition of lŏgŏs; the "Christ" or Holy Ghost part of lŏgŏs; seems to also describe a complete process such as: "Let there be light" and there was light. Again there is equal and opposite reactions as the result of the exercise of will.

Some of this "Word," (lŏgŏs), is contained in the Bible; most especially in The, (believed by many to be ten), Commandments. Some of this Word is in Science; some is in Mathematics; and some is found in Justice. In fact; wherever there is truth—therein is found the Word (lŏgŏs) of God.

Omniscience means that; among other things; there is nothing to learn. The enemy is not omniscient. [The temptation to state "in any way omniscient" is resisted here, as omniscience is a binary.] Ergo; the enemy can and does learn. When he encounters "judicial punishment" attacks via the "dirk or knife of the soul—which is 'the Word of God;'" he remembers to: "Be careful with that one. He's crazy. He 'knows what time it is,' and he fights back—and it hurts. I've still got the scars to prove it."

This will have a serious effect at the applied "voltage," forcing him to return at a more opportune time. It must remembered that in order to *return*, he must first *depart*. . . shall we say *retreat*?

The basic premise of Chiropractic; is that there is a Vital Life Force or "Innate Intelligence" which maintains the human body. According to Chiropractic, this force is 100% perfect; 100% of the time. It needs no help, but any interference results in disease, (dis-ease). There are analogous beliefs in acupuncture, and homeopathy—albeit each with different means of "remediation."

Chiropractic is concerned primarily with *material* interference to this VLF or Innate Intelligence. Thus; Chiropractors find levels of *material* interference to the expression of this *immaterial* intelligence, and remove this material interference. This material interference occurs *after* this immaterial intelligence enters the material realm of the body, and for Chiropractors, this is the nervous system.

As previously addressed, this intelligence is contained in this "breath of life" referenced in Genesis: *"and breathed into his nostrils the breath of life; and man became a living soul."*

Thus this VLF or Innate Intelligence originates in the *immaterial*, and by design is then received in the *material*; with its purpose being to maintain the material human vessel in a state of "health." When *material* interference occurs; such as in the nervous system by mechanical pressure; Chiropractors remove this material interference.

Years ago, Chiropractors had an interesting "joke," or perhaps a "ha-ha" would be a better description.

"Subluxation Above Atlas" was an intra-professional term that referred to various levels of mental insanity. This was generally stated in friendly manner. Since the atlas is the first vertebra, "Subluxation Above Atlas" referred to interference with that which was *above* the first vertebra, meaning a problem with the mental processes. [Practitioners of *craniopathy* excluded here.]

However; there may have been some degree of serendipitous wisdom in this term—

Is it such a certainty that interference with the VLF or Innate Intelligence can only take place in the *material* realm? *Material* things can interfere with the expression of the VLF or Innate Intelligence at the *material* level—but what about interference to this VLF occurring at the *immaterial* level?

Is there something in the immaterial realm that *would* or *could* benefit from causing *immaterial* interference to this immaterial VLF or Innate Intelligence in "hosts" (H. Sapiens); who according to the

Bible; are by design, brought into existence primarily to wage war against said entity?

The answer to the "would" part of course is a resounding yes. After all what entity would not wish to decrease the productivity and longevity of *its* enemy? Surely there is ample motive.

But with regard to the "could" part, although this *seems* a bit more complex; in actuality only requires "connecting the dots" that have already been addressed.

Ask any competent physician: "When does sickness or disease occur?" The answer is when the external invasive forces overcome the internal resistive forces. Generally this involves the *material* realm: e.g.; invasive microorganisms. This can also be said of various types of physical trauma such as fractures.

This very same rule applies in the *immaterial* realm, as was previously addressed in Ohms law.

As previously stated:

> *"However; just as in Ohm's law, in order for this to work, there must be the load, and that load of course is the host. But being made in the image and likeness of God; that load (host) is not a particularly good conductor for the enemy's "current;" which necessarily means that the host is a particularly good resistor. In order to maximize the current flow for a given voltage; the enemy will also lower the host's resistance."*

It is important to understand the (true) actuality of "sin." The Greek word for "sin" often used in the New Testament is:

> "264 hamartanō; perh. from 1 (as a neg. particle) and the base of 3313; prop. to miss the mark (and so not share in the prize), i.e. (fig.) to err, esp. (mor.)..."[31]

The *reality* of sin, or that which is *perceived*; is generally limited to the action or inaction itself. However; again, it is the *actuality* of sin which truly exists, and "it is what it is;" independent of any limitations of *perception*, resulting in insufficient *reality*.

Here with *hamartanō*, we have the true twofold explanation of "sin." Not only is there error involved, but there is a subsequent and necessary *result* of this error. Here in this definition, the same being: "and so not share in the prize." The "and so" here reasonably meaning: "and so therefore because of this."

Thus this definition of *hamartanō*, tells us that the actuality of sin is twofold. Sin is not just the act of lying stealing, etc.; but rather both that portion and also the "and so therefore because of this." However; in this particular definition, to "not share in the prize," implies that a "zero" is possible. Meaning; that the consequence of sin could be merely to not obtain something of positive value. However this would necessarily require that there would be *no* "MA" for the "F;" no equal and opposite reactions; unless the "F" was positive in nature. Hence if this were true, one would reap what was sown if and only if it was positive; and reap nothing "no sharing in the prize" for negative actions.

Any and all actions, (and sometimes inactions); represent an actuality with two distinct but related components. The first being the *perceived* action; and the second being the, (secondary but necessary), *result(s)* of that action. Simply because the result is not contemplated matters little. One cannot have any action, without an equal and opposite reaction. Opposite here meaning: *towards* the source of the original action.

Thus; choosing the sinful behavior is always a matter of choosing the *twofold* actuality of sin; and not any erroneous *partial* perception—as ignorance of these laws changing nothing. When one chooses the actuality, one receives the actuality.

The laws of the universe care not one whit about any deficient perceptions. Sin is always a "package deal." Whatever behavior one chooses; one is also choosing and is bound to the *result*, as they are inextricably linked.

This is not to say that nothing can be done to mitigate any undesired result(s), as the creation of additional forces; e.g.; repentance, prayer for forgiveness, restitution etc.; can often mitigate circumstances. What is important to understand and remember; is that they *always* come together as a unit.

Following is a short excerpt from *"MeekRaker Beginnings. . .,"* Chapter 9: *"Job's Predicament."*

"The following is likely the first great misconception which is purported to be in the Book of Job; as appearing in Job 1:8:

> *"The LORD said to Satan,*
> *"Have you considered My servant Job?*
> *For there is no one like him on the earth,*
> *a blameless and upright man,*
> *fearing God and turning away from evil."*[MR1]

"In this passage, God appears to be offering up Job to the devil, and inquiring as to whether or not the devil would be interested in Job; this being precisely what many believe to in fact to be the case. But this really does not make any particular amount of sense. Firstly, God is not going to help the devil by suggesting or offering up Job. And secondly, an omniscient God would have known from the beginning of time what Satan's answer to this question was to be; as well as the very reason for which the devil was approaching Him at this time.

"In all fairness, it must be noted that some of the versions do contain a footnote to 1:8; which indicates that the original words that were correctly translated as "set thy heart on," were for some reason later supplanted by the word "considered."

"The *Interlinear Bible* confirms this: "Have you set your heart on" translation, as the correct translation of the original verse.[MR2]

"Now it is also fair to say, that the same argument as to why God asked Satan something that God already knew, can be raised with respect to the proper translation and understanding of this question. (And as though somehow Satan would actually tell God the truth.) In fact, the very same question is repeated, and again asked of the devil again in Job 2:3.[MR3] Of course God knew the answer to this question. It was not asked twice or even once because God was in need of this or any other type of information from Satan; neither is Satan known to be a reliable source for truth.

"The most reasonable explanation being that this was actually offered as a warning to the devil, in a question form. "Have you set your heart on my servant Job?" A more contemporary translation or translations being: "Are you really sure you want to do this?;" or; "Can I change your mind about doing this?," etc. Most people being given this type of warning by God would immediately reconsider. But not the devil, instead he starts complaining about how God is protecting Job etc.

"Job 1:9-12 tells us:

> "*Then Satan answered the* LORD,
> "*Does Job fear God for nothing?*
> "*Have You not made a hedge about him*
> *and his house and all that he has,*
> *on every side?*
>
> *You have blessed the work of his hands,*
> *and his possessions have increased in the land.*
>
> *But put forth Your hand now*
> *and touch all that he has;*
> *he will surely curse You to Your face."*
>
> *Then the* LORD *said to Satan,*
> "*Behold, all that he has is in your power,*
> *only do not put forth your hand on him."*
> *So Satan departed from*
> *the presence of the* LORD."[MR4]

"This represents classic Satan behavior. First he pollutes Job's mind with all of this doubt and subsequent fear. Then, after falling for Satan's meanderings, Job becomes terrified about the welfare of his sons, makes these continual burnt offerings; which establishes the **f₍t₎**, and then Satan comes to God for permission to deliver the **ma**. And deliver this **ma** he did."[32] [Excerpt from: "*MeekRaker Beginnings...*" Chapter 9: "*Job's Predicament.*" © 2016 QPG, LLC All Rights Reserved. Reprinted by permission]
[It must be noted that the lower case "f," rather than the upper case "F" was utilized. The use of the lower case represents the "force of *fear*."]

Here in Job, the enemy is instructed that all he (Job) *has* is in your, (the enemy's), *power*; but to "*not put forth your hand on him,*" (Job). If it were the case that the enemy was generally *not* permitted to "*put forth your* (Satan's) *hand on*" a host; there would be little or no need for this instruction. Ergo; this ("*not put forth your hand on him*"), represents an *unusual* situation.

Thus; no other reasonable explanation exists other than the *usual* situation, is that Satan *is* in fact permitted to: "*put forth your* (his or Satan's) *hand*" on a host, as a result of said host's behavior.

How is it that an immaterial entity such as Satan; is in any way capable of putting his "*hand*" upon a material host, or anything material for that matter? Immaterial entities are not known for having any "hands." [Neither are *snakes*, (nachash), known to have legs or feet. But that is another matter. (see Genesis 3:14)]

It is interesting that Strong's provides no original Hebrew word for the word translated here as "hand" in verse 12—there simply is nothing listed. However the *Interlinear Bible* indicates that this word translated here as "hand" is: "3027 yâd."[33]

Strong's defines yâd as:

"3027 yâd; a prim. word; a *hand* (the *open* one [indicating *power*, *means*, *direction*, etc.]. in distinction from 3079, the *closed* one)..."[34]

Therefore; the "unusuality" of this situation, is that Job is being protected from the usage of Satans's yâd; or his "power, means, (and) direction;" upon him *directly*. Instead Satan is only permitted to use the same only upon *"all that he has."* Indirect attacks were okay here; but *direct* attacks were strictly forbidden.

Unlike the "normal" situation where Satan *is* permitted to "put on" or use his "hand" or "yâd... power, means, direction, etc." directly; here Job is being protected by God and God makes this quite clear to the enemy.

And we are or were told why earlier in Job 1:8: *"For there is no one like him on the earth, a blameless and upright man, fearing God and turning away from evil."*

So unless one fits the above unique: *"for there is no one like him on the earth"* description of Job, one should not expect the same type of protection. Meaning: that the result of sin will likely be that Satan *is* permitted to "put on" or use his "hand;" (albeit an *open* and not a *closed* "hand"); or "yâd... power, means, direction, etc.;" *directly* upon us most, or at least some of the time. In a sense, here again the *actuality* of sin, includes the enemy having "permission to attack" or "judicial punishment;" as is also the case when attacking the *enemy*.

The universe respects the free will of H. Sapiens. When one chooses sin, the "sin" is always accompanied by the result [equal and opposite] of this sin. So it is understood that the "chooser" is in fact choosing the "undesired" result, as well and as the "desired" part of the "sin." [Again, "opposite" here in this usage, means *toward* the active party.]

As clearly seen in Job, behavior alters the *hedge* or *resistance* of H. Sapiens or hosts. And as previously seen in "Ohms law," and as seen with respect to *disease*; lowered resistance permits the entrance of undesirable and dangerous forces. Too low resistance in an electrical circuit permits an increased flow of electrons; which can damage or destroy the components. Too low *physical* resistance can permit the entrance of pathological microorganisms, which can damage or destroy the physical body. And too low a *"spiritual"* or *"immaterial"* resistance, can permit the entrance of the "hand" or "yâd... *power*, *means*, *direction*, etc." of the enemy—something from which Job was protected.

The enemy has the *motive*.

The enemy has the *means*.

What he or it *lacks* and is looking for; is the *opportunity*. And it is the lowered resistance or hedge; which is part of the "other side" of the actuality of sin; that provides him or it with this opportunity.

This is balance. The rules that apply with regard to attacking the enemy with the "the knife of the soul;" which is the "*Word of God*" in all of its forms; and even in a sense the "judicial punishment;" also apply to the enemy with respect to attacking H. Sapiens. The fact that most people simply "read over;" and therefore *miss* these *offensive* instructions *against* the enemy notwithstanding.

After all, if the enemy is subject to "judicial punishment" as the direct result of his choosing to act against the will of God; then this rule is the same for any other entity who chooses to act against the will of God. The main difference is that the enemy knows the rules, and collects. Those of "faith" generally do not know "the rules," and therefore generally do not collect. And often even those that do *know*, do not *understand* that this is *war*.

Satan means adversary; but this is only with respect to God; as despite Satan's wishes and beliefs; God cannot be killed. With respect to man however, the name "Satan" represents an understated term; as Satan can and in fact does cause the *physical*; (and he hopes also the *spiritual*); death of hosts. But Satan cannot ever do it alone.

God is about order and balance. Satan is about disorder and imbalance; i.e.; "creating chaos."

There are many types of "disorder" and "chaos" for which Satan is responsible. However the subject here is *immaterial* interference to the VLF or "Innate Intelligence," and the role of this interference in causing disease, and "premature" physical death.

If the "miracles" contained in the Bible are carefully analyzed, they fall into two categories: Those that actually violate natural law; and those that only *appear* to violate natural law. A miracle can only be a miracle—*if it violates natural law*.

With respect to the "miracles" of the "healing of the sick," the same is true. Again, the key difference is generally evidence of immediate physical changes. If a withered hand *instantaneously* is no longer withered; then this violates natural law and is a true miracle. However if disease is cured without any evidence of violation of natural law; then this represents not a miracle; but a matter of *authority* and *force*. And simply because this mechanism of "authority and force" is not known or understood; this does not necessarily or automatically cause the event to rise to the level of a true miracle.

This "authority and force," is merely the removal of the interference to the VLF. Once the interference is removed, then "normal" healing processes ensue.

It would be remiss to not address the following, which appears in Genesis 6:3.

Genesis 6:3 tells us:

> "And the LORD said, My spirit shall not always strive with man, for that he also is flesh: yet his days shall be an hundred and twenty years."[35]

Two approaches can be taken with respect to this verse:

The first would be that this translation means precisely what it seems to say. Namely; that man is supposed to live to one hundred and twenty years—which is precisely how long Moses is believed to have lived.

It must be noted however, that although this falls far short of the lifespan of many of those in the early Biblical passages; this, (120 years), represents an increase in longevity of about 50% over today's average lifespan.

The second approach would be that it means something else. The same of course meaning; that this translation, or the "common understanding" of this translation, is less than accurate.

If this passage; Genesis 6:3; is examined in *context*; i.e.; by examining the two verses *preceding* Genesis 6:3, and the verse immediately *following* it; perhaps some clarity can be obtained:

Genesis 6:1 tells us:

> *"And it came to pass,*
> *when men began to multiply*
> *on the face of the earth,*
> *and daughters were born unto them,"*[36]

Here in verse 1, is described what many would consider as a "no-brainer." As man, (*"men"*), would begin to *"multiply on the face of the earth,"* one would reasonably expect that approximately 50% of this "multiplication" would be female.

However; that, (the "no-brainer"), is not what the passage is actually stating. Rather; this passage is setting up the timeframe, or the "when" for the introduction of an event described in the very next (Genesis 6:2) verse:

Genesis 6:2 then tells us what this event was:

> *"That the sons of God saw the daughters*
> *of men that they were fair;*
> *and they took them wives*
> *of all which they chose."*[37]

Here in verse 2, other participants are introduced into the event. These are in addition to the *"men"* and *"daughters"* referenced in verse 1—with this reference to the same now being these *"sons of God."* Here at this juncture; (the "set up" for the beginning of the previously cited verse 3); there are actually now *three* groups or classifications present. Here these are the original *"men,"* the *"daughters;"* and now there are the *"sons of God."*

A clear distinction is being made here with respect to those who were *bearing* the "daughters," (*"men"* representing both genders of course); and these *"sons of God"* who *"took them wives of all which they chose."* Here it was not the *"daughters"* of the *"sons of God"* whom these "*sons of God*" were "taking;" but rather the "*daughters*" of "*men.*"

Who were these "*sons of God?*"

The very next thing that follows these two verses, is the "120 year rule" from the aforementioned verse 3: "*And the LORD said, My spirit shall not always strive with man, for that he also is flesh: yet his days shall be an hundred and twenty years.*"

The verse appearing *after* this "120 year rule" contained in Genesis 6:3, is Genesis 6:4; and provides some pertinent information.

Genesis 6:4 tells us:

> "*The Nephilim were on the earth in those days, and also afterward, when the sons of God came in to the daughters of men, and they bore children to them. Those were the mighty men who were of old, men of renown.*"[38]

The following is an excerpt from "*MeekRaker Beginnings. . . Chapter 10: 'The Slanderer:'*"

"This is a very interesting, but easily misread passage. Nephilim is the word: "5303 nephiyl, or nephil, from 5307; prop., a *feller*, i.e. a *bully* or *tyrant*: - giant. 5307 naphal, a prim. root; to *fall*, in a great variety of applications (intrans. or causat., lit. or fig.)..."[MR5]

"The way this verse is normally interpreted, demons (fallen angels) had sexual relations with human women, and giants were the offspring of this union. These giants thus representing beings which were half human and half demon. This is the passage that is generally used to substantiate this theory.

"The problem with this theory; is that this passage in no way reasonably substantiates any such thing. It states that the Nephilim were on the earth already and afterwards, when the sons of God had sexual relations with daughters of men. It does not state when *they* (the Nephilum) had relations, but rather when the *Sons of God* had relations; thus making a distinction between the two. The *"them"* then referring to the Sons of God, to whom the children were born; and not the Nephilim.

"This demon theory also must presuppose that demons are to be considered "Sons of God." An argument would then logically follow that Messiah was the only begotten demon; which of course makes no sense. It also then follows that these Nephilim, half human half-demon beings are the ones who were of old and renown.

"An alternate read would be that the mention of the Nephilim is merely to state the relative time when the events of the rest of the verse occurred. Thus in this reading, the Nephilim were on the earth, but are otherwise unrelated to the remainder of the passage. It would then actually be those from the other side (the Hebrews) who were these Sons of God; who then had sexual relations with the gentile daughters, or daughters of the (gentile) men, and bore children to them; the children then being half gentile and half Hebrew."[39] [Excerpt from: *"MeekRaker Beginnings..."* Chapter 10: *"The Slanderer"* © 2016 QPG, LLC All Rights Reserved. Reprinted by permission]

Thus it seems that these referenced *"sons of God,"* are or were those Hebrews; (ones from the "other side" of the *gan* or garden); the offspring of Adam, who (Adam), was *formed* by God from *something,* and not *created* from *nothing*—and within the past ten thousand years. These Hebrews were God's *chosen* people, because they were *chosen* for the bloodline for Messiah.

And these referenced *"men,"* are or were the offspring of

those (the gentiles) who were *created* by God from *nothing*, perhaps hundreds of thousand of years ago.

Today "gentile" is synonymous with "non-Jewish," and in a certain very limited sense this can be true. However; the actual meaning of gentile refers to those "men" who were *created* and their offspring; such as the original *Chaldeans* who attacked Job; who lived on the earth long before, (and long after), the formation of Adam. This is why there is so much *Chaldean* in the Hebrew language.

Thus the *"man,"* (singular of "men"), referred to in Genesis 6:3 stated to have a lifespan of 120 years, is or are the *gentiles*; and not the *"sons of God"* or Hebrews.

Why is it that God seems to be playing favorites here? If it is assumed that being exempt from this "120 year rule" is simply a matter of genetics; then this would appear to be the case. After all, precisely how is it that one's parents are chosen?

However it is not a matter of *genetics*, but rather a matter of *knowledge*. It is *knowledge* of God's system, (and working within it), that increases longevity; and it is not merely a matter of one's ancestors. Through His Word one learns the system. And it was the Hebrews who at that time had this knowledge.

Perhaps a more modern translation of:

> *"And the LORD said, My spirit shall not always strive with man, for that he also is flesh: yet his days shall be an hundred and twenty years."*

would be:

> "I can only provide truth. If after 120 years of 'striving,' and they still insist on worshiping these false and dead "gods;" then that's it. I can only go so far in trying to get them to understand the rules, and it would be unfair and create a substantial imbalance to even try to do any more. After 120 years of being a hard head, (non-Meek—cannot be Raked); it "aint a gonna" soften."

Another view from a different perspective—

When the word *Kabbalah* in any of its various spellings is mentioned, generally ideas of some evil religion that should be avoided come to mind. The fact is that Kabbalah is actually not a "religion;" has nothing to do with "voodoo;" and simply means *"to receive."*

It is true that Kabbalah professes many things that are inconsistent with Judeo/Christian tenets. The best example being the Kabbalistic view of Satan; which Kabbalists pronounce as "Suh-tan"—which is different from the Judeo/Christian pronunciation of "Say-tun." The Kabbalistic view seems to be that "Suh-tan" is actually deliberately provided as a means of human self-improvement.

This view is inconsistent with the Judeo/Christian belief that man was created in the image and likeness of God, and thus needs no improvement because of faulty design.

One might try to argue that this "image and likeness" is only the case in the first incarnation, and thus in subsequent incarnations improvements are required because faults are passed on with subsequent incarnations. Although this is clearly beyond the scope of this monograph; one would nevertheless be left asking the *cause* of the need for *any* improvements to a being *initially* created in the image and likeness of God. [See *"Reincarnation —A Reasonable Inquiry"*]

Thus either way; it seems that any need for improvement of H. Sapiens arises because of H. Sapien's succumbing to Satan's previous attacks. Satan is thus the *cause* of the need for improvement; and is *not* deliberately provided to assist in the correction of any "pre-existing conditions."

It is true that one can improve one's state by learning from one's mistakes—particularly as a result of the arrival of the "equal and opposite reaction" to sin. But without previous attacks; (as was the case with Adam for some period of time); there would simply be no need.

Nevertheless; the Kabbalistic concept of *Tikkune* merits some consideration. *Tikkune* is essentially the process of correcting one's faults.

It is unclear "Kabbalistically" whether *Tikkune* represents the correction of an individual's faults, or the discovery of an individual's true purpose in life; or both—meaning that the correction and the discovery of one's true purpose are two aspects of the same actuality. It is also unclear "Kabbalistically," as to whether said true purpose in life; according to Tikkune; represents anything beyond the correction of these personal faults.

If so; that is; that fault correction represents the true and only purpose of life; this also can conflict or not conflict with Judeo-Christian tenets. If it is supposed that the Bible is a book about *redemption*; which is something that is generally considered to be true; then one should reasonably and logically inquire as to precisely what it is that is to be redeemed.

If it is believed that it is only man himself that requires redemption; then this would be consistent with what this possible "true purpose" often suggested as the "true purpose" of Tikkune may represent. However; there seems to be no logical reason as to why God would have set up this type of system.

If however, the position is taken that redemption goes beyond personal redemption, and in fact includes the redemption of the earth; then things begin to make a bit more sense. But again, most erroneously believe that Genesis 1:2 merely represents a part of the *process* by which earth was created.

Genesis 1:2 tells us:

> "And the earth was without form, and void;
> and darkness was upon the face of the deep.
> And the Spirit of God moved
> upon the face of the waters."[40]

However; there is a much more compelling argument that this is not so, and that the earth was actually completed at the end of

Genesis 1:1—as after all, that is precisely what is stated. [see "*MeekRaker Beginnings* . . ." for irrefutable evidence in support of this position.]

Thus with this latter position, the redemptive process of the earth actually began in this second sentence of Genesis 1:2. At some unspecified time, God then created man as hosts or tsâbâ', to continue this redemptive process. This was due not to any lack in God's *capabilities*, but rather a matter of *authority*.

Tikkune is at a minimum, concerned with the removal of what Kabbalists call *Klipot*; or shells, rinds, husk's etc. According to Kabbalah, these Klipot block "the Light," or God.

If it can be stipulated that these Klipot are created as the result of behaviors inconsistent with will of God, and/or his rules; then these Klipot are created as a result of man's behavior. If it can be further stipulated, that these Klipot block "the Light" or God; then an interesting and pertinent illustration arises.

When Klipot are created because of what most would call "sinful behavior;" then there exists some blockage of "the Light" or God; including all of the emanations of God; which necessarily includes the VLF or Innate Intelligence.

Thus although this VLF or Innate Intelligence is 100% perfect 100% of the time at the source of its immaterial *transmission*; these Klipot can interfere with its *reception* by the desired person. Thus the immaterial *reception* of these blocked or interfered with emissions is less than 100% perfect. Since these emissions are responsible for maintaining the health of the human physical vessel, the result would then necessarily be physical sickness, and/or physical death.

It must be asked as to whether this Tikkune process can remove currently existing Klipot; and if so whether or not *all* currently existing Klipot; and whether they are removed partially or completely; or if it is the case only future Klipot can be prevented. It must also be asked if any of this actually matters.

The reason why this might not actually matter, is that H. Sapiens are under constant *attack* by Say-tun, and are not being in any way directly or indirectly *assisted* by Suh-tan. In order to prevent *all* future Klipot, any given H. Sapien would have to immediately achieve *perfection* in behavior; which is essentially impossible when under constant attack, and in fact was only ever achieved by One. The same can be said for removing any existing Klipot. If there is a mechanism by which Tikkune could remove all currently existing Klipot; the same level of perfection would likely be required for sustaining the complete removal.

Thus at this juncture; physical life and death represents a binary; and physical death is a certainty; as any level of Klipot will block a corresponding amount of VLF or Innate Intelligence. And the result of any amount of VLF or Innate Intelligence blockage results is some degree of physical dysfunction, and thus ultimately physical death.

However; neither longevity nor physical health are a binary. The more upright the behavior, the fewer Klipot. The fewer Klipot; the less interference. The less interference, the greater the reception of the 100% VLF or Innate Intelligence. The greater the reception of the VLF or Innate Intelligence, the healthier one is, and the longer one lives.

CONCLUSION

There is an immaterial world or realm. There must be. This is a necessity, from both the scientific and the "spiritual" viewpoints.

Science refers to the creation of the material universe, with said *process* commonly referred to as the "Big Bang" theory. The creation of the *material* universe necessarily represents an *effect* of something else. Science has no reasonable idea what that "something else" might be. That "something else" is of course necessarily the *cause* for the *effect* known as the creation of the material universe. [Just as an aside; this is where difficulties ultimately arise, as eventually there must be a *primium movens* or prime mover, or the *initial* cause. God is considered to be the causeless effect, which then caused everything else to be brought into existence. It seems that science currently has no plausible equivalent.]

Since the cause for this effect known as the creation of the universe: AKA: "The Big Bang;"" had to have existed *before* the manifestation of the effect; said *cause* had to reside *in*, and be delivered *from*, "somewhere." Since it could not have resided in the yet to be created material universe, it must have been "somewhere," other than the yet to be created material universe. Hobson's choice is that the source of this cause had to be an, or the, *immaterial* realm.

Even a Bible skeptic knows that the Bible tells us that God created the heavens and the earth. Where was God when He created the heavens and the earth? The answer is not stated. However as previously concluded; He could not have been in the material realm, ("the heavens and the earth"); until He created them ("the heavens and the earth"). Ergo; He was in, ("Who art in"), *an*, or *the immaterial* realm, prior to the creation of the *material* realm.

As previously discussed, any time a decision is made to act or even sometimes to not act is brought into fruition, this represents two causes or imbalances. Thus there are two effects:

One effect is the balancing of the imbalance created in the *material* realm: "I threw the rock." Where the rock ended up is a simple material vector analysis. [A vector is a quantity with both magnitude and direction.] Thus as long as these factors are known, the rock's path and destination can be scientifically predicted. A spacecraft being sent to the moon, is essentially throwing a big rock—albeit with incredible force and precision.

The other effect is concerned with *why* one threw the rock. Depending on what the reason(s) is or are, different *causes* or *immaterial* imbalances are created. "I was mad and wanted to hit it in the head;" and "I had to stop that wild animal from attacking him;" represent entirely different causes. Thus even though the *material* forces might in fact be exactly the same; the imbalances created in the *immaterial* are entirely different. Thus the *effects* (equal and opposite reactions) of these created *causes* likewise will be entirely different.

Newton's "equal and opposite reactions," which apply in the *material*; also apply in the *immaterial*. This is sometimes referred to as *karma* or "reaping what one sowed." Jesus was advising on proper behavior, and not trying to provide analyses when he said to: "Do unto others as you would have them do unto you." The reason for this: is that whatever one does do unto others, will in fact ultimately also be done to him.

Here actions and reasons are being treated as two separate (material and immaterial) causes; but in fact they are actually one. Choosing to throw that rock in the material, includes also choosing, (as the result of the *reason*), the immaterial effects—effects which will ultimately; but not necessarily immediately; return to the material.

We are told that man is initially brought into existence in "the image and likeness of God." This can be represented by "A." This is not to say that this "image and likeness" represents in any way the *totality* of God; but rather that whatever man is when brought into existence, is entirely consistent with God. Man or "A" is a subset of that set which is known as "God." Man may only represent a *partial* expression of God, but this partial expression is entirely consistent with the totality—for at least a nanosecond.

If it can be stipulated that the enemy wishes to change the "nature" of man, he must introduce these desired, (by the enemy), changes. These changes can be represented by "B."

What is this "B?" "B" is anything that is *not* consistent with this image and likeness of God. Thus "B" represents the *polar opposite* of anything that is in the image and likeness of God.

And just as man or "A" does not represent the *totality* of God; "B" rarely if ever can represent the opposite of the *totality* of mans portion of the "image and likeness" of God or "A." This is not because the enemy *would* not have this "B" be of the same magnitude as "A;" but simply and solely because he *cannot*, as opposed to "*will not.*"

Thus it may *seem* that this could be expressed as "A - B = C;" with the resultant, or man's *condition* at any given time represented by "C."

However; given the actual circumstances it seems prudent to be better to always express this "B" in "A - B = C;" as "−A" to some extent in terms of *quality*, or *polarity*; but not in terms of *quantity*, or *magnitude*. Thus this: "A - B = C" equation does not hold; as: "A" − "-A" would in actuality be: "A" + "A." It is better understood as: "A + (-A) = C." This may seem unimportant, but it must be remembered that the enemy *introduces* factors that neutralize that which is of God.

Man spends very little time as "A." The overwhelming majority of the time man is "C." In fact for all practical purposes "A" can be ignored; and the status of man is "C." However this "C;" unlike a strictly numerical equation; retains any and all of the original "A" that was unchanged by the addition of "B, (−A)."

With the addition of "B," (or what is actually by design equal to "−A,"), to the original "A;" there is a "neutralization" of some of the magnitude of the original "A." This is what results in man's condition at any given time, or "C." If the enemy is able to add a negative; say neutralizing the "thou shall not steal" part of man, and the man is now a thief; this may not have any effect whatsoever upon the man telling a falsehood—although in many ways lying is in fact theft.

Neither is there any guaranteed permanency to the particulars of a given "C," at any given time. The thief may get arrested and punished, and not steal again. (Some of the best addiction counselors are former addicts.) Or a thief may steal a copy of this very Monograph, read it; and then understand that any perceived benefits from stealing are only temporary, and will ultimately be removed—likely with substantial interest charged.

This same "fluid" state exists with *immaterial* attacks on Innate Intelligence or the VLF. The actual percentage of the 100% perfect VLF *immaterially received* by man, (as opposed to reductions because of any subsequent VLF *material* interference); is a *variable* which depends upon how much of this "B" the enemy is able to introduce into the host, as per "Ohm's law."

Although it is essentially impossible to truly know, (science); or to truly understand, (wisdom); the immaterial realm—at least as of this writing; this nevertheless provides no license for not trying to derive some semblance of the processes, as well as the rules involved. Simply because something is not known or understood, in no way changes the fact that man must deal with the emanations from this realm—both "good" and "bad."

This *immaterial* interference to the VLF or Innate Intelligence likely occurs in two *direct* forms:

The *first* and easiest to visualize, would be the reduction of the amount of VLF received by the host. This would be analogous to, a simple blockage of the transmission, resulting in less than 100% reception of this force. This is similar to "closing the blinds," in order to reduce (block) the amount of light entering a room. This is similar to the *classical* explanation of *material* nerve interference by chiropractors. But chiropractors are concerned with *material* interference of this immaterial VLF, which is different than the *immaterial* interference under discussion.

The *second* direct form, would be to introduce *additional* emissions. Unlike a *blockage*, the creation of these additional emissions is like "jamming" a radio signal. The introduction of additional emissions produces errors; and likely produces them in two ways.

First is simply by the reception of these nonsense emissions. These are unnecessary and unwanted *additions* to the VLF which are simply nonsense; and thus disrupt the functioning of the VLF.

This is the *actual* belief of many chiropractors, in that in addition to *material* nerve interference *blocking* nerve impulses, *aberrant* impulses are created at the site of this mechanical impingement. But again, chiropractic is concerned with *material* interference, which is different than *immaterial* interference to the VLF.

And the *second* way these spurious "additional emissions" cause error; is likely the mixing of these nonsensical signals with both themselves and normal signals; (heterodyning); producing two *additional* signals; one equal to their sum and one equal to their difference.

There are three ways with which this *immaterial* interference to the VLF can be dealt:

The first is to do nothing. This is the predominant method, as here there is no general recognition of this *immaterial* VLF interference. Rather; the *material results* of this interference are "treated;" but unfortunately can only be treated up to a certain point.

The second is to modify the nature of these interfered with VLF signals at the site of reception. Meaning; that the VLF is modified by some type of "treatment" directly on or to the person. Homeopathy and Traditional Chinese Medicine [particularly Acupuncture, Moxibustion etc.] represent examples of this.

The main problem with the latter; (Traditional Chinese Medicine); is their current belief in "Deism" rather than "Theism." Since unlike Theism, which purports that there is an *active* God; Deism purports that although there is a God, He is currently not active. Why does this matter? Because without an active God, the *source* of the VLF is thus necessarily *internal*, or from within; rather than *external*, or from without. In fact; because of this change, that which used to be known as "Tao" was changed, and is now referred to as "Dao."

The third method is to remove the interference at its source. Christian Science touches upon this concept; however Christian Science is a *religion*. This is stated with no disrespect to religion in general, or Christian Science in the particular. But any religion represents a system; which although is generally formed based upon belief(s); is involved in many other activities and aspects of the lives of its members.

Modern day Christianity is almost exclusively involved with He who is the Anointed one, (Jesus); and not the *Anointing* Itself, (Christos), or the *source* of this anointing, (The Holy Ghost). "Christ" was not Jesus' last name. He is known as "The Christ," because of this Anointing—Jesus the Christ means Jesus the Anointed One.

The Holy Ghost, or the *third* part of The Trinity provided the

Anointing to the Son, or the *second* part of the Trinity; with said anointing being known as "Christos." A fair read of The Book Acts shows that the concern at that time was in fact largely this "Christos" or anointing by the Holy Ghost or the third part of the Trinity, and *not* almost exclusively the Son—hence the name: "Acts."

Nevertheless; major religions today are grouped under a title, (Christianity); that was named such because of the capabilities of the Third part of the Trinity, and not the Second part of the Trinity; but are now almost exclusively concerned with the *Second* part of the Trinity, or the Son. This *inclusion* of the Son is both necessary and good. It is the virtual *exclusion* of the Holy Ghost that is the problem; as this, (Third Part) is where; even for Jesus, (Second Part); true miraculous power (dunamis) is found.

But how does one "remove the interference at its source?" In order to answer this question, a distinction must be made. There is a clear difference between *ectoparisitosis* or oppression; and *endoparisitosis* or possession—albeit with the point of transition often unclear.

Bacteria and demonic forces are both ubiquitous. In the material, if one is not careful, bacteria; being opportunistic entities; can and will *oppress* a host, creating a *parasitic* relationship between itself and the host. Meaning; that the bacteria will derive benefit at the expense of the host.

This parasitic relationship can be superficial and largely a nuisance, such as a small skin wound that has become "infected." Like with most battles, if the host engages in activities that the "parasite" does not like; this then begins a "reverse parasitic" relationship, in that the *host* is now acting in a manner believed to be to the benefit of the host and to the detriment of the bacteria. Keeping the area clean, and applying antiseptic will usually cause enough disturbances, that the tissue will heal faster than the invader can repair itself and its colony, or *nidus*. Here the microorganism is attacking from without, and is trying to get inside.

Or; this parasitic relationship can *increase* to the benefit of the invader with commensurate damage to the host. Impetigo, (from

Latin *impetere* to attack),[41] is substantially more serious than "a small skin wound that has become infected," even though the same microorganism; *S. Aureus*; may be the "attacker." Here not always, but often; more serious and much more aggressive measures are required; including intervention by a third party, and often with the introduction of restricted chemical substances such as antibiotics. Here again the microorganism is attacking from without, but its "foot is in the door" and it is trying to get inside.

Once this or any other invading microorganism can truly get inside; i.e.; infectious systemic disease; matters change dramatically. At this juncture; unlike the previous two examples; the microorganism is now *within* and is attacking outward from within. Normally the VLF or Innate Intelligence is considered to operate "ADIO"—Above, Down, Inside, Out. Once infectious disease reaches a certain point, and subsequently begins to act from inside out; this can supplant the normal "IO" portion of "ADIO."

The first two examples above, represent material *ectoparisitosis* or oppression. The third example represents material *endoparisitosis* or possession—again, with the actual point of transition often unclear.

There are *immaterial* equivalents to the above three examples of material attack, or *impetere*. Just like bacteria, demonic forces attempt *ectoparisitosis*, or *oppression*, on an ongoing basis. As previously stated, it is when the external invasive forces overcome the internal resistive forces that sickness or disease occurs—both in the *material* and in the *immaterial*.

In the case of the *material*, these external invasive forces can increase simply as a matter of environment. Meaning; that if one spends time in an enclosed room with a large group of people who have contracted an infectious disease, the external invasive forces are dramatically increased. Thus it becomes quite likely that the normal internal resistive forces will be overcome, with the result being the "contraction" of this disease.

In the case of the *immaterial*, it is a bit different. As one behaves in a manner consistent with the Will of God; this will attract that which is *not* of God; e.g.; *demons*.

This may seem similar to the change of environment provided

by the enclosed room full of sick people. However; here it is the case that the invasive forces are brought to the host, and it is not the host going to that environment.

However; as seen with Satan "complaining" to God about Job; there is simultaneously provided a "hedge" to protect this host. The nature of this hedge; (how high, how thick, how impenetrable); is determined by, and is the necessary result of, the balancing of the host's actions. *Materially*; this would be similar to a unexplained sudden increase in the internal resistive forces commensurate with the threat.

There is an interesting "side-effect" to this phenomenon. If it is so stipulated that there are a finite number of angels, and that the enemy took one third with him, (which is actually not true); then either way there are a finite number of these working for the enemy. To the extent that some of these are wasting their time "banging their heads" against a hedge, and likely complaining about it; they are incapable of mischief elsewhere. And even these mere *attempts*, set into motion forces that will return to them much to their dislike. The end result of this, is similar to an attack upon them.

Thus "upright" behavior necessarily results in increased demonic activity, with a concomitant increase in protection, (hedge), from that demonic activity. This results in the immediate and automatic provision of "Haz-Mat" protection. A host's resistance is not lowered, but raised. Again; this was the initial case with Job.

It is the willful engaging in "non-upright" behavior that then results in the provision of a "portal of entry," which permits successful immaterial *ectoparisitosis* or oppression, and/or *endoparisitosis* or possession. This *result* is not due to merely any increased demonic activity. And unlike upright behavior which raises the internal resistance; non-upright behavior lowers the resistance and thus this provides this portal.

Usually this portal of entry is provided because of emotional or *pyritic*; (Author's terminology, as iron pyrite known as "fool's gold."); decisions. These types of decisions are made because it "feels good" in the short term; with either no knowledge of equal and opposite reactions; or a transitory lack of concern, because it "feels good."

As long as the ectoparisitosis remains as such, a host's behavior can continue to alter the resistive portion; and thus things can change as a direct result of subsequent decisions regarding behavior.

However; just as is the case with material systemic diseases such as tuberculosis; once ectoparisitosis or oppression becomes *endoparisitosis,* or *possession*; this generally cannot be ameliorated or undone by the infected host. A discussion of this is beyond the scope of this monograph. [A rather exhaustive discussion of this phenomenon is contained in an upcoming new book—currently in post production.]

Years ago; in the attempt to obtain the utmost accuracy and precision; scientific weighing instruments were often enclosed in a vibration proof glass cabinet. These devices were such that they resembled the "Scales of Lady Justice," except that the two plates were supported from below not from above.

The weights to be placed on the one side were of such high precision, that if the tops of these weights were opened, tiny round spheres of metal were visible. The weights were cast slightly under the specifications, and these tiny spheres were then added for precision.

"Ms. X" decides she wants to make pound cake; [traditionally a pound of flour, a pound of butter, a pound of eggs, and a pound of sugar]. So to make sure it is "just right," she decides to use the aforementioned precise balance.

She places the highly precise and accurate one pound weight on the left, and begins to weigh the components on the right. However; when she weighs the sugar, she find out that she only has one half pound of sugar available. So she takes then a *half* pound weight, and places it on the left side, with the half pound of sugar on the right. And voila, there is perfect balance.

But she later discovers that no one seems to like the pound cake. This creates another imbalance, so she then convinces herself that the real problem must be that her guests must either be "gluten free;" or so "full" from the excellent meal, that they simply cannot eat any more.

Ms. X had (other) alternatives:

She could have simply made half of a pound cake, as here the sugar was the "limiting reagent." But then what would the guests have thought of her serving that tiny pound cake—that obviously was not enough to "go around?"

She could have borrowed a half pound of sugar from the neighbor next door; but then what could the neighbor possibly think of her then?

She could have gone to the market, but she was in the middle of cooking, and did not want to wait.

So instead; she did what "hosts" do on a regular basis. Huck Finn or Tom Sawyer would likely say that she *"let on"* that there was a pound of sugar; even though there was not.

The difference here being; that for children to *"let on"* that there are pirates in the cave, is necessary merely for the fun of the *process* of being children; and without any concern for the end *result*. But it is unclear precisely what end result it was that Ms. X expected, or could reasonably have expected; other than precisely what it was that happened.

"It all turned out for the best;" often results in both an *absolute* and a *relative* definition of "best." It is true that "best" is a superlative, and a superlative can neither be diminished nor augmented. "Almost best" or "better than best" are meaningless terms—despite any common usage.

"It all turned out for the best;" is usually stated as some sort of apology or acceptance of that which is less than "best." Ms. X might state this and provide some sort of justification(s) as to why this is so. But although the pound cake was better than it would have been had she used only one quarter pound of sugar, and thus when comparing the two, the disaster she baked was "better" than it could have been; it was only "best" if given only these two alternatives. This reminds one of when the former Soviet Union would lose a two team sports competition with the US. They would report the outcome as: "USSR came in second; and the US came in next to last."

The correct way to state "It all turned out for the best;" would be: "Given my ignorance, hardheadedness, stupidity, and belief that something is so simply because I say so—irrespective of what actually exists; it all tuned out as best as I would allow." Another might say that this actually represents one possible definition of "mercy."

When one chooses, one must choose from what is available. One cannot choose sin and not also choose the wages of sin. One cannot choose upright behavior and avoid the wages of upright behavior. Although the effects of the *immaterial* wages of sin have been removed by justification; *material* wages are very much alive, present, and quite active.

Understanding this, and acting in accord with this understanding; will allow, and arguably *force*, the "wages" of one's actions to be that which is beneficial—including a longer and healthier life.

Many do not understand how it is that Radical Islamic Terrorists could possibly ever come into existence. This is because the process is not understood. It is in fact the very same process encouraged by God when He gave us The Commandments—but here perverted to entirely different ends.

SHÂMAR TO SHARIA

Radicalization—a term seemingly incessantly in use today. Bantered back and forth, most assume that this word; or perhaps better stated, the *result* of this *process*; (that of being radicalized; i.e.; that state or condition of being a radical); is well understood by all who participate in these discussions. However; in order to truly understand the result, (that of being radicalized or a radical); one must understand the *process*. And in order to understand that process, one must understand precisely the process for which that particular process, (radicalization), is being proffered as a substitute.

Irrespective of whether or not the result, (radical), is the correct terminology; and thus likewise whether "radicalization" is the correct term for the process; it nevertheless *is*, and *remains* in use. However "radical" is a tricky term, with seemingly mutually exclusive meanings.

If it is assumed that the origin is the Latin "*radix*," then this would indicate the *origin* or *source* of something. But *radiate* generally means to be in or at a place anywhere *except* at the source whence it came. Politically speaking, radicals are rarely called centrists.

"Fundamental," generally refers to a base or foundation. But to be "fundamentalized," and thus resulting in the state of being an "Islamic fundamentalist;" does not seem to sound quite as impressive.

It must be asked precisely how those "radicals," who having become a radical as the direct result of "radicalization;" can be both at the source; and yet at the same time having become "radiated" away from the source?

The answer of course is a matter of perspective. Facts can often be stubborn and unpleasant things. One can argue whether it is a mere preponderance of evidence, clear and convincing evidence, or proof beyond a reasonable doubt; but a fair argument can be made that Islam is or was largely based upon Judaism; but Judaism according to Ishmael, and not Abraham. However; to state that Islam is an *outgrowth* of Judaism would be incorrect. Nevertheless it seems at least arguable that what today is called Judaism; again at least via Ishmael's version of Judaism; provides or provided the basis for what ultimately became Islam. This is a not new concept, as much has been written about it. It is well beyond the scope of this monograph to delve into this theory.

It must also be remembered that in order to truly be anti-Semitic, one must also hate Arabs, as this, (Semitism), is based upon *language* and not *religion*. This is to be distinguished from Zionist, as this is from the Hebrew meaning a *fort* or *stronghold*; i.e.; the State of Israel.

Thus one who is an Islamic fundamentalist, can be characterized as a "radical" meaning being *at* the source, if *Islam* is considered to be the source. However, at the same time he or (she) can be characterized as a radical in the sense of being *away* from the source; if it is understood and so stipulated that the true source of Islam is or was Judaism. It must again be stated that although the *source* of Islam is or may have originally been Judaism, Islam is in no way any type of *outgrowth* of Judaism.

Practically everyone knows that there are Ten Commandments; written in stone; which we all have been commanded by God to obey. After all, they are called *commandments* and not suggestions. Thus it would seem clear that God has commanded us to obey them.

There are two problems with what here is universally considered to be *epistémē*, or certain knowledge; but what is in fact actually *doxa*, (less than certain), knowledge:

The first; is that in fact there are not and have never been Ten Commandments—at least contained in Exodus 20; but rather there actually are, and have always been only nine. For example: In one attempt to get to ten, it seems that at some point some person or persons, for some reason or reasons; chose to "bust out" the coveting of a wife from the rest of the coveting, thus providing an additional "Commandment."

This likely happened prior to the "modern" era, as it is "wife," and not "spouse" or "partner," that appears in the translations. Others break up the first Commandment into two; with the "no other Gods" and "graven images" parts receiving their very own separate Commandment status and number. Except for perhaps some numerological or Kaballistic concerns, this appears to be a relatively minor point and not particularly germane to the subject at hand—at least at this time.

The second problem; is the purported *requirement to obey* these commandments, which of course is another matter. This is not to say that God does not want us to obey these Commandments; that He would not prefer that we obey these Commandments; or that there are not serious repercussions each and every time these commandments are not obeyed. Rather, the issue is whether or not He actually told or "commanded" us to obey them.

There is a difference between stating what the laws are; and asking or requiring one to obey them. The former is *informative* in nature; with the latter being at least arguably *manipulative* in nature.

The Commandments appear for the first time in Exodus 20.

In Exodus 20:6 (KJV)we are told:

> *"And shewing mercy unto thousands of them that love me, and keep my commandments."*[1]

One might reasonably first ask what need there would be for mercy to be shown, (shewn), to those who both love God and also keep, (i.e.; obey), (His) commandments? Mercy generally refers to not getting what one deserves, (usually in the negative); as opposed to grace, which is getting what one does not deserve, and is usually in the positive. So then it must be asked that if "keep" means obey, then why would there be any need for any type of mercy to be shown to those "thousands" who are obeying said Commandments? The answer of course: is that by definition there would be no need whatsoever for any such mercy.

The actual Hebrew word translated here as "mercy" is:

"2617 checed; from 2616; *kindness*;..."[2]

"2616 châcad; a prim. root; prop. perh. to *bow* (the neck only [comp. 2603] courtesy to an equal), i.e. to *be kind*;..."[3]

"2603 chânan; a prim. root [comp. 2583]; prop. to *bend* or stoop in kindness to an inferior; to *favor bestow*..."[4]

A distinction is made here with regard to the roots of the Hebrew word originally contained in Exodus 20:6 which is translated as "mercy," (*checed* from *châcad*). It seems that the actual definition of *checed*, is concerned with showing or providing kindness or courtesy to an *equal*; versus the similar word *chânan*, which is concerned with providing kindness to an *inferior*.

Thus it remains unclear as to why the translators chose "mercy" as the English translation of *checed*; as this seems antithetical to its actual meaning. More precisely; generally in order to show "mercy," one must necessarily be in a position of superiority with regard to the potential recipient of any "mercy"—at least with respect to that particular situation. Here with the use of *checed* a position of equality is required.

In Exodus 20:6 it is God who is or was communicating, so it seems likely He would have known which Hebrew word to choose to convey His precise meaning. And He chose the word *checed*, and not *chânan*. Thus what is clear, in at least in this regard; is that from this standpoint; (with regard to showing kindness in *this* context); He (God) considers or considered us to be equals—else He would have used *chânan*—which He did not.

This may be disturbing to those who attempt to reconcile that which is originally and by design brought into existence in the "image and likeness of God, (H. Sapiens);" with their view of the actual, (real time), current state of the same. This is the inevitable result of conflating the original pure and perfect product, with the current polluted result.

But it seems there is an additional requirement in order to obtain said kindness from the standpoint of being shown kindness as an equal and not as an inferior; as it must be remembered we were told: "*And shewing mercy unto thousands of them that love me, and keep my commandments.*"

This can be rephrased as a reversed "if then" declaration: "

> "I, (God), will show you kindness from the standpoint of an equal, if you both love me, *and* also keep my commandments."

The actual Hebrew word translated as "love" is:

> "157 'âhab or 'âhêb; a prim. root: to *have affection* for

(sexually or otherwise): - (be-) love (-ed, -ly, -r), like, friend."⁵

Thus the translation as "love," seems reasonably straightforward.

The answer to this "obedience" matter, lies in the actual word which is translated here as "keep."

The actual Hebrew word translated here in Exodus 20:6 as "keep" is:

> "8104: shâmar; A prim. root; prop. to *hedge* about (as with thorns), i.e. *guard*; gen. to *protect, attend to*, etc.: - beware, be circumspect, take heed (to self), keep (-er, self), mark, look narrowly, observe, preserve, regard, reserve, save (self), sure, (that lay) wait (for), watch (-man)."⁶

As can easily be seen, the Hebrew word *shâmar*, does not in any way mean obey; but rather to *protect* as though surrounded by a "hedge" of "thorns."

In fact, according to Strong, *shâmar* is not translated as "obey" anywhere in the entire Bible. (See the above provided list of words after the ": -," as these represent all of the Biblical translations of *shâmar*.)

Perhaps God made an error, in that He actually meant to use a word that meant "obey," but was just preoccupied with the ongoing follies of His Chosen Ones at the time.

Or perhaps in fact He actually did use a word that meant "obey," and somehow an error just cropped up in the translation.

Or perhaps Moses actually spoke Hebrew with a serious "Brooklynese" accent, and thus just misunderstood God.

The first of course is impossible. The second is possible; but the problem with this, as well as the latter "perhaps;" is the pesky matter of the "written in stone" part for the content. If God was that serious about not being misunderstood about the rules, He would likely be just as clear about what to do with them.

Much later, Jesus addressed this same issue of love and "obeying" the Commandments.

In John 14:15 (KJV) Jesus tells us:

> "*If ye love me, keep my commandments.*"[7]

So it seems clear that Jesus is merely saying: "If you love me, then show it by obeying My commandments."
Or is He?
Here the actual Greek word translated as "keep" is:

> "5083 tērĕō; from tĕrŏs (a *watch*; perh. akin to 2334); to *guard* (from *loss* or *injury*, prop. by keeping *the eye* upon..."[8]

Thus the Greek word *tērĕō*, is very synonymic to the aforementioned Hebrew word *shâmar*. And neither *shâmar* nor *tērĕō* is even remotely concerned with obeying the Commandments, or showing *obedience* to anything else.

It is clear that Jesus was not asking for, or even addressing *obedience* either.

In Exodus 20:6, when the Father addressed the matter, He said to shâmar His Commandments—meaning that we should *protect* His Commandments as though to surround them with a hedge of thorns.

Then when Jesus addressed this same matter in John 14:15, the best Greek word for whatever Aramaic word it was that Jesus actually spoke, was the Greek word *tērĕō*—meaning to watch or guard from loss or injury by "keeping the eye upon," His (My) Commandments. In neither case was any type of actual *obedience* to the Commandments sought.

So when God referenced keeping his commandments: "*And shewing mercy unto thousands of them that love me, and keep my commandments*; what is under discussion with regard to His Commandments, is to *protect* (them) as though surrounded by a hedge of thorns. And much later Jesus essentially stated the very same thing.

What possible good are the Commandments if H. Sapiens are not required to *obey* them, but only asked to *guard* them? In truth; at least in this passage; is that He did not even *require* us to guard them; but rather advised us as to what would happen if we loved Him, and if and when we did *shâmar* or guard or protect said Commandments. And why is it that God will show us kindness *as though an (His) equal*, if we merely shâmar His commandments; irrespective of whether or not we actually obey them?

Can it be stated that God does not care if we obey His Commandments? Of course not, as He cares very much whether or not we obey His Commandments—else why would He have provided them. If for no other reason; He cares because of the matter of what is often referred to as *karma*. [This subject is addressed in great detail in the "Second Intermission" of "*MeekRaker Beginnings...*" This mechanism is therein analyzed, and explained on a strictly scientific basis; with the application of the Newtonian laws of F = MA, inertia, and equal and opposite reactions.]

What is much more important to God than H. Sapiens *obeying* His Commandments; is H. Sapiens *choosing* to obey His Commandments. There are two primary things that drive the universe: The first is *free will*; and the second is the aforementioned equal and opposite reactions; i.e.; *karma*.

Many have stated that the entire existence of man consists of nothing more than decision making, or perhaps better stated: "a series of decisions." And of course many have also stated that whatever position(s) a person finds themselves in at any given time, the same is the direct result of all of the decisions one has made up to that point.

Irrespective of whether or not one considers either or both of these beliefs a bit hyperbolic; it nevertheless remains the fact that in the course of one's life, one is forced to make many decisions; including all too often, making the decision to not decide.

But in order to make quality decisions, one requires quality information. This is why with regard to the Commandments; it is *shâmar* that is the concern, and not *obedience*.

What God was saying in Exodus 20:6 is that if we love Him and guard his Commandments as though surrounded by a ""hedge of thorns," he will show kindness to us as though an equal. And later Jesus essentially said the same thing about "guarding." This means to place these Commandments firmly in our intellect; and to protect or guard them; and then to refer back to them when making all decisions. As long as these Commandments are well understood and integrated into the decision making process; said decisions will tend to be the correct ones.

But what about this "as an equal" part?

Genesis 1:28 (KJV) tells us:

> "And God blessed them,
> and God said unto them,
> Be fruitful, and multiply,
> and replenish the earth, and subdue it:
> and have dominion over the fish
> of the sea, and over the fowl of the air,
> and over every living thing
> that moveth upon the earth."[9]

The actual Hebrew word translated as "replenish" is:

> "4390 mâlê'; or mâlâ' (Esth. 7:5),; a prim. root, to *fill* or (intrans.) *be full* of, in a wide application (lit. and fig.)..."[10]

It is unclear as to why Esther is referenced here, as mâlê' in Esther 7:5 is translated as "presume" in the KJV.[11]

The actual word translated as "subdue" is:

> "3533 kâbash; a prim. root; to *tread* down; hence neg. to *disregard*; pos. to *conquer, subjugate, violate*: - bring into bondage, force, keep under, subdue, bring into subjection."[12]

A slight variant of this Hebrew word is seen in current English vernacular, although it is spelled *kibosh*.

The actual Hebrew word translated as "dominion" is:

> "7287 râdâh; to *tread* down, i.e. *subjugate*; spec. to *crumble* of: - (come to make to) have dominion, prevail against, reign, (bear, make to) rule, (-r, over), take."[13]

There are two points contained here in Genesis 1:28 worthy of "considerable consideration:"

The *first*; is that it is clear that it is God's will that man have dominion over the earth. God is establishing and instructing His wishes with regard to man's relationship to the earth, *and* all the life forms upon the earth.

God told man to: "*subdue it*," and "*have dominion.*" Thus this refers to both the earth itself, "*subdue it;*" as well as to "*have dominion*" over all the other various life forms—"*over every living thing that moveth upon the earth.*" [Note that the members of the "audience," appear to be deliberately *excluded*, in terms of man's dominion over any other man, at least at this time.]

In Revelation 7:14 and 19:16 Jesus is referred to as: "King of Kings"[14] and "Lord of Lords."[15]

Given that this appearance is in Revelation, these "kings" or "lords" are generally understood to mean political or quasi-political leaders in the "end times;" of which of course the book of Revelation is actually concerned only in a relative manner. This is usually presented only in the *negative* sense, in that these same kings and lords are, (will be), no match for Jesus; which of course is true.

However; Jesus is also "King of Kings," and "Lord of Lords," in a *positive* sense. This refers to the instructions given to man by the Father in Genesis 1:28. In order for man to have just dominion over the earth and all the life forms upon it; it was necessary for the *Creator* of the earth and all the life forms upon it, who duly had such authority; to grant said authority to man—which is precisely what He did in Genesis 1:28.

Thus from the standpoint of man's relationship to the *earth*; man has an authority similar to God's authority over the universe *as per His will and instructions*. It is for this reason that the kindness He will show us with regard to the Commandments is as an equal, and not an inferior; *checed* and not *chânan*. Thus with regard to the earth, H. Sapiens by design are "little gods." However it must be remembered that there is also the requirement that one must also *love* Him in order to obtain this treatment as an equal.

At this juncture, it would represent gross negligence to not address the "controversial" contents of Psalm 82:6-7, and John 10:34-35:

Psalm 82:6-7 tells us:

> *"I have said, Ye are gods;*
> *and all of you are children of the most High.*
> *But ye shall die like men,*
> *and fall like one of the princes"*[16]

From just these two verses, it is not clear who is speaking; and at first it seems to be God. However; upon further reading of Psalm 82, it becomes clear that it is likely that it is the author; believed to be Asaph; who is speaking.

If for the purpose of analysis, it can be stipulated that Asaph is in fact a prophet; and is speaking as such here, (on God's behalf); then it is clear that in this passage, H. Sapiens are considered to be described as (little) "gods."

The actual Hebrew word translated here as "gods" is:

> "430 'ĕlôhîym; plur. of 433; *gods* in the ordinary sense; but spec. used (in the plur. thus, esp. with the art.) of the supreme *God*; occasionally applied by way of deference to *magistrates*; and sometimes as a superlative: - angels, x exceeding, God (gods) (-dess, -ly), x (very) great, judges, x mighty."[17]

This statement in Psalms 82:6 is considered to be highly controversial, as many are uncomfortable with the notion that H. Sapiens are in any way to be considered "gods."

Since Psalm 82 is generally considered to be a rebuke of unjust judges, many prefer to believe that the "occasionally applied by way of deference to *magistrates*" translation should apply. This then supplants "gods" with "judges." This then solves their problem of H. Sapiens being declared in any way "gods."

However it must be noted that this is the very same Hebrew word for God, ('ĕlôhîym); that appears in Exodus 20:2 where God Himself states:

> "*I* am the LORD thy God ('ĕlôhîym), which have brought thee out of the land of Egypt, out of the house of bondage."[18]

Others; those who accept "gods" as the correct translation here; then rely on Psalm 82 verse 7 to disprove H. Sapiens being any type of "god," as again it states:

> "But ye shall die like men, and fall like one of the princes."[19]

This is where the context; i.e.; the audience of corrupt judges, becomes significant. Rather than disproving that *'ĕlôhîym* actually means "gods;" this is instead a statement of what will *become* of that which originally and by design were *'ĕlôhîym* or "gods," because of their subsequent behaviors.

And then John 10:34-35 tells us:

> "*Jesus answered them, Is it not written in your law, I said, Ye are gods? If he called them gods, unto whom the word of God came,*

> *and the scripture cannot be broken;*"[20]

The actual Greek word translated here as "gods" in "Ye are gods" is:

> "*2316* thĕŏs; of uncert. affin.; a *deity*, espec. (with *3588*) the supreme *Divinity*; fig. a *magistrate*; by Heb. *very*: - x exceeding, God, god [-ly, -ward]."[21]

Here again is the *figurative* use for a magistrate.

According to Strong, this very same word, (thĕŏs), appears again in the included phrase: *"word of God."*[22]

Thus; the same word used to describe God in *"word of God,"* is used to describe H. Sapiens in the preceding *"Ye* (H. Sapiens) *are gods."*

As an aside, there is an interesting use of the first person by Jesus asking about what He "said," as contained in their written "law." Psalms is considered to have been written many centuries prior to Jesus' birth.

And *secondly*; there is that inescapable point which it seems is almost universally overlooked. Most consider the creation of the earth to be a process, with Genesis 1:2 et. seq. simply representing or describing a part or a stage of this creation process. The "without form, void, and dark" therefore being considered a *transitional* state, ultimately resulting in the creation of the final product: earth.

Many or most consider the conditions and events which appear after Genesis 1:1, as a mere *recapitulation* of events occurring in Genesis 1:1—which they are not. This is despite the fact that Genesis 1:1 ends with the word earth, and Genesis 1:2 begins with earth, right after the "pickup notes." Litigating this error is beyond the scope of this monograph. However, this extremely significant widespread error is rectified in great referenced detail in the initial chapters of *"MeekRaker Beginnings..."*

If it were true that "without form, void, and dark" were merely transitional states in the process of the creation of the earth; there then would be one inescapable fact. The same being: that according to God's instructions as contained in Genesis 1:28; God necessarily must have created a final product for man, (the earth), that required in English; "putting the kibosh on;" or in Hebrew; *kâbash*(ing). This is certain because God Himself instructed man to "kâbash; a prim. root; to *tread* down; hence neg. to *disregard*; pos. to *conquer, subjugate, violate*: - bring into bondage, force, keep under, subdue, bring into subjection" the earth—arguably in order to be able to live on it. As though somehow God was incapable of creating an earth that did not require *kâbash*(ing).

One alternative explanation would be that although God *could* have created a world where *kâbash*(ing) was not necessary, He nevertheless chose not to. The more this possible explanation is pondered, the more absurd any such contention becomes.

The truth; is that the end of Genesis 1:1 represents a statement of completion; of the final product; of the creation of the earth—which is exactly what is stated.

Genesis 1:2 onward is not any type of "flashback" to some point in time in the middle of Genesis 1:1; but rather describes the condition of the earth at some unspecified point in time after time *after* its creation or completion. Although most of the more popular translations/versions do not contain this, the *Interlinear Bible* includes "she became," prior to the subsequent description of "without form, void, and dark" condition of the earth.[23]

It is clear in literal reading of Genesis, that God subsequently intervened in the altered condition of the originally completed earth; but intervened only to a certain point—which is why it was that man was *created*, and then instructed by God to subdue or *kâbash* the earth in Genesis 1:28. This was not because God *could* not do it, but rather because He *would* not do it. This was the result of the allocation of His *authority*, and had nothing to do with His *capabilities*.

The only *"primum movens"* or prime mover is God. God is the only entity that exists without a cause. This is a major problem for science regarding the cause of the origin of the universe. Genesis 1:1 is merely a description of the result of the "Big Bang," with the responsible party, (cause), stated therein. Any and all other entities except God are either results or causes; and are at the same time both. When the earth *became* without form, void and dark; this was a result that required a cause; and this cause clearly was not God.

Without getting into too much detail, it is clear that there exists an entity that is active in opposing the will of God. Although there seems to be a plethora of *doxa* about this entity; there is a paucity of *epistémē*.

What is known, is that this entity was "thrown down" to the earth; likely at some time between Genesis 1:1 and Genesis 1:2. (For much greater detail on this, see: "*Ostium Ab Inferno—The Opening From Hell*") What is also known is that man is to have dominion over "all the life forms upon the earth." This includes that which was "thrown down."

What is not known is the actual origin of this opposition entity. Any serious and logical contemplation of the actual origin of this opposing entity necessarily leaves one in a bit of a conundrum, and thus is beyond the scope of this monograph. Although the *results* of the infection are described; neither the original *source*, (possible tautology noted), nor the *vector* is known.

What is also important and germane here, is that in keeping with this; i.e.; in the consideration of *shâmar* (H), or *tērĕō* (G); there is a clear unmistakable implication—arguably a requirement—of or for something to *guard* these Commandments *from*.

Said entity—by all of its various names, is in the overall business of opposing the will of God in the general sense; and violently opposed to *man* carrying out the will of God in the specific. Said "adversary" to God, and "enemy" to man, basically has two choices:

The first; is to be involved on a "case by case" basis in interfering with each and every decision being made by those in the "*image and likeness*" of God; if and when said decision would be in furtherance of the will of God. The enemy can "go to lunch," if the decision appears to be against the will of God, as it is pleased with this. However this "case by case," is a very messy and very "time consuming" process, requiring many "demon-hours" of effort. It will do this seemingly incessantly, but this is a grossly inefficient process.

The *second* method; and the one that is much more efficient for it, (the enemy or adversary); is for it to carefully attack that which is utilized as the principles by which one makes decisions. It is against this very attack that God wishes us to *shâmar* or *tērĕō*, that which is contained in His Commandments.

For example: If one fully understands: "Thou shall not steal," and incorporates this in the decision making process; then usually one is not likely to take that which rightfully belongs to another. In order for the enemy to win, it then has to wage a battle each and every time the opportunity for theft arises.

If however, it can successfully attack this: "Thou shall not steal" principle, by getting through that protective hedge of thorns, (via either inadequate *shâmar*, or overwhelming force); and then supplant this with something such as: "Stealing is okay, as long as you do not get caught;" then most or all future battles regarding stealing itself suddenly become unnecessary.

The target or victim of this attack will now *shâmar* this new "principle;" and behave in a manner consistent with this "new rule." Going forward; it no longer will be the issue of *stealing* being a wrongdoing to be avoided; but rather the issue of *getting caught* being the wrongdoing to be avoided, which then guides the behavior. So although *stealing* was once an abomination; it has now become acceptable, with only the prospect of *getting caught* now being that which is abominable.

One only need look at automobiles to see the regression of the quality of that which is *shâmar*(ed) currently in the United States. As late as the early 1960's, automobile ignition switches had a "lock," and an "off" position. This "off" position was a means by which when the engine was shut off and the key was removed, the vehicle could still be started and driven without the key—by design. Today, anti-theft devices are extremely complicated and complex. This was not done because of any overall decrease in the incidence of auto theft.

That which is *shâmar*(ed) by H. Sapiens in the US has changed dramatically; shifting from principled rules, to self-centered thinking. This was not only predictable, but done by design by those in power whose goals are antithetical to the will of God—the same being His primary desire for the *free will* of man. Once this is understood, many seemingly inexplicable actions; particularly by political leaders; begin to make perfect sense.

Often cited as justification, this concept of "separation of church and state;" which appears nowhere in the US constitution; *should* be utilized to prevent a theocracy, and not to justify serious infringements on the 1st Amendment to the US Constitution. "Someone might be offended," grossly falls far short of a "clear and present danger," or any similar subsequent test. In fact it was primarily for religious and political expression that the 1st Amendment was ratified.

If there is any legitimate use for "separation of church and state" rule; this should be utilized to prevent the government from religious proselytizing, not to be used to justify 1st Amendment restrictions on US citizens, simply because of a money trail purportedly providing the government with jurisdiction—i.e.; the *authority*, but not the *right*.

To the extent that God and His rules for behavior can be removed, made inaccessible, or determined to be "uncool;" then His rules are necessarily then supplanted by man's rules, which over millennia simply did not work. Clearly one cannot *shâmar* what one has never read or understood. This is not an unintended consequence, but rather the main objective of those who are making access to God's word as difficult as possible.

The inevitable result of this, is a government that can, (now must), become ever increasingly involved with regulating what H. Sapiens *can* do, because what H. Sapiens *will* do has changed so dramatically. This change is the direct result of deliberately and with malice, making God's rules as inaccessible as possible. Automobile ignition switches are merely one result or symptom.

What is even more dangerous; is that the current, (modern), state of behavior of H. Sapiens; is generally viewed as an *end* of a process, and not merely a snapshot of a *stage* in a process. Meaning; that unless something dramatically changes, behavior will continue to degenerate until there is little to no freedom left. But then again, that is and always was the intention of those; who unlike God; find the free will of man not only repulsive, but often times abominable. It is far better to be in quicksand, and know one is in quicksand; than it is to be in the very same quicksand, and not even realize it.

There are two main differences between so called radicalization of Islamic terrorists, and what is happening in the US today.

In the so called radicalization of Islamic terrorists, whatever the "recruit" may have previously *shâmar*(ed), is supplanted by what someone said someone else said, about what someone said someone else said. . ., ad nauseum; about what someone may have written circa 700AD. The "recruit" is rapidly forced to *shâmar* what he/she is told to *shâmar*, based upon said hearsay, from this "original" source.

And although said "original" source, "originally" was Judaism, (via Abraham); this newer "original" source, Judaism, (via Ishmael); is at a minimum highly questionable. But it is nevertheless God and His purported will, which provides the motive for Islamic "radicalization;" and the subsequent actions of the resultant Islamic radical.

The ultimate determination of success of the "radicalized," is that individual working what was previously a "measure of faith;" but now by requiring all others to obey what he was recently commanded and chose to *shâmar*. Should anyone, (infidel), choose to *shâmar* what he or they believe God said to *shâmar*; and not what the "radical" now commands them to *shâmar*, they simply are killed. And said terrorist is not only willing to die him or herself as a consequence of the furtherance of this process of killing what he now considers infidels; but welcomes the opportunity, as he has also been told and now considers his death in killing others as an honor.

Islamic terrorists actually believe that they both *know* and are zealously *obeying* the will of God. As insane as this, (the Islamic terrorists'), interpretation of the will of God may be, this nevertheless remains manipulation by *commission* with respect to

God; as all of this is done in what is believed to be in furtherance of the same.

It also seems clear that in Islam, there is this extreme misunderstanding regarding the coming of Messiah. It is difficult to determine with any degree of precision the nature of this misunderstanding. It seems that the Islamic Mahdi is analogous to Judeo/Christian Messiah. Whether it is believed that the 12th Imam is the Mahdi, or Islam's Messiah; or will merely *accompany* the Messiah, is difficult to determine. Likewise it is difficult to determine precisely who it is that may have been hidden, (occultation), for perhaps some 1200 years.

Although conflated by many in Christianity and Judaism, the Bible references to Messiah as the "fuller's soap," and the "great and dreadful day" of the Lord;" are references to two different events. The former refers to the first coming, and the latter to the second coming of Messiah.

A fair argument can be made that in Islam, it is not believed that the first coming, (for salvation and redemption), has yet happened; as is also the case with Judaism. Or perhaps better phrased; that which is required for salvation has not yet occurred, irrespective of who it is that may currently be involved in any "occultation." If it can be so stipulated that this is *incorrect*—meaning that when Messiah comes it will be the *second* time, then some degree of sense can be made out of this.

Mainstream Christianity believes that the first coming has already occurred, and there will be a period of tribulation prior to the *second* coming of Jesus. Many believe that this will be preceded by the rapture, where current believers will be taken up to heaven *in corpus*. If this is so, this will result in only non-believers being left on the earth at that juncture. If this, (rapture), is not so; both believers and non-believers will experience the tribulation.

Either way, there is to be a period of tribulation on earth; the purpose being for a final opportunity to accept Messiah, and thus be "saved." During this time, "believers" will be persecuted and killed by the enemy of God. At some point; (the end of the tribulation); there will be the return of Jesus.

"Anti-Christ" or not, in Christianity it is the *enemy* who is responsible for persecution of believers; as well as providing the ensuing chaos which Jesus ultimately resolves.

In "radical" Islam, it seems things are a bit backwards. The "radicals" are killing *non-believers*, (by their standards); leaving only believers; (again by their standards). Thus by their standards, to the extent they succeed; only Islamic "believers" will be left at the Christian second coming, or it seems what may be the Islamic *only* coming.

Since Islam does not seem to be particularly big on the idea of reincarnation, those who do not accept radical Islam are knowingly; (according to radical Islam); being sent to eternal damnation. This is not by their own choice to not believe in Messiah; but rather by the *deliberate* choices of those very same Islamic "radicals" who kill them.

The purported purpose of the Tribulation, is to provide such overwhelming evidence for choosing to accept Messiah; that one can make no other *logical* decision, other than to *choose* to accept Messiah.

The purpose of Islamic "radicals," is by the threat of immediate physical death, to force belief in Islam; or to forever be denied the option of salvation; (according to the killers understanding).

It must be asked which belief it is that represents a loving and just God?

The ongoing degeneration of behavior of H. Sapiens in the US, is a bit different. Here there are and have been "progressive," and thus long term attempts to; unlike the terrorists; *remove* the entire concept of God; and let behavior be determined by whatever it is that one "chooses" to *shâmar*; that is: *as long as it is always the case that God's rules are not considered.* This is the same reason why it is a crime in many Muslim countries to possess, study, or preach the Bible?

It must be remembered that *progressivism*, (in the political context), is not a political ideology; but rather is a tactic or strategy, depending upon its use.

To characterize one's self as a "progressive" *politically*, merely means that one believes in placing the frog in a pot of cold water and placing the pot on the stove; rather than placing the frog in boiling water; because the frog then could and likely would simply jump out.

The enemy is and has been an expert at this type of progressivism. In fact it can be reasonably argued that he (it) invented it.

In the US, God's rules are, and have for quite some time, been progressively removed; so that they are not readily available for consideration when making choices. Instead of concrete, (written in stone), rules for behavior; what one *shâmar*(s) has become an ongoing "learning" process, and is subject to changes and modifications.

This is; in contradistinction to the terrorists; manipulation by *omission* with respect to God.

Long term karmic, (equal and opposite reactions), are the basis for God's rules. But man's rules today are largely based upon the short term, particularly *feelings*; (as commonly defined). Things that make one "feel good," are now acceptable; and things that make one feel bad; or sometimes make or may make another feel bad, are not. Giving a student the failing grade that they earned, is frowned upon because of how it could make the student *feel*. What is the likelihood of long term success, when failure is rewarded in the short term and shortsighted concern for feelings?

This is a supplanting of the objective with the subjective. Meaning; that the rules that God stated are based upon the objective—the quantity and quality of that which is or will be the actual result of one's choices. But these supplanting factors are largely not based upon what will *actually* happen, but rather based largely upon what is *believed* will happen to *me*.

This then concomitantly results in the supplanting of actuality with reality. Actuality being here defined as that which "actually" exists; as opposed as to reality being that which is perceived and *believed* to exist. When the appropriate reality, (that which is consistent with actuality); ultimately collides with subjective and self-centered reality, things become anything but boring.

God's will for the free will of man is both an absolute and non-absolute. It is an absolute in the sense of man being completely free to make whatever choice(s) he wishes. And it is also an absolute, in that whatever is sown will ultimately be reaped.

However God's will for man's free will is also a non-absolute, in that interfering with another's free will provides the boundary. Thus free will, as is the case with many things, must be kept in balance.

1 Corinthians 8:9 (KJV) tells us:

> *"But take heed lest by any means this liberty of yours become a stumbling block to them that are weak."*[24]

This "subjectivation," can be seen with the longstanding, but seemingly now obsolete, "clear and present danger et seq.," tests for infringing upon one's free speech. There was a time where imminent actual harm to another was required, (interference to another's will to remain unharmed), before free speech could be infringed.

This has changed dramatically. There is an ongoing war about infringing upon free speech in an attempt to supplant "clear and present," with "may or might;" and supplanting "danger," with "hurt the feelings" of someone in disagreement with these words. This is extremely dangerous; and clearly inconsistent with both the US Constitution, and the will of God.

Another difference between so called radicalization and progressivism is the time factor. "Radicalization" is accomplished in a relatively short period of time.

Political progressivism however, has been at work for well over a century, (see Woodrow Wilson). Said progressivism is at this time not quite eugenics, as that became taboo because of adherents such as Adolph Hitler. It is currently much more about gradually obtaining *control* than destruction—at least for now. Given that the

US was originally based upon free will and Judeo-Christian principles, slow and methodical changes are required by the "progressives"—lest the frog jump out. [See: *Statists Saving One*"]

The result of Islamic Radicalism and concomitant "sharia law;" is the predictable, (and deliberate), effect of a cause. That cause being the supplanting of that which God desires us to *shâmar*, with something contrary to the concept of free will entirely. It must be noted that much of sharia is merely *derived*.

Thus; quite unlike the actual Judeo-Christian Commandments; sharia is not even proffered to be the literal Word of God. Instead it is proffered as "what He really meant" (according to me); as opposed to *what He actually said*.

God can never have it both ways, and neither can the Islamists. Unfortunately; this derivation is not unique to Islam. It could reasonably be argued that the Muslim Hadith, the Jewish Talmud, and various Christian "pronunciamentos" all have this "derivation" issue in common.

But what is to be done about it?

As most know; whether or not it is known that it is known; initially, the attacks of the enemy are oppressive. This oppression is similar to an infestation or *ectoparisitosis*.

For example: attacks upon the person who has chosen to *shâmar*: "Thou shalt not steal;" are attacks that are situation specific, (oppressive); attacks from *without*. ("Go ahead and take it, no one is looking.") And although some may succeed "short term;" they generally do not succeed long term. This is because these attacks have little long term effect upon what it is that *guides* the behavior. There is an imbalance created between the thoughts ideas and suggestions comprising the attack; and that which is protected or guarded, ("Thou shalt not steal," via *shâmar*.

The attack, (TIS attack; thoughts, ideas and suggestions), may succeed either totally or partially; but there nevertheless remains the unbalanced force created by the imbalance between the suggested action, (the attack), or the action itself; and that which is guarded or protected. And this unbalanced force must eventually be balanced.   Said imbalance can be balanced by outright rejection. Here the hand grenade is quickly hurled back at the attacker: "Here if you like it so much; and if it is such a good idea, you take it."

However; to the extent that the attack succeeds, there is created an imbalance which must be subjectively balanced. In the use of progressive techniques, (including and most especially political progressivism); the idea is to balance this imbalance by a change, even if only a slight change, in that which is *shâmar*(ed).

"It was only a dollar, so it is fine;" or "It was only a white lie." Here the definition of stealing or lying, is changed from an absolute to a relative. Initially, taking the *property of,* or the *truth from,* another was wrong; but now it becomes relative, in that below a certain threshold, it is not now considered actually stealing or lying. The purpose of the next attack of course, will be to again raise the threshold. Eventually one finds themselves robbing banks, and does not even know how they got there.

These *subjective* imbalances, are to be distinguished from the *objective* karmic or "equal and opposite reaction" imbalances, created by any and all actions.

However; for a variety of reasons beyond the scope of this monograph; this oppressive and *infestation* like ectoparasitosis, can "progress," to possessive and *infection* like endoparasitosis.

This can be on one area, or many areas. This can be constant or intermittent. This can be constant in one area for a time, and absent in another. This variation is determined not as much by the intensity of the attack, but rather largely by the resistance of the host. Infectious disease operates in a similar manner. Any time the external invasive forces overcome the internal resistive forces, "disease" is the result.   This is the rule in both the material and immaterial realms.

To suggest that the Islamic terrorists represent the *most* heinous result of the supplanting of that which should be "*shâmar*(ed)" with that which is not of God; would likely reveal an inexcusable ignorance of history. Nevertheless, it would be both naive and dangerous, to not recognize the presence of this level of evil now present in the world.

It seems that there are only two ways in which this menace can be remedied:

The first would be to find a means by which to "un*shâmar*" that which these individuals have chosen to shâmar. However there are some problems associated with this approach:

1) Unless these terrorists can be taught of their own free will to *choose* to remove that which they currently shâmar, (by their own previous choosing); this would then be *manipulative* in nature. Thus even though the techniques involved would in no way resemble the terrorist techniques, at the root nevertheless remains manipulation—which would be just as much against the will of God as the manipulation by the terrorists or anyone else.

2) Even if this approach were possible, the free will of the *victims* of the remaining or unconverted, (still radicalized), terrorists; would continue to be under attack by terrorists during the process. This would then mean that the free will and God given rights of the terrorists; who after all *are* the active and menacing parties; would be placed higher than the rights of these innocent victims who just want to exercise *their* free will and God given rights.

3) In terms of raw numbers, the actual number of "conversion" of current terrorists, would have to exceed the number of those who are being "radicalized" or "recruited." The positive or negative "delta" or difference would then be the measure of success or failure. With the number of Muslims currently in the world today, even a very small percentage as a "recruitment rate" represents a rather large number—an amount which would likely increase as news of mass (re)conversions spread.

Unfortunately; the only alternative at this time seems to be complete and total destruction of each and every Islamic terrorist on a consistent and ongoing basis.

1 Samuel 15:18:

> *"And the LORD sent thee on a journey, and said, Go and utterly destroy the sinners the Amalekites, and fight against them until they be consumed."*[25]

> *"Excessive free will easily becomes manipulation"*—Emma B. Quadrakoff

Most agree that the Bible is a book about redemption. But few understand these implications. There is that which the Father redeemed beginning in Genesis 1:2. There is that which man must redeem beginning in Genesis 1:28. And there is that which the Son redeemed. It is about that which the Son redeemed; much of which remains unknown even today; that this work is focused.

Calvary's Hidden Truths

From *man's* perspective, the three most significant events in all of history are the *creation* from *nothing*, (H. bârâ), of the original hosts or tsâbâ', (Genesis 1:27); the *formation* from *something*, (H. yatsâr), of Adam in the garden or gan, (Genesis 2:7-8); and the birth of Jesus. It is more than arguable that the second event is or was inextricably linked to the first; and that the third event is or was inextricably linked to the second.

Most regard the Bible as a book about redemption, but few understand what this actually means. From man's self-centered position, this redemption; and thus the very purpose of the Bible; strictly and solely refers to the redemption of man—with perhaps some minor historical information provided, along with a salting of wisdom.

But there is a much greater story in the "redemption department." If correctly read, Genesis 1:2 and onward for some time, represents the beginning of the redemption of the earth by God. Contrary to common belief, Genesis 1:2 onward, represents the condition of the earth at some point in time *after* its completion; and is not a recapitulation of what happened in Genesis 1:1—as it simply cannot be.

The same error occurs in the belief that the *formation* of Adam, represents merely a recapitulation of the *creation* of the original hosts. This also cannot be so, as the means of causation are mutually exclusive. The *creation* or *bârâ* of the original hosts, requires that they were brought into existence from *nothing* material; and the *formation* or *yatsâr* of Adam, requires that he be *formed* from *something* material. And we are even told what that "something" was: *'âphâr*; often translated as "dust."

Genesis 1:2 literally tells us the condition of the earth *after* its completion; and is *after* the subsequent event of the enemy being "thrown down" to the earth.

The *first* part of Genesis 1:2 represents the situation "on the ground," as the direct and indirect results of the enemy's activities or "works" perpetrated upon the previously completed earth.

The *second* part of Genesis 1:2 describes the beginning of the redemptive process with God's "moving." [Litigating these facts is far beyond the scope of this Monograph. An exhaustive analysis of all of this can be found in *"MeekRaker Beginnings..."*]

For reasons also beyond the scope of this Monograph, after God redeemed what He redeemed; He then *created* man to continue this redemptive process.

This is known because of God's description of man as tsâbâ', which is defined as:

> "6635 tsâbâ' or tsᵉbâ'âh from 6633; a *mass* of persons (or fig. things), espec. reg. organized for war (an *army*); by impl. a *campaign*, lit. or fig. (spec. *hardship, worship*): -

appointed time, (+) army, (+) battle, company, host, service, soldiers, waiting upon..."¹

This is also known, because of the instructions God gave to these tsâbâ' in Genesis 1:27 (NAS):

> *"Be fruitful and multiply, and fill the earth, and subdue it; and rule over the fish of the sea and over the birds of the sky and over every living thing that moves on the earth."*²

But God was now in what was an impossible situation—except for God. Each and every individual member of His army had been exposed to the enemy, and none survived his or its onslaught unscathed. If the "mark," was living physically on earth; and carrying out God's instructions perfectly; and never even once succumbing to the influence of the enemy; collectively all, and individually each, had "missed the mark."

The Greek word *hamartano* appears often in the Bible, and is generally translated as "sin."

Hamartano is defined as:

> "264 hamartanō, perh. from *1* (as a neg. particle) and the base of *3313*; prop. to *miss* the mark (and *so not share* in the prize), i.e. (fig.) to *err*, esp. (mor.) to *sin*; - for your faults, offend, sin, trespass."³

The "prize" in this particular context, refers to reconnection with God at the end of physical life. Hence the need for what is often referred to as "salvation," "redemption," or "justification;" generally used interchangeably as though synonyms—which they are not.

This currently is, and always was an unfair war, and God knew this beforehand. The tsâbâ', (hosts), *were* and *are* exposed to the attacks of the enemy 24/7, with no limits on what the enemy *would* or *will* do, the only limits being what the enemy *could* or *can* do. God is required to play "fair" lest he violate His own rules; but the enemy was and is not. It is this imbalance, which "paid for," or balanced "justification;" i.e.; what God would do to allow man to be reconnected to Him. Past tense is used here, because from God's position: "it is finished"—man need only accept it; notwithstanding any *religious* claims to the contrary.

Thus the need for man's "redemption," represents a previously known, but unintended consequence, of man's role as redeemer of something else. God knew what He wanted to do; but He had to do it in a manner consistent not only with the rules of the *immaterial* realm, but the rules of the *material* realm as well. This means that the consideration of time, space, and matter was required.

The *formation* of Adam began this justification process, and occurred relatively recently. Although it is not known when the original created hosts came into existence, science tells us that it was some hundreds of thousands of years ago.

No major religion seems to dispute that Adam was formed approximately six thousand years ago, and this is likely correct. Their *error*, is the unwarranted assumption that Adam was the first human, made in the first literal week, and therefore that the earth must be about the same age. Although this is not widely known; Adam lived approximately 800 years *after* he left the garden or *gan*, and lived to about 930 years of age.

The reason for the formation of Adam as God did, was to begin the "rescue" plan for mankind. Adam (and Eve), represented the first in the bloodline for Messiah. Although the story of Adam & Co. was written in Hebrew; the truth is that we know not what language Adam spoke; or if he in fact even spoke any verbal language at all while *in* the gan.

When Adam was what essentially amounts to as banished, he found himself outside of this gan; but the outside of the gan was then already occupied by the descendants of the original created hosts, including the true Chaldeans. Since Adam & Co. were now on the *other* side of the garden or gan; it seems likely that those who saw them exit, or saw them afterwards, knew they were from the other side of the gan.

So it would seem natural for Adam & Co. to be named by these people in a manner commensurate with their origin; i.e.; whatever word in their, (those always outside the gan), language meant: "one from the other side."

The name Adam & Co. were given, was "Hebrew;" which in fact means "one from the other side." This is why when researching Hebrew words, one finds so many Hebrew words that have Chaldean origins. Adam, the very first *Hebrew*, likely learned the language of those already outside of the gan, rather than expecting them to learn his language—assuming he had one. So Adam's language of *Hebrew*, originated with the language of those outside—most especially the Chaldeans.

The reason that Hebrews are often called "God's chosen people;" is because through Adam and his descendants, they were *chosen* as the bloodline for Messiah. This term is merely a statement of superior suitability for a particular purpose; and should never be extrapolated to any other area of superiority.

About four thousand years later, there was a birth of a boy named Yeshua, in various spellings.

The first part of this name refers to the tetragrammaton YHWH, also with various spellings. YHWH is generally considered to be the usually unspoken or ineffable name of God. But this is only partially true. YHWH represents the *structure* of that which we refer to as God. The term God itself is more *function* related. YHWH is utilized because as soon as something is named, limitations are placed upon it. Since God himself is infinite, that won't work. Ineffable essentially means something that cannot be described with, or in, words.

The second part of this name refers to salvation. So *Yeshua* means: "*YHWH* is salvation." This is in contrast to *Elisha*, which means *God* is salvation.

And so this Hebrew boy named Yeshua, today with the English spelling of *Jesus*, was born. He is sometimes referred to as "The last Adam," and for good reason. For once it was "finished," there need not be any more Adams—at least for the redemption of man.

The Apocrypha

The period of time beginning with Gethsemane, and ending with the Crucifixion, is a relatively short one. Thousands of years of both planning and acting by God, largely culminating in a series of events; many of which occurred in this relatively short time frame. This is *not* in any way meant to diminish the importance of any events that occurred outside of this time. But rather, in a time relative sense; to note that the *understanding* of many of these events, as well as the *significance* of these events; all of which happened in this short duration of time; requires a bit of careful reading.

There is an interesting initial thing to consider: What do the "Star of David," the Masonic "Square and Compasses," and the cross have in common? The Masonic "Square and Compasses," is or are in reality a hidden or veiled version of the "Star of David;" thus there are really only two symbols; the "Star" and the Cross.

This "Star" is really not a star at all. It is a symbol of interlaced triangles. This is despite the fact that it is usually shown as two *superimposed* triangles; they are not supposed to be superimposed, but are in fact supposed to be *interlaced*.

A triangle with the base down, is generally considered to be a symbol of the *material* realm; and when it is the point or apex that is pointed downward, this generally symbolizes the *immaterial* realm. Thus when they are interlaced, this symbolizes complete harmony between the material and the immaterial. This is a very ancient symbol.

Symbolically, the cross quite similar. The vertical part of the cross symbolizes the *immaterial* realm; and the horizontal portion symbolizes the *material* realm. Thus the intersection represents the intersection of these two realms, with Jesus right in the middle.

"Jesus took the punishment for our sins, He died for our sins because he loves us."

The first part of this statement is not exactly true. There are two main results of sin; with one occurring in the material or *natural* realm, and the other occurring in the immaterial or *supernatural* realm.

The *material* results, although having immaterial, (F and MA) components, we call the law of compensation or karma. "We reap what we sow." Had Jesus actually taken this, (our), material punishment; He then necessarily would have also repealed the law of compensation or karma; if and when said compensation was the result of sinful behavior—at least from Calvary going forward.

In addition; if this had actually happened, then God's mercy would no longer be necessary for sinful behavior. *Mercy* meaning intervention by God so that we *do not* get what we *do* deserve; and *grace* meaning intervention by God *to* give us what we *do not* deserve. This of course is not so; we still require mercy.

Secondly, the law of *compensation*, or *karma*, is not punitive in nature by design. It is in a sense, neutral. When we choose to sin, we choose the results of sin. Likewise, when we choose to engage in upright behavior, we choose the results of upright behavior. Where the real trouble occurs, is when we think that we can mix and match these to our own liking. We think we can sin, and yet somehow not only *not* receive the karmic results of sin, but instead; somehow receive the results of upright behavior, and often it may actually appear that way to us at first.

This of course being the "bait;" bait which is often very effective when we choose to do it our way, (usually with significant help from the enemy); and not do it "God's way." It is interesting that no one ever seems to expect the reverse, that is; to engage in upright behavior, and yet somehow receive the wages of sin; as though that situation, and that situation alone would somehow uniquely be unfair.

Jesus did not die for our sins. In a sense, He died *because* of our sins. In common usage, "for," and "because," are considered synonyms.

This is more than just a semantic exercise. Because of our sin, we were disqualified from being (re-)connected to God; and thus the physical death, (disconnection), of Jesus was necessary. Not in order to make the *material* results of sin irrelevant, but to restore the possibility of a *spiritual* reconnection.

If Jesus brought us eternal life, then why do people still die? Because; it is this *immaterial* and eternal soul to God connection that He brought; and not an eternal *physical*, or soul to body connection. Thus, at least for now, we still must die physically; but there is no longer any need to remain spiritually dead by maintaining spiritual disconnection.

"Jesus loves us." Very few people can have any idea what this actually means, because most people are not personally familiar with this *agape* or unconditional love—except perhaps in rare, and short duration episodes.

Agape is complete unconditional love; a love that is never diminished no matter what the object of this love may do to you. Some may experience this in times of crisis; but it soon diminishes when the crisis passes. This love or agape that Jesus has for each and every human being is 100% and runs 24/7. The word agape also can mean opening in a wide manner, as in one's mouth when one is in total amazement.

Luke 22:39-46 (NAS) tells us:

"And He came out and proceeded
as was His custom to the Mount of Olives;
and the disciples also followed Him.

When He arrived at the place, He said
to them, "Pray that you may not
enter into temptation."

And He withdrew from them
about a stone's throw,
and He knelt down and began to pray,
saying, "Father, if You are willing,
remove this cup from Me;
yet not My will, but Yours be done."

Now an angel from heaven

> *appeared to Him, strengthening Him.*
> *And being in agony He was praying*
> *very fervently; and His sweat became*
> *like drops of blood,*
> *falling down upon the ground.*
>
> *When He rose from prayer,*
> *He came to the disciples and found*
> *them sleeping from sorrow,*
> *and said to them,*
> *"Why are you sleeping?*
> *Get up and pray that you*
> *may not enter into temptation."*[4]

This was a pivotal moment. The first thing and the last thing Jesus said to his disciples in these passages referred to temptation. Clearly temptation was on His mind. This was the last real chance the devil may have had to change the course of events. What was about to happen, was not and would not ever be a matter of brute force. The events that transpired after this encounter would be a matter of His choosing; and would not in any way be any type of victory by the devil. At some point, the enemy put together what was actually happening, and it was likely around this time when he did so.

When Mel Gibson's *"The Passion of the Christ"* was released, he was of course criticized by many of the secular movie reviewers. Some of this criticism was because he had placed Satan in Gethsemane. There were claims that this inclusion of Satan in Gethsemane was Scripturally inaccurate, because the Bible does not actually state such. Clearly this was a time of temptation for Jesus; as Satan realized what was about to transpire, and was not pleased with the circumstances. And if not from Satan, then whence came this temptation?

It was just a very short time before this, at the "supper," when the devil had actually entered Judas.

John 13:25-27 (NAS) tells us:

> *"He, (John) leaning back thus on*
> *Jesus' bosom, said to Him,*
> *"Lord, who is it?"*
> *Jesus then answered,*
> *That is the one for whom I shall*
> *dip the morsel and give it to him."*
>
> *So when He had dipped the morsel,*
> *He took and gave it to Judas,*
> *the son of Simon Iscariot.*
> *After the morsel, Satan*
> *then entered into him.*
>
> *Therefore Jesus said to him,*
> *"What you do, do quickly."*[5]

At that (supper) juncture, Satan was going full speed ahead. His plan of course, was to have Judas betray Jesus to the authorities. There is no evidence that Satan was having any second thoughts at *this* time; else why would he have entered Judas at *this* same, (supper), time? And we know that Jesus knew this, because of the inclusion of the word *"therefore."*

But here in *Gethsemane*, Jesus is asking the Father, (arguably three times), if He would, (not could), change the course of events to follow; but if not, then Jesus would be willing go through with it. And just at that very time, an angel appeared from heaven; it states to *"strengthen him."*

It is difficult to imagine what must have actually happened when this angel appeared. The story seems a bit "underreported." It does not state that this angel and Satan had "a few beers," and talked about old times; as this could probably not be farther from the truth.

The Scriptures do not state who the angel was, but since it was Gabriel that God had sent to Mary; when any angel might have arguably worked just as well; it is likely that this particular angel, if not Gabe himself, clearly would have been a member of the "A Team."

It does not state what Satan did at that time, but it does not seem likely that he was around very long after that. Had he in fact remained, there would likely have been the recounting of a rather spectacular battle included in the story. Likely he fled—hoping to return at a more "opportune time."

Here in Gethsemane, the only begotten Son of God is now being attacked by Satan, in order to try and stop Him from going through with the crucifixion. It was just a short time ago that Satan entered Judas in furtherance of his plan—likely quite pleased with himself. Now it seems he is suddenly trying his best to get Jesus to *not* go through with it.

One reasonable explanation being, that here in Gethsemane, Satan was attempting, (a tempting?), to get Jesus to sin. Had Jesus refused to go through with it, then He arguably would no longer be "without sin;" and thus all else would have become irrelevant. Satan; likely believing that any such refusal would not change the *course* of events; but would drastically alter the *significance* of said events. Meaning: that Satan believed that Jesus would still be "killed;" but without providing redemption, salvation, or anything else.

Another explanation, would be that this represented what probably would best be termed as an *"evilation;"* (authors' terminology); meaning a combination of the words evil and revelation; but revelation from deductive reasoning and not divine guidance. Satan is not so much concerned with always being wicked; but he is very concerned; some would say obsessed, with always being evil; with evil being defined as anything that is contrary to God's will. If God were wicked, which of course He is not; then Satan would probably be a "very nice guy;" because then wickedness would be God's will.

No Scriptural evidence can be easily found with respect to the nature of this "evilation." At some point between entering Judas, and Jesus' decision to go to Gethsemane; Satan must have realized that all of his evil was playing right into God's hand. He likely did not know this at the time of the "Last Supper," or perhaps termed the "Last Seder," else he likely would have done things differently.

Satan may have sensed an interesting relationship between

what was transpiring at this time, and something that had transpired in the past.

The reason for the common confusion about the day of the crucifixion; and thus the subsequent "three days and three nights" discrepancy; is related to the fact that this particular "Sabbath," was to be "The Passover," and not the usual Saturday, (beginning at sundown on Friday), Sabbath.

Up until this time, Passover related to the blood of a lamb being placed over the door posts and lintel; in order to have the "angel" of death pass over, and save the first born children from *physical* death. This lamb had to live among the family for a week; and the lamb had to be killed at twilight; and had to be eaten.

This particular Passover, it was the Lamb of God who was to give his blood, (more about this later); in order to save all those who believe; from *spiritual* death, or *spiritual* disconnection from God. Jesus had lived among the people, and thus was killed sometime around twilight; this being the time in that culture when the new day began.

The word "save" can also mean *except*, or the making of an *exception*. It is easy to confuse the words "savior" and "salvation." *Savior* relates to the exception being made; and *salvation* refers here to the salvaging or restoration of a previous relationship. Acceptance of this *exception* results in *salvation*; and each of these have specific meanings that are different than redemption.

It was likely because of this relationship, that Jesus addressed the issues of His body and blood; as well as the remembrance—with this being the *new* Passover to be remembered in lieu of the old.

Shortly after these events, they came to arrest Him, and John 18:4-6 (NAS) tells us:

> *"So Jesus, knowing all the things*
> *that were coming upon Him,*
> *went forth and said to them,*
> *"Whom do you seek?"*
>
> *They answered Him, "Jesus the Nazarene."*

> *He said to them, "I am He." And Judas*
> *also, who was betraying Him,*
> *was standing with them.*
> *So when He said to them, "I am He,"*
> *they drew back and fell to the ground."*[6]

This is a very important event. A crowd comes to arrest Jesus with torches, lanterns, and swords; and Jesus merely speaks: *"I am He,"* and they all fall to the ground.

They did not just fall, but drew back first; and likely because of the magnitude of the force. There is no evidence to suggest any limits with respect to how many times this would have worked. When they arose, if Jesus had again said the same thing, it seems likely that they would have all fallen to the ground again. This could, and likely would have continued until each and every member of the crowd either starved to death, or died of old age. The importance being, that Jesus could not have been arrested *against* His will, but He in fact *chose* to go with those who were sent to arrest Him.

It is always a spectacular scene in a movie, when the bad guy gets shot by the good guy; and the force of the 44 magnum handgun projectile is so great, that the force of impact alone knocks the bad guy to the ground. The problem with this is that this is generally impossible in real life.

The reason for this, is the law of "equal and opposite reactions." If the bad guy gets knocked to the ground, then since an equal but opposite force is imparted to the shooter; the good guy would also necessarily have to be knocked to the ground. This would be so, unless there was a tremendous disparity in their masses, or a means of deflecting the force and preventing it from being imparted to the shooter.

This is why large caliber weapons are often bolted down. In a way, it is something like trying to move a refrigerator in stocking feet. The person slides backwards, but the refrigerator does not move.

But here, simply by Jesus simply saying: *"I am He;"* an

entire crowd draws back, and falls to the ground. There is no evidence that Jesus in any way moved. This by definition was a miracle, as it defied natural law. Likely this force came from the Father, and through Jesus.

Jesus knew: "*all the things* (plural) *that were coming upon him.*"

There are two relevant concepts which merit some attention:

The first is that of substitution. We saw this earlier in the Old Testament, with the use of the scapegoat. The idea of placing sin on the goat as a substitute for the actual sinner, represented a shadow of the mechanism that was to come; with Jesus as the vehicle for salvation.[7]

The other, is very much like the Homeopathic: "Law of Similars." In Homeopathy, "Like cures like." A substance which is known to produce certain symptoms in a healthy individual, is used to cure an individual with those same symptoms. Although in actual practice this is not quite as simple as it sounds; both because actual diagnosis is quite complex, and appropriate methods of "dilution and succussion" are also employed.

This Homeopathic law is immaterial in nature. The lower the concentration of the actual substance by dilution, and subsequent succussion; the more potent is the remedy. At some point in the dilution process, the likelihood of even one molecule of the original substance being present approaches zero; thus an inverse relationship existing between concentration and potency. It is the *vibrational* essence, and not the *chemical* characteristics that provide the efficacy.

There are actually at least three separate processes involved with events surrounding Calvary: There is the general process of *saving*, or making an exception of those who believe. There is also the matter of *salvation*; as well as the matter of *redemption*.

If the a store clerk is asked for assistance in *salvaging* a coupon, they would likely offer adhesive tape.

If the same store clerk were instead asked for assistance in *redeeming* a coupon, they would likely be concerned with some type of a discount; or exchanging the coupon for some benefit to the consumer. Although an argument could be made that salvation is a type of redemption, they are not the same.

The salvation aspects of the events of Calvary are generally understood in terms of *results*; even if they are not completely understood in terms of the actual *process*. Basically, God did something so that He could stand to be connected to us.

The *redemptive* events, although similar in this regard, generally are another matter.

Firstly, there is the redemption of or from sickness or disease.

The last line of Isaiah 53:5 (NAS) tells us:

"And by His scourging we are healed."[8]

"The Interlinear Bible" version of Isaiah 53:5 is:

*"and with His wounds
we ourselves are healed."*[9]

The actual Hebrew word translated as "scourging" and "wounds" is:

"2250 chabbûwrâh, or chabbûrâh, or chăbûrâh, from 2266; prop. *bound* (with stripes), i.e. a *weal* (or black - and - blue mark itself): - blueness, bruise, hurt, stripe, wound."[10]

The word 2266, is the same root relating to the actual word for "waters," appearing in early Genesis:

"2266 châbar, a prim. root; to *join* (lit. or fig.); spec. (by means of spells) to *fascinate*: - charm (-er), be compact, couple (together), have fellowship with, heap up, join (self, together), league."[11]

It is interesting to note the relationship between these two words: *chabbûwrâh* and *châbar*; with one, (chabbûwrâh), meaning injuries of various sorts; and the other, (châbar), the *root* of *chabbuwrah*, relating to joining, "to *join* (lit. or fig.);" fellowship, fascination etc.

As in Genesis, fascination necessarily implies the existence of some type of entity capable of successfully engaging in fascinating or charming. The idea of fellowship also requires another entity with which to have fellowship; and in this context does likely not mean God; else what was God doing in early Genesis while he was hovering over the surface of this seam.

Hence this reasonably supports the fact of the relationship between the existence of maladies, and the involvement of another entity in "joining;" and is likely the enemy.

The actual Hebrew word translated as "healed" is:

"7495 râphâ', or râphâh, a prim. root; prop. to *mend* (by stitching), i.e. (fig.) to *cure*: - cure, (cause to) heal, physician, repair, x thoroughly, make whole."[12]

Proverbs 20:30 (NAS) tells us:

"*Stripes that wound scour away evil,
And strokes reach the innermost parts.*"[13]

"The Interlinear Bible" version of Proverbs 20:30 is:

"*The stripes of a wound cleanse away evil;
and strokes the inward parts of the heart.*"[14]

The "*stripes*" translation used here in these Proverbs 20:30 translations; is same word as "*scourging*" and "*wounds,*" (chabbûwrâh, chabbûrâh, or chăbûrâh), previously seen in Isaiah 53:5.[15]

The original Hebrew word translated as "scour" and "cleanse" is:

"8562 tamrûwq, or tamrûq, or tamrîyq, from 4838; prop. a *scouring*, i.e. *soap* or *perfumery* for the bath; fig. a *detergent*: - x cleanse, (thing for) purification (- fying)."¹⁶

In Malachi 3:2 (NAS), God is speaking about Jesus, and He tells us:

*"For He is like a refiner's fire and like fullers' soap."*¹⁷

The original Hebrew word translated as "fullers" is:

"3526 kábac, a prim. root; to *trample*; hence to *wash* (prop. by stamping with the feet), whether lit. (including the *fulling* process) or fig.: - fuller, wash (-ing)."¹⁸

There is no need to go into the details of the beatings and the scourging of Jesus prior to the crucifixion, as this is well known. Based upon the above, a fair conclusion is that it is these stripes; the ones inflicted upon Jesus; which are the very stripes referred to in the aforementioned passages.

By the appearance of *"His scourging"* in Isaiah, and *"He is like"* in Malachi, with both being capitalized; it is clear that this refers to deity; this deity being *Messiah*, or The *Christ*. The one main problem is that Messiah or The Christ, by definition, uniquely had no evil to "clean up." Were this not so, He could not have been Messiah.

Back to the Homeopathic "Law of Similars." It is by the infliction of these wounds on Messiah; who up until that time has no recorded history of ever being sick or ill; being made ill by the same; that would provide curing, healing, or a remedy for those of us who were, are, or ever would be ill. Hence: "we are healed."

This represents a kind of intercessory healing, by the principles of the: "Law of Similars;" perhaps better termed: "Law of Intercessory Similars;" and likely could only have been accomplished by Jesus. But this is only a part of it. This is one result, albeit a very important one, of the cleansing away of the evil.

At this juncture Satan had lost his *right*, but not his *ability* to inflict sickness upon us. There is sickness in the world today, not because Satan has any "right" to inflict it upon us; but because he still has the ability to inflict the same upon us; however he *cannot* any longer do so *unilaterally*.

The above definition of the word that is translated as "healed," this word *râphâ'*; also includes the meanings of: "...repair, x thoroughly, make whole." Thus, there are other areas associated with this event other than physical illness. The "evil" which is "cleansed," also has to do with any other state of man's circumstances which are against God's will for us.

Usually, God's will is only considered from a rather Narcissistic viewpoint: "What am I going to get in trouble for doing or not doing?" But God's will for us is not just about laws and rules. The 23rd Psalm is usually reserved for funerals and the like, but a reading of this outside of the funerary context can provide some insight into God's will for us.

In addition to redemption from sickness, there are some other clues in the events surrounding Calvary, thathich are consistent with this intercessory "Law of Similars" process, including:

> 1. They stole from Him, hence we are healed from poverty.
> 2. When faced with false accusations, he remained silent. Jesus' silence then, gives him the just authority now, to be the mediator that was cried out for in Job. When the devil goes to God regarding to what he is "entitled" to because we sinned, just as he did with Job; for believers, Jesus now can just say; "case dismissed."
> 3. The crown of thorns restored our kingship; part of which was lost as result of sin. It is important to remember that thorns and thistles were not originally enemies of the food supply, back when the mist "used to rise." The presence of these "weeds" in agriculture is the direct result of the transfer of some earthly authority to the enemy because of sin. Certainly we still have thorns;

but this is about the kingship lost, and then restored by the King of kings; the use of the crown of thorns being a clue to this area of redemption.

Probably the most spectacular redemptive event, was Jesus' blood contacting the ground. When God breathes into our nostrils the "breath of life," and we become living beings, as per Genesis 2:7; this essence resides in the blood. In the case of Jesus, this essence was the Father Himself. When that blood containing the essence of the Father "hit the ground," over which Satan had been given, (delivered); a large amount of authority because of sin, literally "all hell broke loose."

Generally, the movies depict the sky becoming darkened at the time of Jesus' physical death—arguably as a direct result of his death. This is generally perceived as the wrath of the Father, because of the murder of His Son. Many believe this darkening was the result of a perfectly timed solar eclipse.

According to Matthew, this darkening or "solar eclipse," as many believe; actually occurred from the sixth hour to the ninth hour.[19] Other accounts agree with this.

The earliest time that can be determined for Jesus' physical death, would be sometime during the "ninth hour;" the same generally *assumed* to be 3:00 PM. This of course would then necessarily be at the time of the *ending* of this darkness, and not the *beginning*.

With regard to this "solar eclipse" theory, it is quite problematic. According to *Wikipedia*: "The longest total solar eclipse during the 8,000-year period from 3000 BC to 5000 AD will occur on July 16, 2186, when totality will last 7 min 29 s."[20]

Solar eclipses are a phenomenon of short duration; and even this record eclipse in 2186, will clearly be much shorter than the three hour duration of the darkness implied in the Bible.

The sun travels 360 degrees in 24 hours. This amounts to 15 degrees per hour. Thus 45 degrees of solar motion would have had to occur in this three hour period. This (45 degrees) of solar motion would represent one fourth of the total motion of the sun (approximately 180 degrees) during daylight hours. This would have then have been an eclipse, the duration of which is far beyond the duration of any known eclipses.

In addition, according to *mreclipse.com*: "An eclipse of the Sun (or solar eclipse) can *only* occur at New Moon when the Moon passes between Earth and Sun;"[21] and other sources agree with this requirement.

The date of Passover is determined by the date of the first *full* moon, after the vernal equinox; and Easter is determined by the first Sunday, after the first *full* moon, after the vernal equinox. This makes perfect sense, as it seems reasonable that the Exodus would occur when the moon was full. However, since one cannot simultaneously have a full moon and a new moon; the possibility of this darkness at Calvary being the result of an "solar eclipse," appears to be zero.

Ergo; it can be conclusively proved that whatever it was that caused this darkness, was not and could not have been a solar eclipse.

The actual Greek word used here translated as "darkness" is:

> "4655 skŏtŏs, from the base of 4639; *shadiness*, i.e. *obscurity* (lit. or fig.): - darkness." "4639 skia, appar. A prim. word; "*shade*" or a shadow (lit. or fig. [darkness of *error* or an *adumbration*]): - shadow."[22]

This word *skŏtŏs*, seems to be a member of the "skoteinos" family of words, meaning tent or covering. The word adumbration contains the same root of umbra; from which we derive the word umbrella.

Thus, just as in the darkness referenced in early Genesis, again we see this concept of not just darkness as merely the absence of light; but rather the darkness existing because of shading or a cover. The concept of a shade implies there is light, but it is blocked; with the resulting area of *less light* described as shade. Even today, we refer to the victim of a dishonest scheme as being kept "in the dark," by a "shady" character.

Some *secular* sources try to place place the birth of Jesus somewhere in the range of approximately 3BC to 3AD. This error may very well be due to referencing when the known solar eclipses occurred, and then counting backwards approximately 33 years.

This 3:00 PM time of His death is uncertain for several reasons. There is the matter of removal of the bodies from the crosses because of the approaching Sabbath.

The Jewish time for the beginning of the day is *sundown*, and not midnight or sunrise.

The sixth hour is generally *assumed* to be six hours after sunrise, or approximately at noon. The ninth hour is *assumed* to be nine hours later, or at 3:00 PM.

If this were all so, then Jesus "died" at 3:00 PM; and then the body must have been on the cross for approximately three hours from the time of death; this being from 3:00 until sundown, the time when this "Sabbath" was to begin.

But in that culture, the 24 hour day was broken up into *three hour* segments. The night segments were called *watches* and the day segments were called *hours*. These were named by the times they began; either after sunrise or sunset.

The *first watch* began at sunset or about 6:00 PM, and lasted until about 8:59PM, followed by the *second* watch.

The *first hour* began at sunrise or about 6:00 AM, and lasted until 8:59 AM; but unlike the night watches, was actually followed by the *third*, (not second), hour beginning at 9:00 AM.[23]

Thus, when the Bible speaks of the "sixth hour," or the "ninth hour;" it is not necessarily referring to the time that would appear on a clock, or the hours counted from sunrise; which is presumed to be at 6:00 AM. Rather it is referring to a *period* of time of three hours, which merely *begins* at that time. The "sixth hour" would then be a period of time lasting from approximately 12:00 noon until approximately 2:59 PM; and the "ninth hour" would then be a period of time lasting from approximately 3:00 PM until approximately 5:59 PM.

According to Mark, the crucifixion of Jesus actually began at the "third hour."

Mark 15:25 (NAS) tells us:

> *"It was the third hour when they crucified Him."*[24]

Thus, according to Mark, this would be between 9:00 AM and noon.

According to John, the events leading up to crucifixion of Jesus, actually *began* at the "sixth hour."

John 19:14-15 (NAS) tells us:

> *"Now it was the day of preparation
> for the Passover; it was about the sixth hour.
> And he said to the Jews, "Behold, your King!"
> So they cried out, "Away with Him,
> away with Him, crucify Him!"*
>
> *Pilate said to them,
> "Shall I crucify your King?"
> The chief priests answered,
> "We have no king but Caesar."*[25]

Thus, according to John, these "preliminary" events *began* between noon and 3:00 PM. From these passages, the precise time of the separation of Jesus' soul from His body, cannot be determined.

However, the aforementioned *darkness*, cannot definitively be placed at the beginning of the crucifixion or in the middle of it; but what can be said, is that it did not begin *after* His death.

John was an eyewitness to these events. We know this because Jesus spoke to him from the cross as stated in John 19:26.[26]

Here in John 19:31-34 (NAS), he tells us:

> *"Then the Jews, because it was
> the day of preparation,
> so that the bodies would not remain
> on the cross on the Sabbath*

> *(for that Sabbath was a high day),*
> *asked Pilate that their legs might be broken,*
> *and that they might be taken away.*
>
> *So the soldiers came, and broke*
> *the legs of the first man and*
> *of the other who was crucified with Him;*
> *but coming to Jesus, when they saw*
> *that He was already dead,*
> *they did not break His legs.*
> *But one of the soldiers pierced His*
> *side with a spear, and immediately*
> *blood and water came out."*[27]

Here the Jews are asking that the legs of all three be broken so that *they*, not *He*, could be taken down and/or away, because of the *"high day."*

One theory for this request, is that this would accelerate death.

Another theory would be that this was to insure that none of them would be able to escape once taken down from the cross; and they did not want them hanging on the cross on this *"high day."* Generally, crucifixion is believed to have been invented by the Romans; however—

Deuteronomy 21:22-23 may be related to both their desire for crucifixion, and their request for the leg breaking; because of concerns about them being taken away:

Deuteronomy 21:22-23 (NAS) tells us:

> *"If a man has committed a sin*
> *worthy of death and he is put to death,*
> *and you hang him on a tree,*
> *his corpse shall not hang*
> *all night on the tree,*
> *but you shall surely bury him*
> *on the same day (for he who is*

> *hanged is accursed of God),*
> *so that you do not defile your*
> *land which the* LORD *your*
> *God gives you as an inheritance."*[28]

    When it was seen by the soldiers that Jesus was already dead, His legs were not broken; so either theory would support this.

    He was *"pierced,"* likely to make certain that He was in fact "dead then," as a kind of "insurance," in case had He not actually been dead before this. This is also likely the reason why they *"looked at whom they pierced,"* to make certain that He had exsanguinated; the soldiers not realizing that their acts fulfilled two Messianic prophesies. (Actually three, if *not* breaking His bones is considered.)

    It is not stated if the Jews took away the bodies of the other two. It is possible they did; and they may or may not have still been alive. It seems likely that Golgotha was actually named such because of the collection of skulls from those who were crucified and whose bodies were merely left there. Of course the more modern explanation of the origin of this name; is that this hill resembles a skull, hence its name.

    Nevertheless, and despite the additional requirements of Deuteronomy 21:22-23; they did not take away the body of Jesus for burial. It seems obvious that they were unconcerned with any aspect of proper treatment of the dead; instead being concerned only with the fact that he was dead.

    This *"high day"* Sabbath, is also a source of confusion regarding the Resurrection. It is generally assumed that this Sabbath is the normal Saturday Sabbath; which would begin Friday at sundown. Thus it is believed that the death must have occurred on Friday, at or sometime prior to sundown. But this was not the normal Sabbath. Rather, it was the case that *"that Sabbath was a high day."* This particular "high day" Sabbath was Passover, and not the normal Friday at sundown until Saturday at sundown Sabbath.

    In Matthew 12:40 (NAS), Jesus is speaking and tells us:

> *"for just as JONAH WAS THREE DAYS*
> *AND THREE NIGHTS IN THE BELLY*
> *OF THE SEA MONSTER,*
> *so will the Son of Man be three days*
> *and three nights in the heart of the earth."*[29]

Thus if you "back out" from Sunday at dawn three days and nights; then Friday around sundown being the time of His death simply will not work. Neither will this work if the resurrection occurred at dawn; no matter what day is used as a starting point.

If the "death" occurred at or near sundown, which seems a certainty; then the resurrection must have occurred three days and three nights later; at or near sundown.

John 20:1 (NAS) tells us:

> *"Now on the first day of the week*
> *Mary Magdalene came early to the tomb,*
> *while it was still dark,*
> *and saw the stone already*
> *taken away from the tomb."*[30]

The *"first day of the week"* was *Sunday* in that culture, and it was *"still dark"* when she discovered that He was gone. Ergo; the Resurrection had already occurred while it was dark, and not at dawn, early or otherwise.

Thus it had to be on Wednesday, sometime between 3:00 PM and sundown that was the actual time of His "death." The Resurrection must have occurred three days and three nights later, on Saturday sometime between 3:00 PM and sundown.

There are those who will go where the most facts lead, and there are those who will not. But as will be shortly seen with the misplaced man-added comma; similarly here, *"still dark"* logically precludes that which defines dawn.

Mark 15:42-44 (NAS) tells us:

> *"When evening had already come,*
> *because it was the preparation day,*
> *that is, the day before the Sabbath,*
> *Joseph of Arimathea came,*
> *a prominent member of the Council,*
> *who himself was waiting*
> *for the kingdom of God;*
> *and he gathered up courage*
> *and went in before Pilate,*
> *and asked for the body of Jesus.*
>
> *Pilate wondered if He was dead by this time,*
> *and summoning the centurion,*
> *he questioned him as to whether*
> *He was already dead.*
> *And ascertaining this from the centurion,*
> *he granted the body to Joseph."*[31]

It seems likely that at this juncture, that Pilate did not initially know what was going on; including whether or not Jesus was taken away alive, left there alive with His legs broken, or if he was dead.

Pilate had previously agreed to permit having all their legs broken, so that they could be "taken away." But he did not seem to know that Jesus was already dead, and subsequently pierced to make certain.

The *King James* version of Mark 15:42-44 substitutes the words "*any while dead*" for "*already dead.*"[32]

This KJV version makes it appear that Pilate was also concerned with how long Jesus was dead; as though beyond a certain period of time Pilate would be safe.

Perhaps a more contemporary phraseology would be: "Is he dead enough?"

Alternately, since death from crucifixion generally required several days; perhaps it was merely that Pilate was surprised that

Jesus was dead. This could be contradicted however, because the breaking of the legs was also a death accelerant.

There is an issue with the conversation between Jesus and one of the thieves on the cross; which as commonly believed, makes little sense if taken literally as it appears. The citation for this appears in Luke.

Luke 23:42-43 tells us:

> *"And he was saying,*
> *"Jesus, remember me when*
> *You come in Your kingdom!"*
>
> *And He said to him,*
> *"Truly I say to you, today*
> *you shall be with Me in Paradise."*[33]

As it appears, this seems quite easy to understand. Here the thief believed Jesus was the Christ, and was asking to be saved. It is interesting that two men were crucified alongside Jesus, and their names are not even mentioned.

Clearly this thief was not referring to any physical kingdom. But the problem with this citation; is that the answer given by Jesus, as written, cannot possibly be true.

The word "paradise," comes from para-deity, which roughly means "next to God." Obviously, Jesus had said this to the thief while He was still alive. If it is true, that as in the case of the Passover lamb, Jesus actually died at sundown; then this would have technically been the next day. Thus, Jesus would still have been alive the entire day He made this statement, and could not have gone to "*Paradise*" on that day.

If it is believed that he died *before* sundown; clearly before the beginning of the next day; then He did not go to "*Paradise*" on that next day either.

This is known because in John 20:17 it states:

> *"Jesus said to her,*
> *'Stop clinging to Me,*
> *for I have not yet ascended to the Father;*
> *but go to My brethren and say to them,*
> *I ascend to My Father and your Father,*
> *and My God and your God."*[34]

This statement was made by Jesus *after* the resurrection.

The problem with the previous citation, (Luke 23:43): *"Truly I say to you, today you shall be with Me in Paradise.;"* lies with the placement of the comma. The comma belongs after the *"today,"* and not after the *"you."* Thus it should read: "Truly I say to you *today*, you shall be with Me in Paradise."

The *today* refers to when the statement was being made, and not when the thief would be with Jesus; as Jesus would not be in *"Paradise"* until 40 days had passed.[35]

It is believed that the original Biblical writings were written in continuous form, and contained no punctuation. Thus this misplaced comma was added later.

There is scant information about the earthquake contained in the four Gospels. It seems that Matthew is the only one of the four who provides any substantial amount of information.

Matthew 27: 50-54 tells us:

> "(50) *And Jesus cried out again with a loud voice,*
> *and yielded up His spirit.*
>
> (51) *And behold, the veil of the temple*
> *was torn in two from top to bottom;*
> *and the earth shook and the rocks were split.*
>
> (52) *The tombs were opened,*
> *and many bodies of the saints*
> *who had fallen asleep were raised;*
>
> (53) *and coming out of the tombs after*

*His resurrection they entered the
holy city and appeared to many.*

*(54) Now the centurion, and those who
were with him keeping guard over Jesus,
when they saw the earthquake and the
things that were happening,
became very frightened and said,
'Truly this was the Son of God'!"*[36]

These five verses arguably span at least forty days; that being approximately the duration of time from the crucifixion to the resurrection.

But if verse 53; ("*and coming out of the tombs after His resurrection they entered the holy city and appeared to many;*") were temporarily removed, the chronology seems reasonably consistent.

In verse 51, three things are happening. These seem to be related in terms of cause and effect, but this may not necessarily be so.

Firstly: "*The veil of the temple was torn in two.*"

It is easy for the mind to create an image of what this veil was—perhaps similar to a larger version of what a bride wears. Tearing it in half seems like no great effort. But this veil in no way resembled such a veil.

It is not clear from this passage alone, if this "veil" is the "screen" which was the entrance to the *tent*; or if it was the veil that separated the holy room from the inner room, or the "Holy of Holies."

The original Greek word translated as "veil" is:

"2665 katapĕtasma, from a comp. of 2596 and a congener of 4072; something *spread thoroughly*, i.e. (spec.) the door *screen* (to the Most Holy Place) in the Jewish Temple: - vail."[37]

Thus it appears that this veil was the inner veil, separating the "Holy Room" from the "Most Holy Place."

Exodus 26: 31-33 describes this veil:

> *"You shall make a veil of blue and purple*
> *and scarlet material and fine twisted linen;*
> *it shall be made with cherubim,*
> *the work of a skillful workman.*
>
> *"You shall hang it on four pillars*
> *of acacia overlaid with gold,*
> *their hooks also being of gold,*
> *on four sockets of silver.*
>
> *"You shall hang up the veil under the clasps,*
> *and shall bring in the ark of the testimony*
> *there within the veil; and the veil shall*
> *serve for you as a partition between*
> *the holy place and the holy of holies."*[38]

Thus this veil was large, and substantial enough to require four pillars on which it was to hang. In the case of an earthquake, it seems more likely that the pillars would have fallen, rather than the veil being torn in two from top to bottom. Yet, this is not what happened.

The Interlinear Bible version of Matthew 27:51 states: "was torn into two, from above *until* below."[39]

The original Greek word translated as "until" is:

> "2193 hĕōs, of uncert. affin.; a conj., prep. and adv. of continuance, until (of time and place): - even (until, unto), (as) far (as), how long, (un-) til (-l), (hither-, un-, up) to, while (-s)."[40]

Thus, there is a clear implication that this tearing was not instantaneous. The use of the phrase *"from top to bottom,"* strictly indicates the location of the tear. The term *"from above until below,"* suggests that both time and location were factors.

Perhaps this was a slow motion tearing, beginning at the top and continuing downward; a rather unusual sight—unless one is familiar with Doberman Pinchers and upholstered furniture.

It is difficult to imagine what it must have been like to watch this veil tear itself in half, from the top to the bottom. With the human mind likely comprehending this tearing, as though a pair of invisible hands were tearing this substantial fabric in half.

According to Scriptures, God had "resided" on the other side of this veil. And: "This most sacred enclosure had only one item of furniture, the ark of the Covenant."[41]

Only once a year, on the "day of atonement," was a human even permitted to enter this Holy of Holies. Yet, upon the death of Jesus, this veil was completely torn. Was this so that God could get out?

The answer is no. God could have easily "gotten out" without the tearing of this veil. The veil was torn in this manner, so that all would *know* he had gotten out.

Upon the death of Jesus, a substantial portion of the world was "un-handed-over" to Satan. Prior to this; God the Father had license to be present on the earth only under certain circumstances, with the ark being one. But all of this had just changed.

In the following passage from Luke 4:5-7 (NAS), the "he" is Satan; and the 'Him' is Jesus:

"And he led Him up and showed
Him all the kingdoms of the world
in a moment of time.

"And the devil said to Him,
'I will give You all this domain and its glory;
for it has been handed over to me,
and I give it to whomever I wish.

"Therefore if You worship before me,
it shall all be Yours.'"[42]

Given the circumstances, it is likely that it was only because of the nature of Jesus, that his answer to the devil was not: "Why should I do that? I am going to get it all back anyway?"

It would probably make the most sense to take another look at Mathew 27:54 and the centurion, in order to get some insight into the verses that precede it.

This can fairly be treated as a type of conclusive statement, which was based upon the real time observation of events: *"Now the centurion, and those who were with him keeping guard over Jesus, when they saw the earthquake and the things that were happening, became very frightened and said, "Truly this was the Son of God!"*

A centurion is not just a Roman soldier. He is the leader of a large group of foot soldiers; possibly as many as one hundred—hence the name.

A centurion was likely quite used to "killing people and breaking things," which is generally the main task of any military organization; as well as countless times being an eyewitness the same. It was a centurion who was going to "examine," (by scourging), Paul; until he found out that Paul was a Roman citizen.

This was a man who had seen much. He was entrusted to "guard" Jesus; keeping in mind that of course there are two types of guards. One type of guard, such as a *bodyguard*; is there to insure that the person he is guarding *is* able to do what he wants to do. The other type of guard, such as a *prison* guard; is there to insure that the person he is guarding *is not* able to do what he wants to do. [The same can be said of "chaperones," but that is another matter.]

What would or could it take to not merely frighten such a man, but to make him *"very frightened?"*

In verse 54, Matthew had told us that they: *"saw the earthquake and the things that were happening."*

The actual Greek word that is translated as earthquake is:

> "4578 sĕismŏs, from 4579; a *commotion*, i.e. (of the air) a *gale*, (of the ground) an *earthquake*: - earthquake, tempest."[43]

Thus this word "sĕismŏs," is a general term denoting commotion; which can be applied to the air, the ground or a storm, or anything else. The decision to mistranslate a word denoting *general* commotion, into the *specific*—earthquake; leads the reader to an unwarranted conclusion. This was likely translated as such because of the English word "seismic," usually relating to earthquakes. There is a difference however, between an earthquake and the earth quaking.

The former is a specific event, usually tectonic in origin; which often causes the crust of the *earth* to "quake." The latter is a condition of the mere quaking of the earth, which could be caused by many other phenomena as well.

As written, this "sĕismŏs" does not necessarily relate to the ground, but likely is also assumed to be so because of the following statement, which actually precedes the "earthquake" translation in Matthew 27:51.

"And the earth shook and the rocks were split."

This would have been another opportunity for the translator to have translated the word as earthquake; yet at least in this verse, he, she, or they did not.

The original Greek word translated here as "earth" is:

> "1093 gē, contr. From a prim. word; *soil*; by extens. a *region*, or the solid part or the whole of the *terrene* globe (includ. the occupants in each application): - country, earth (-ly), ground, land, world."[44]

The original Greek word translated as "shook" is:

> "4579 sĕiō, appar. a prim. verb; to *rock* (*vibrate*, prop. sideways or to and fro), i.e. (gen.) to *agitate* (in a any direction; cause to *tremble*); fig. to throw into a *tremor* (of fear or concern): - move, quake, shake."[45]

Neither "sĕiō" nor "sĕismŏs" specifically relate to an earthquake, but rather motion or commotion respectively. However the use of the "gē," indicates that "seio" in this passage was related to the ground.

Thus it seems that a fair interpretation that it was both

the soil or ground; *as well as the occupants*; ["whole of the *terrene* globe (includ. the occupants in each application"]; which were rocking or vibrating either sideways or to and fro. It does not state that anyone fell down during this time.

Back in Matthew 12:40, when Jesus told us *"the Son of Man be three days and three nights in the heart of the earth,"* many people believe this refers to His time in the tomb. But does this refer to Jesus' *body*; or does this refer to Jesus' *soul*?

Jesus tomb was not actually in the heart of the earth, either literally or figuratively. Thus His *body* was not even in the ground, but rather in what essentially was a cave.

Ephesians 4:9-10 tells us:

> *"(Now this expression, "He ascended,"*
> *what does it mean except that*
> *He also had descended into*
> *the lower parts of the earth?*
>
> *"He who descended is Himself also*
> *He who ascended far above all the heavens,*
> *so that He might fill all things.)"*[46]

So we have some confirmation that the *"heart of the earth,"* as likely meaning *"the lower parts of the earth."* It seems that when Jesus; (Jesus' *soul*, but not *body*); descended into the heart or lower parts of the earth, the ground above and the occupants began to move. [As an aside, was this part of the earth the same area relating to the prohibited likenesses or images in Exodus 20:4?]

To suggest that this was in any way an earthquake in the normal sense; takes away from the significance of the events going on between the forces of light, and the forces of darkness. It would be unfair to characterize this as an underground battle, as the battle had already been fought and won. It is likely this was more an *enforcement* issue.

It is also interesting that the rocks were split.

The word "split" is

"4977 schizo, appar. a prim. verb; to *split* or *sever* (lit. or fig.): - break, divide, open, rend, make a rent"⁴⁷

This does not say crushed.
"The tombs were opened, and many bodies of the saints who had fallen asleep were raised"
The actual Greek word translated as "tombs" is:

"3419 mnēmĕiŏn, from 3420; a *remembrance*, i.e. *cenotaph* (*place of interment*): - grave, sepulchre, tomb."⁴⁸

The actual Greek word translated as "bodies" is:

"4983 sōma, from 4982; the *body* (as a *sound* whole), used in a very wide application, lit. or fig.: - bodily, body, slave."⁴⁹

The actual Greek word translated as "saints" is:

"40 hagiŏs, from hagos (an *awful* thing) [comp. 53, 2282]; *sacred* (phys. *pure*, mor. *blameless* or *religious*, cer. *consecrated*): - (most) holy (one, thing), saint."⁵⁰

The actual Greek word translated as "asleep" is:

"2837 kŏimaō, from 2749; to *put to sleep* i.e. (pass. or reflex.) to *slumber*; fig. to *decease*: - (be a -, fall a -, fall on) sleep, be dead."⁵¹

The actual original Greek word translated as "raised" is:

"1453 ĕgĕirō, prob. Akin to the base of 58 (through the idea of *collecting* one's faculties); to *waken* (trans. or intrans.), i.e. *rouse* (lit. from sleep, from sitting or lying, from disease, from death; or fig. from obscurity, inactivity, ruins, nonexistence): - awake, lift (up), raise (again, up), rear up, (a -) rise (again, up), stand, take up."[52]

There seems to be no way around the fact that the only reasonable read on this passage, is that this must have actually happened as described. The word "tomb," tends to make one think only of a mausoleum, but *mnēměiŏn* seems to refer to *any* place of interment.

It must be noted that there seems to be a time lag between when these were *raised*, (at the crucifixion); and when they actually *came out* of their tombs and *entered* the city, (after the resurrection). This may be a translational error, but this is how it reads.

Here is what appears to be the likely situation: The centurion guard is on the hill close to the crosses, likely facing Jesus, (Mark 15:39). It is unnaturally dark. Nearby him is the crowd that is mocking Jesus, (Mark 15:29). Farther away are the followers of Jesus, (Luke 23:49).

As previously stated, this hill is named Calvary or Golgotha, meaning skull; allegedly called such because the hill resembled a skull; but again more than likely named so because of the remaining skulls of most of those who were crucified there.

This centurion is making sure that no one, especially Jesus, gets off the crosses and escapes; in case His reputed powers actually existed; or in case He had obtained assistance. Those around him are taunting and mocking Jesus.

Then at some point, the darkness lifts and Jesus in a loud voice gives up his spirit. This likely surprises them, because the actual cause of death by crucifixion at that time was prolonged, and believed to be by either suffocation or exhaustion.[53]

Then this veil gets slowly ripped in half, from top to bottom; with no one appearing to be tearing it. Then the ground shakes as though an earthquake, but the crosses do not fall. Then graves and tombs open up and those previously interred, may or may have not come out of their tombs and started walking around. At this point, the centurion came to the conclusion that the "Jews" had been wrong.

Luke 23:48 (NAS) tells us:

> *"And all the crowds who came together for this spectacle, when they observed what had happened, began to return, beating their breasts."*[54]

It seems that once the crowd saw that Jesus was dead; and since the "fun" was all over, they had begun to leave. But when they observed what had then subsequently happened, something was not "right;" or at least not what they had expected, or had come to usually expect. So they began to return to the area. At this point they, like the centurion, had become very frightened.

This beating of the breasts is important.

This Greek word for "beating" is:

> "5180 tuptō, a prim. verb (in a strength. form); to *"thump"*, i.e. *cudgel* or *pummel* (prop. with a stick or *bastinado*), but in any case by *repeated* blows; thus differing from 3817 and 3960, which denote a [usually single] blow with the hand or any instrument, or 4141 with the *fist* [or a *hammer*], or 4474 with the *palm*; as well as from 5177, an *accidental* collision); by impl. to *punish*; fig. to *offend* (the conscience): - beat, smite, strike, wound."[55]

According to *"Illustrated Dictionary of the Bible,"* beating one's breast was a sign of intense sorrow.[56]

As a reference; earlier in Luke 18:13 Jesus is speaking and it states therein:

> *"But the tax collector,*

standing some distance away,
was even unwilling to lift up his eyes
to heaven, but was beating his breast,
saying, 'God, be merciful to me, the sinner!'"[57]

Today there is much confusion regarding precisely who Jesus was, and what this all means. Some major religions have attempted to place a "price tag" on salvation, by requiring certain types of behaviors or prohibiting certain types of behaviors, in order to maintain "saved" status. This then necessarily relates "salvation" to "works." [See: "*Statists Saving One*" Chapter 10: "*The Pseudo-Statists*"
But Ephesians 2:8-9 tells us:

"For by grace are ye saved through faith;
and that not of yourselves: it is the gift of God:
Not of works, lest any man should boast."[58]

So as can be seen, "works-dependent salvation" is not what God in any way said; at least according to Paul; who after all, did in fact write approximately one third of the entire New Testament.

If this "works-dependent" position reminds one of the: "And we'll send you a second for free – just pay a separate fee" commercials, there are good reasons for this. It remains unclear as to what Scriptural basis could be utilized in making the determination that works can in any way, means, or manner, affect salvation. It is quite clear that it is a *"gift of God: not of works;"* and not "of" but rather "for" ourselves.

Said salvation or saving is a binary, meaning; that if it is simply accepted, [and that (faith) is all that is required]; then one has it. To try and determine the magnitude of the sinfulness or *hamartano* of an individual is not only impossible, but irrelevant. No man can assign levels of sinfulness from God's perspective, and even if one could, it matters not. This is because the *need* for salvation is also a binary. Any sin, even so much as one "little" sin; "contaminates" that immaterial part of man; and thus he or she cannot ever be reconnected to God in that condition. God cannot ever allow Himself to be *contaminated* by man's transgressions.

Hence man's need for salvation; or perhaps better termed *justification*—just as though one never sinned. Others with different faiths may disagree, but there is *no* other way back to God other than justification, and there is only one giving it away.

If one cusses and fusses prior to obtaining said justification, he or she is free to cuss and fuss afterwards; and this has no effect on salvation/justification. Such behavior will affect the "cusser and fusser's" *earthly* conditions, because of "equal and opposite reactions;" i.e.; *karma*; but this will not affect salvation/justification one whit—at least according to His word.

Those who in any way attempt to place price tags, (except faith), on what God clearly offers for free; cannot avoid also necessarily being considered as those who believe that ends justify means. And on that path always lies destruction—*always*.

There is also a major attempt to "mis-portray" Jesus. Any one who proffers that Jesus was 'killed" by "anyone;" either does not understand the story, or does not believe it. Jesus was not "killed," and could not be "killed" by anyone. Many had tried and failed. The reason for this appears to be His lack of sin. This is the subject of another Monograph: *"It's Not Just a Theory."*

As one deviates from the *source*, one becomes prone to errors. The US Supreme Court spends way too much time looking to what others have said about the Constitution, rather than concerning themselves with what the document actually states.

Bible "scholars" are often guilty of the same. In the *Foundation* series, Isaac Asimov wrote about an archeologist who could not pronounce his r's, who saw no need to ever visit an archeological site. Being familiar with the writings of other was sufficient in his mind to be an archeologist.

Calvary was an amazing event. To understand what actually

transpired, requires the understanding of what those who were *present*, or at least *alive* at the time it happened, have to say about it.

Man sometimes sees one when there are two; and sometimes sees two when there is but one. The first error is seen with perception of that which is alive. The second occurs when evaluating man's actions. That which is referred to as karma, is not a separate entity; but rather is inextricably contained in the original action—whether admitted or not.

INEVITABLE BALANCE

What is *balance*?

If used as a noun, this represents some type of device utilized for balancing. Of course using a word in its definition helps little. But if it can be so stipulated that balance is derived from the Latin *bi*, meaning two; and the Latin *lanx*, meaning "dish or plate;"[1] then an image of the "scales" such as those representing the "scales of justice" comes to mind.

But much more importantly, balance as a noun can also represent a state of *equilibrium*.

If used as a verb, this then represents the act of achieving the second meaning of the noun—equilibrium. So here when one expends effort in order to *balance* something; the desired result is *balance*.

Kinetic energy is the energy that "a thing" has because it is in *motion*. Depending upon one's perspective, it can be said that a thing in motion is in actuality in the act of *attaining balance*. Or it could also be said that a thing in motion *is* in balance. Hit a baseball with a bat, and the ball then has kinetic energy from the force imparted to it by the bat. The ball will travel until other forces act upon it and bring it to a stop—most particularly gravity and wind resistance. [However due to the *inertia* of the ball, or any thing "in motion," the same will remain in motion until acted upon by another force, such as said gravity and wind resistance.] Thus this motion or kinetic energy could also be considered as a form of balance, but generally not in the material world. Even the planets are believed to be slowing down, however gradually.

Potential energy is energy that is *stored*. Here; again depending upon perspective; either a *balanced* or an *unbalanced* situation is present, and will remain present, unless and until the potential energy is released. A rock perched on the very edge of a cliff has potential energy, representing both a balance and an imbalance. Should the vibrations from a thunderstorm be sufficient to dislodge this perched rock, this potential energy then becomes kinetic energy as the rock is then in motion. Once the rock comes to a rest, that particular potential energy no longer exists. However, unless and until the rock is dislodged laterally by some force, it is also in a sense balanced.

Potential energy can be converted to kinetic energy, and kinetic energy can result in potential energy. Just ask the child who threw the ball that ended up "stuck" on the roof. If he could just dislodge it with a stick, it would fall to the ground. Or in the case of a pendulum; when moving; the pendulum has kinetic energy; and then potential energy when it stops, just before changing direction. Older watches require "winding," which is introducing kinetic energy, which produces potential energy in the spring. This potential energy is then released slowly as kinetic energy, moving the hands of the watch, until insufficient potential energy remains in the spring.

This kinetic-potential-kinetic conversion process is a very important concept, as along with free will; represent what could very well be considered as the "key" or the "keys," to, or of, the universe—assuming any such "keys" exist.

There are many forms of *material* potential energy, even that which is contained in the atoms that undergo fission or fusion in a nuclear reaction. Batteries and electric power represent material potential energy.

There is also *immaterial* potential energy. If this sounds a bit insane, then purposely insult, (stimulus), someone until they respond, (response). As these insults continue, there is immaterial potential energy being "created" and "stored" in the mind of the recipient of the insults. This immaterial potential energy exists until released, and is largely; although not necessarily exclusively; released as *material* kinetic energy, if and when there is a response.

Materially; there can be both internal as well as external responses to the insults, in attempts to achieve some degree of balance. The material *externals* are somewhat easy to detect— often verbal or physical. Increase in heart rate, respiration, and blood pressure can be considered as material *internal* responses.

Assuming the response is verbal; immaterial potential energy will subsequently then build in the *recipient* (source of original stimulus) of this response. And even when the response is physical; (better duck); the same holds true. And back and forth this can go until some degree and some type of balance is achieved.

It is also quite possible that this immaterial potential energy might not be released at that time. "Revenge is a dish best served cold," being a prime example.

Immaterial potential energy is by no means limited to the above. Terms such as "drive," "passion," and "determination;" all represent examples of immaterial potential energy, and there are many more. "I'm going to give him a piece of my mind;" or "I want satisfaction;" or "Who does she think she is?;" each represents evidence of immaterial potential energy. These potential energies will generally either become material kinetic energy, or will "dissipate" over time, causing changes elsewhere. Said "dissipation" can often result in health issues. This is one main reason why forgiveness is important. Forgiveness is not necessarily for the benefit of the perpetrator; as the same might not know, care, or even *believe* that there is anything requiring forgiveness. Forgiveness helps channel this immaterial potential energy elsewhere, often to the benefit of the "forgiver."

How much *immaterial* potential energy is there present in the above "insult" scenario? There are infinite possibilities of answers. The actual immaterial potential energy "created," is the result of many subjective and objective factors; but what is always the case, is that it is a "difference of potential."

The same is true materially with the flow of electricity. A charged 12V battery has the voltage or "difference of potential" of 12V, and electrons (I) will flow according to the resistance of the load (R) in this DC (direct current) circuit. A completely discharged battery essentially has a difference of potential of zero, and nothing will flow; unless and until the battery is "charged."

In fact, the use of the word *charge* itself in many contexts relates either to the imposition of an imbalance; or sometimes can refer to the actions undertaken to balance an existing imbalance.

The discharged or "dead" battery is a balanced phenomenon. It contains little or no potential energy, or difference of potential. The act of *charging* a discharged battery causes an imbalance, by providing a difference of potential between the two contacts. It is then the subsequent *balancing* of this imbalance; that is by design the purpose of the battery. The imbalance of a charged battery represents stored or potential energy, for the very purpose of discharging this energy, until the battery again becomes balanced or discharged.

A *criminal* charge causes an imbalance that will be balanced by some type of adjudication. This imbalance can remain for some period of time. There is a prosecutor that generally initiates this imbalance.

In fact the very word prosecutor itself alludes to this. The prefix "pro," generally means *before*; and the "secutor," appears to be related to *sequence* or what follows.

Inevitable Balance

The prosecutor expends energy to create this imbalance *before* whatever *follows*; e.g; punishment. Thus the very term *prosecutor* indicates *causing* an imbalance. Why does the prosecutor cause this imbalance? This is normally done, because the accused is believed to have previously caused an imbalance to another by his or her actions, or lack thereof. The prosecutor creates imbalances, in order to balance a previous imbalance or imbalances.

Juries are *charged* by the judge, by instructing them as to the law; and then after conclusion of the matter or mistrial are *discharged*. In a sense, the obligation for balancing the imbalance caused by the prosecutor, is transferred to the jury after the presentation of all facts. The jury's imbalance or burden is the determination of guilt or lack of guilt; (not guilty as opposed to *innocent*); based upon facts as presented and the law.

Whatever it is that is determined, this then transfers the imbalance back to the judge for sentencing and then to "corrections" if guilty; or transferred back to the prosecutor if unable to reach a verdict, or released if acquitted.

The imbalance of a "hung jury," is then placed upon the prosecutor with regard to a retrial; or in the case of an acquittal, this imbalance is partially balanced by some degree of diminution of the reputation of the prosecutor.

One who is *in charge*, has the responsibility, (imbalance), of managing something; e.g.; "Who is in charge here?;" or "the boss is charged with . . ." Or; when one is placed *in the charge* of another, said other has an imbalance placed upon him or her by being given the responsibility for another person.

"Charge" can also be the balance for the imbalance created by purchase or consumption of goods or services, often used in lieu of "price" or "cost." From the *consumer's* standpoint, monies due on a "charge account" represent an imbalance, which must be balanced. From the *creditor's* standpoint, a charge account is unbalanced when there are no monies due; as this is the business they are in. Thus when there are monies due, this is "carrying a balance;" and when no monies are due, there is "no balance."

An alternative explanation being, that "carry" here means a burden that must be met. Thus here "carrying a balance" represents an imbalanced state to the borrower.

As an aside, it is not difficult to attribute "death measurement" as a literal definition to the word "mort-gage." Creditors prefer to receive interest payments for the entire remaining life of the borrower, so they then tailor the loan to the borrower's life expectancy.

Immaterial Kinetic Energy

Thus far; *material* potential energy, and *material* kinetic energy were addressed, along with a brief mention of *immaterial potential* energy. There is something else which was deliberately left "un-addressed" until now. The same being, whether or not there exists the phenomenon of *immaterial kinetic energy?*

In order to understand the answer to this, a closer examination of immaterial *potential* energy is helpful.

In an unrealistic "all other things being equal" sense, an immaterial *potential* energy or difference of potential *increase*, represents the *difference* between the existing level of "balance" *prior* to the introduction of the new stimulus; and the magnitude of the *total* imbalance, including that which was caused by said new stimulus.

With respect to the "insult" scenario; since no one is completely "balanced," *relative* degrees of imbalance must be utilized.

It is true that the level of any prior imbalance can disproportionately affect the increase in imbalance caused by a new stimulus; but that is "on the recipient." Meaning; that if it is true that "he's just crabby," or "she's just upset about something else;"

disproportional increases in immaterial potential energy will exist, but not necessarily having been solely caused by that stimulus.

This Δ or change, (here increase), in *imbalance* from that level which existed prior to the new stimulus; represents the immaterial potential energy *increase* for that particular new stimulus. Thus the increase in "difference of potential," is this Δ for that particular new stimulus.

$$IPE_T = IPE_O + IPE_S$$

or

$$IPE_S = IPE_T - IPE_O$$

Here the total immaterial potential energy, is equal to the *original* immaterial potential energy, (IPE_O); plus the additional imbalance created by the *new* stimulus, (IPE_S).

Or; the increase in immaterial potential energy due to the stimulus, (IPE_S); is equal to the "post stimulus" total, (IPE_T), minus what was originally present prior to the new stimulus, (IPE_O).

Just as there are virtually unlimited possibilities for this Δ, or increase in immaterial potential energy because of differences in the perceptions of people and situations; the same can be said for that which then becomes the *kinetic* energy (response).

Thus the ultimate *balancing* of the increase in immaterial *potential* energy, is also subject to these same possibilities. What can and should be said however; is that the sane *objective* of any response should be *justice*, with the *goal* being *balance*.

When there is an obviously disproportionally large kinetic response to a given stimulus; this is often referred to as "petty." Meaning; that the *kinetic* response to a stimulus was much greater that that which would be considered as reasonable. When this kinetic response is disproportionately high, this is likely due to, (the balancing of), a disproportionately large immaterial *potential* energy change. The question is why?

If a given stimulus is considered as *s*, and the response is considered *r*; it must be asked as to why there can be such a variety of possible *quantities* and *qualities* for *r,* with each being a response to the very same stimulus, or the same given *s*?

Stated a bit differently, A x B = C; here with A representing the *stimulus*, B representing the person or *recipient*, and C representing the *reaction* of the recipient.

In a room full of people, all who are receiving precisely the same stimulus; both the *quantity* and *qualitiy* of C will be different for each person receiving this same stimulus. Therefore since A is a constant, the plethora of different responses cannot be a function of A. Thus any variations in C; must then necessarily be the result of variations in B; or the individual recipient.

The answer is that which is universally so; and yet produces the confusion. The same being; that *all* human beings act from the standpoint of *reality*—as there is no other choice. This is stated with the understanding that the term "all" is quite inclusive. How can this be so?

This answer lies in the definition of *reality*. *Reality* is what is *perceived* or *believed* to be so. This is in contradistinction to *actuality*, which is what (actually) *is* so.

That which is a mirage; but is not known to be a mirage; represents a *reality* of water, with an *actuality* of "not water;" e.g.; sand. This *reality* of water will be acted upon by traveling a great distance; only to then ultimately find that the previous reality, and the actuality, are quite different; producing a new *reality* for this very same actuality.

The seemingly disproportional response by the "petty" person, is considered as such; because of the different *realities* produced by the same stimulus, (an *actuality*). Even words that are considered as innocuous by most; can cause massive increases in immaterial potential energy in those, who for whatever reason(s), are sensitive to these terms.

And obviously this increase in this immaterial potential energy, is likely to produce a much larger, (kinetic), response. The observers of the "petty" person, know not of the reality produced in others;

but know only of that which is produced in themselves, and thus do not understand this reaction.

Here it is not so much the *actuality* that is responsible, but rather that the *reality*, as is the case with the mirage, is disproportionately altered; but here likely because of some past experiences.

This forms the basis for "politically correct" speech. Some person or group of persons makes a determination as to what their particular sensitivity is to be; and then requires all others to then use terminology that is "sensitive" to these purported "sensitivities."

Surely there are *legitimate* sensitivities to certain words or phrases, as a result of past experiences; and the same, if known, should be respected. However these legitimate sensitivities are based upon actualities, and thus do not fall into the category of that which is generally known as "politically correct."

Even seemingly simple actualities are so startlingly complex, that no reality can ever be equal to an actuality. Actuality represents the set, and reality, (if and when accurate), represents merely a subset or subsets. What is vital; is that it is always the case that the subset of *reality*, however small a fraction of the actuality; is always contained within the larger set of *actuality*.

For a material example: The *actuality* of electricity; is generally only perceived by its effects. One does not generally perceive the electrons flowing, or the expanding and contracting fields surrounding the house wiring; yet each is part of the actuality. And the "actual actuality" is that almost all matter is atomic or molecular; and even the atoms, including the atoms comprising molecules, have subsets of "particles."

Thus physicists, chemists, and consumers have different *realities* of the *actuality* known as electricity. And although none represent 100% reality of said actuality; all that is truly "known," (tautology?), represents merely a *subset* of the actuality.

When the *reality* is not part of, or a subset of, the actuality; this then represents a *false* reality. But even those who believe there are "pink elephants" in the room, are nevertheless acting from the *reality* of the existence of said elephants; despite the fact that there is no such actuality.

But once again: "Is there any such thing as *immaterial* kinetic energy; and if so, what does that even mean?"

Probably the best known example of *immaterial* kinetic energy, is that which is often described as the "Big Bang;" or perhaps better stated, that which *caused* the "Big Bang."

Simply put, the "Big Bang" is the *event* of the creation of the universe. The *universe* in this usage refers to the creation of time, space, and matter. Another way to describe the *universe*; would be to call it the *material* or the *natural* realm. So this "Big Bang" event can be called either the *creation* of the *universe*; or the creation of the *material* realm, or the creation of the *natural* realm.

It is inarguable that prior to the creation of matter, there was not matter. Therefore; there could have existed neither *material* potential energy, nor *material* kinetic energy, prior to the creation of the material.

And since the use of material and immaterial to describe two realms is a *binary*—there is either matter contained in a given "realm," or there is not; this leaves *immaterial* potential energy and *immaterial* kinetic energy as the only possible causes for the creation of the universe.

And since potential energy represents only *potential*; but kinetic energy represents *action*, (something's happening); by Hobson's choice, the *cause* of said "Big Bang" had to have been *immaterial* kinetic energy.

This is precisely why no *material cause* can ever, or will ever, be found for the *effect* known as the universe, or the material realm.

Simply put; one cannot find a *cause* for a given phenomenon contained within that same phenomenon, until said, (second), phenomenon exists.

If there were a *material cause* for the effect known as the universe or the material realm; it would had to have emanated from said realm prior to this very realm's existence, Meaning; that said cause would had to have existed in a phenomenon, *prior* to the creation; i.e.; the bringing into existence of; this very same phenomenon.

Inevitable Balance

At the time of the "Big Bang," there was no material realm from which the cause for the creation of the material realm could have emanated.

It must also be asked, if it is possible to have either material or immaterial *kinetic* energy, without having said energy first existing in the *potential* form? Can there be any "action," without first having the *potential* for this action?

Genesis 1:1 tells us:

> "*In the beginning God created the heaven(s) and the earth.*"[2]

It must be remembered that the word here translated as "created," is in fact the Hebrew word bârâ; meaning to bring into existence from *nothing* or "no thing." This is in contradistinction to the Hebrew word yâtsar, generally translated as *formed*; which of course then requires *something* material from which to yâtsar or form.

The Bible tells us that this, (yâtsar), was the case with Adam, as Adam was not brought into existence via bârâ; but rather was *formed* from 'âphâr, generally translated as "dust."

It is from this pandemic misunderstanding of the *process*, that the purported conflict between the scientific and Scriptural age of the earth arises—Adam was *formed*, and thus not one of the original *created* hosts. [A much greater detailed analysis of this can be found in "*MeekRaker Beginnings...*"]

Here in Genesis 1:1 we are told about the *creation* of the universe, or the material realm. If one could have been an observer to the events described in Genesis 1:1, one would have witnessed what is generally scientifically referred to as the "Big Bang."

Some "Bible versions" (note these are not called translations), "translate" "heaven" in the singular. This translation presents a similar problem, because God could not have resided in a yet to be created realm prior to the time when He created said realm.

The use of the term "heaven" in the *singular*, generally refers to the *immaterial* realm where God resides; e.g.; the "heaven" in "Who art in heaven." This refers to the *immaterial* realm.

The use of the *plural* of heaven, "heavens;" generally refers to the space between the celestial bodies, and thus is contained in the *material* realm.

From man's perspective in the *material* realm, where there *is* time, space, and matter; there had to be a *cause* for the creation of the heavens and the earth, ("Big Bang"); which *preceded* this creative event.

From the perspective of the *immaterial* realm, from where, ("whence"), this cause necessarily must have emanated; the same realm where there is no time, space, or matter; any type of *sequencing* is extremely difficult, if not impossible, to comprehend.

Nevertheless; "This is where we are," ("are at").

Most major religions consider God to be *omnipotent*. This could be defined as "all potent;" or complete or unlimited *potential*; the key words here being *potent* or *potential*.

Once again, *all* is a rather inclusive term, leaving little room for debate. Omnipotent refers to one *characteristic* of God. If this characteristic itself is examined, it could be described as "omnipotential," or "all potentials."

But what is or are "all potentials?" That is the set containing all things that are possible. The "all potentials" set, does not include that which is not possible.

Matthew 19:26 tells us:

> *"But Jesus beheld them, and said unto them,*
> *with men this is impossible,*
> *but with God all things are possible."*[3]

If this passage is read as actually written in the KJV, rather than as it is usually interpreted; a qualifier is unmistakably noted. Jesus did not say "all is possible," but rather that "all *things* are possible." (italics supplied)

Meaning that if it is a thing, it is possible; but if it is not a thing, then "it" does not fall into the category of "possible"—at least with respect to this particular passage.

What are "things?" The actual Greek word in this passage translated as "things," could not be found anywhere in the original Strong's.

But if it is so stipulated that "things" means the set of that, (Male/Female/Neuter), which exists or could exist; then the passage tell us that: "All that exists or could exist are possible;" but appears here with a qualifier. Without the qualifier, the statement "All that exists or could exist is/are possible;" would otherwise qualify as merely a tautology, with little or no educational value.

This qualifier is significant, but becomes especially significant if examined in context. *"With men this is impossible," "but with God;"* "All that exists or could exist are possible;" represents two conditions.

Firstly, that this seems to refer not only to what already exists, but what might exist *"are possible,"* in the future.

Secondly, with the contextual use of *"with;"* it is more than arguable that contextually this refers to men acting *"with"* God, rather man acting alone, (*"with men this is impossible"*).

Neither does this seem to refer to God acting alone, and furthermore; that this, (men acting with God), is the very purpose for the statement.

What things are *not* possible even with God? God cannot act against His own *will*. Whatever He chooses; *is* His will.

God cannot arbitrarily change His laws for one entity, while maintaining them for another. Two must remain two, and not be two when one person writes a check; but then be fifteen when this same person deposits another's check in the same amount of two—else the universe might cease to exist.

God must act according to His laws; else he would simultaneously be acting consistent with two different and contradictory, and possibly even mutually exclusive, wills.

Since God has all potentials, how do we know what all these potentials are? The answer is that we don't, and likely could not understand them if we did.

But what *can* be done; is to examine what He has done, and thereby derive what some of these potentials are or were. [*Were* rather than *are* must be included here, as it is unclear that once the immaterial *potential* energy for "a thing" is converted into immaterial *kinetic* energy; whether said *potential* continues to exist in the immaterial realm. This could help explain why Adam was *formed* from matter, and not *created* from nothing, as was the case with the original created hosts.]

Genesis 1:1 tells us what happened, describing the *effects* of this immaterial kinetic energy. Later in Genesis, with the "*And God said let..., and there was;*" again shows us God putting this immaterial potential energy into action.

This is known because prior to the *result*, or the "*and there was;*" clearly there was not. The "let" is the point of conversion of the immaterial *potential* into the immaterial *kinetic*, and we are told the result. This is the expression of free will, and the resultant balance.

As already stated, man is by design an entity capable of *immaterial* potential energy; which in man generally is balanced by or results in *material* kinetic energy.

The question now, is whether man is capable of balancing this immaterial *potential* energy with immaterial *kinetic* energy in any significant way; instead of merely achieving balance with *material* kinetic energy, and if so, to what extent? The true answer exists independent of one's reality, and is solely based upon the actuality.

With respect to *motion*, there is a substantial paradox that lies in the characteristics of the two realms. If it is so stipulated that kinetic energy refers to "a thing" in *motion*; it is inescapable that in order for motion to exist, there must be both time and space. Even mere *vibration* as we know it, requires time and space; as well as "a thing" to move.

"A thing" cannot move without *space* in which to move. Velocity and speed each describe "a thing" that changes its location, with respect to time. Moreover; movement not only requires that "a thing" *be* in a particular "place;" but also that it is no longer in another, the "previous," place"—else movement from where?

It is true that speed generally refers to change in *distance*; and velocity refers to change in *displacement*. But even a circular movement back to the starting point, requires *distance*, even if final displacement is zero.

It is generally understood that: "Two objects cannot occupy the same space at the same time"—at least with respect to gross matter. Thus viewed from the other standpoint, even two neutrons simply cannot exist in a realm with no space. Atoms require space between the primary subatomic particles. Electrons must maintain space between themselves and the nucleus, and require space to orbit said nucleus; as do the celestial bodies.

Generally, this or the "immaterial realm," is considered as such and named as such, because it *does not* contain matter. However; it may in fact be the case that the immaterial realm simply *cannot* contain matter.

Bârâ, or true *creation*, as was done in early Genesis; could be considered as the initial release/conversion of immaterial *potential* energy *from* that which possesses it, *into* immaterial *kinetic* energy.

With *bârâ*, first there is this production of immaterial *kinetic* energy, as a function of the exercise of *will*. But also with bârâ, the desired result of this exercise of will, (particularly if matter); likely cannot exist in a realm with no space.

In order for this will to manifest, this energy; at least after Genesis 1:1; must be transferred to a realm where *space* exists.

After the exercise of this will, and just prior to this transfer of this energy to *this* realm, (the material), which "contains" space; there first exists immaterial *potential* energy, and then immaterial *kinetic* energy.

The problem now is the matter of *time*. There is no time in the realm where this initial process occurs. In fact; as previously stated, it could be reasonable argued that without the existence of time, the very concept of any type of *process* itself cannot possibly exist.

From the *material* perspective of a "hypothetical observer," there is or was the condition when whatever the initial *material* results of bârâ were *to be*; at some time prior to bârâ, the same *was not*.

Before the creation of that which God actually *created* after Genesis 1:1; there were no such entities or phenomena contained in the newly created *material* realm.

But from the *immaterial* perspective, there is no possible sequencing of these two or any other conditions, as there is no time available with which to sequence them.

Thus it seems that there is the choice between two dilemmas:

Either it was the case that the *causative* factor for the creation of a realm with time, space, and matter, somehow nevertheless existed in that same realm before the very realm itself existed—i.e.; the subset existed *prior* to the existence of the set in which it is or was contained.

Or; it is the case, that another realm exists from which this causative factor emanated; but with no ability in this same realm, to distinguish any temporal or spatial differences between when this cause existed as immaterial *potential* energy (prior to the exercise of will); and immaterial *kinetic* energy (the willful release of this potential).

Thus how can any differences be distinguished between the period of "time" when this *potential* energy existed, and *then* became *kinetic* while still in the immaterial; and then "subsequently" "bursting" into the material realm?

The "first one," Genesis 1:1 AKA the "Big Bang;" is a slight bit easier, as time did not yet exist "anywhere."

In fact; neither did any "where(s)" exist—at least as we know them.

But all of the *subsequent* immaterial kinetic energy *effects* in the material realm, must somehow comport with this time paradox. The material *effects* are separated by time on the *material* realm, (duration between events); yet the *causes* of these events exist in a realm with neither time nor space.

To make matters even more complex, again it seems likely that once this "happens;" i.e.; the material result is contained in the material realm; the original or any immaterial *potential* for this same "thing" is no longer contained in the immaterial realm.

It is not clear that a "no thing" in the immaterial realm, remains, or can remain in that realm; after this same "no thing" became "a thing" in the material realm. This particular "no thing," is or was balanced by the appearance of "a thing," in the material.

This would explain why despite common belief, much of what was brought into existence in early Genesis, (after Genesis 1:1); was in fact not true creation or bârâ; and the correct translations, and even the various "versions," are consistent with this.

Thus the truth, is that given the fact that as a matter of logic, that since the first "possibility," (the existence of a subset or member of a set that does not yet exist), is simply impossible; it must therefore be ruled out.

Even if the "worlds without end," (*author's terminology*), position is taken; i.e.; "Big Bangs," then "contractions," and then new "Big Bangs," occur cyclically every ten billion years or so; there nevertheless remains that pesky matter of the first one.

Therefore the second; however *improbable*; must then necessarily represent the truth.

Simply because it appears that man is incapable of sufficiently *understanding* the immaterial realm, should in no way preclude his *attempting* to understand it. Neither should this preclude the establishment of working models—at least to the extent that that they in fact "work."

There are those who prefer to cling to the impossible—such as those who date the earth via the "Adam model" (*author's terminology*).

This position requires conflating or confusing Adam's *formation*, (yatsâr), from *something*, ('âphâr); with the *creation* (bârâ) of original hosts from *nothing*. But these adherents in fact represent the *only* proponents of an earth that is less than 10,000 years old, as the Bible says no such thing. The same is likely the case here with their views regarding material-immaterial relationships.

One such "working model" from the *material* perspective, would be to establish one definition of *immaterial kinetic energy* as: "That which provides the means by which that which is in the *immaterial*, enters the *material*."

Bârâ or true creation is one example of this, but there are others.

Here "the thing" being "in motion," would not be with respect to *space* as is the case in the material realm; but rather would be "realm dependent."

When that which is in the immaterial realm as a *potential*, enters the material; this is the *kinetics* or motion.

Thus *immaterial kinetic,* is motion *between* the realms; i.e.; *immaterial* to *material*; rather than material kinetic motion *within* the *material* realm, as commonly understood.

Although it is interesting to ponder if so called "black holes," will ultimately be determined to be some type of "return path" mechanism from the material to the immaterial; this would represent mere speculation at this time.

John 14:12 (KJV) tells us:

> "*Verily, verily, I say unto you,*
> *He that believeth in me,*
> *the works that I do he shall do also;*
> *and greater works than these shall he do;*
> *because I go unto my father.*"[4]

It is clear and virtually undisputed that these "works" to which Jesus is referring, are not any woodworking projects He may have built as a child. Neither do they refer to any other types of *dynamikós* or *natural* power.

Rather; these "works" refer to *dunamis* or *supernatural* power, and thus the *miraculous* works He did. No mainstream religion disputes this, and the Book of Acts; which chronologically follows John; clearly confirms this meaning.

However with respect to other particulars contained in this passage, there are areas of significant dispute, which generally come down to two:

Firstly: it is often proffered that this passage refers to only the "Apostolic Era." Meaning; that what Jesus said, and to which He was clearly referring, had some type of "expiration" or "best if used before" date—e.g.; "Those were different times. Back then people could do those things—but not today."

There is no Biblical support whatsoever for this "Apostolic Era" position; thus the same likely merely represents an ineffective excuse for the lack of this, (dunamis), ability, on the part of the proponents of this position.

The *second* dispute is centered around the word "greater." Many proffer that what this actually means, is that since today there are so many more who "believe in Him and what He did;" there of course will be greater *numbers* of works, and that this in no way means works of greater *magnitude*.

However; the actual Greek word translated as "greater" that John used was:

"3187 měizōn; irreg. compar. of 3173; *larger*..."[5]

It must be remembered that in here John 14:12 *měizōn* or "larger," is describing *works*, and not the *number* of works. Měizōn refers to *magnitude* of the works, and not the *quantity*.

It must also be noted that neither of the aforementioned disputes, seem to "dispute" *in-toto* the ability of man to engage in miraculous works.

One objects to the applicability today; and the other essentially objects to the idea that man could perform miraculous works that are *měizōn*, or larger than those performed by Jesus—despite the fact that Jesus Himself said so.

It is far beyond the scope of this work to explain the *mechanism* of what Jesus told us, particularly the last phrase: *"because I go unto my father."* [This mechanism is explained in great detail in an upcoming publication, currently in post-production.]

A *miracle* is something that occurs in the material realm, but is contrary to natural law.

In fact in order to be considered a miracle, it *must* contradict natural law or a laws; natural law here meaning the law or laws of the material realm.

If it does not contradict natural law via *supernatural* power, (dunamis), it is not a miracle, but represents merely natural power, (dynamikós)—no matter what it may otherwise seem to be.

A "miracle" is the transformation of immaterial potential energy, into immaterial kinetic energy, which then produces an *effect* in the material realm which defies natural law.

This is precisely what is happening in the early Genesis passages. It *is* the case, that all miracles are caused by immaterial kinetic energy; but it is *not* necessarily the case that all immaterial kinetic energy manifests as miracles in any absolute sense. As it is so that *material* kinetic energy has many manifestations, the same can be said about the manifestation of *immaterial* kinetic energy.

> "When immaterial kinetic energy
> is imparted to the material realm,
> it is generally balanced by some type of
> motion in the material realm."[6]
> —Emma B. Quadrakoff

In the case of bârâ or *creation*, this resultant motion exists at almost all levels, including the atomic and subatomic. All is in motion, with temperature being one way to indicate the amount of motion at the atomic or molecular level.

Absolute Zero is considered to be the temperature at which all such atomic and molecular motion ceases. It is not known if absolute zero exists or can exist anywhere in the material realm. In fact given current technology, it seems that in order to bring and particle of matter to absolute zero; a "freezer" capable of temperatures *below* absolute zero would both required and impossible.

In other material manifestations of *immaterial* kinetic energy, there is generally also some type of movement in the material realm.

Man is a dual being. We know this because of another passage in Genesis.

Genesis 2:7 tells us:

"And God formed man from the dust of the ground, and breathed into his nostrils the breath of life; and man became a living soul."[7]

Although this is a description of how Adam was brought into existence, and not the original created hosts; the same rule applies today. The material vessel is first formed, and then God imparts His "breath" into the vessel. The condition of "physical life" begins with the first breath, and ends with the last.

Thus while "physically alive," man has both a *material* and an *immaterial* component. One is *indirectly* of God, (material); and the other is *directly* of God, (immaterial); often described as *body* and *soul* respectively.

The *material* part is subject to the laws of the material realm, unless acted upon by an immaterial force; e.g.; immaterial kinetic energy. And the *immaterial* part is subject to the laws of the immaterial realm.

Most religions speak of, and are very concerned with "afterlife." This is what happens *after-life*; with life being defined here as that dual condition, or the unity of body and soul. Afterlife is that *severed* condition; and that which happens to the *immaterial* portion, after it is no longer contained within the physical vessel.

But again, when speaking of the realm that has no time; that realm, by definition, has "no time." This is not meant as any type of tautology, but rather as a reminder. If there is no time; then from the immaterial perspective, one could just as easily inquire as to "beforelife," or that condition of this immaterial portion *before* it is "breathed into his nostrils. . . and man became (becomes) a living soul."

Physical, (material), nostrils are required before they can be "breathed into." It seems that the only time that "time" affects this *immaterial* portion, is when it is contained in the physical vessel. "Beforelife" is rarely spoken about by conventional religions.

In very real senses, biology, the study of (the physical portion) of life, is in actuality a study of *miracles*; in that life within certain limits, defies natural law. But we tend to not notice this, because life is so ubiquitous.

The material changes that occur to a corpse, are *consistent* with natural law. The material changes that occur regularly to a living being generally *defy* this natural law. If a corpse is damaged, it remains damaged. If the same body was damaged while alive, it would repair itself; and reverse the damage, again within certain limits. The latter represents an unusual *effect* or a series of *effects*, and thus requires an unusual cause.

The reason or *cause* of this, is what is known as the *Vital Life Force* (VLF) by some, *chi* by others, or *Innate Intelligence* by certain professionals. This "energy" provides the mechanism by which living beings maintain homeostasis; maintaining or increasing the levels of organization of the material body. When this energy is interfered with either *materially*, [see *chiropractic*]; or immaterially, [see: the Monograph: "*It's Not Just a Theory*"); less than optimal organization is the result.

This VLF is another form of immaterial kinetic energy. The origin is the *immaterial* realm; its target is in the *material* realm; and its *purpose* is the maintenance of the *material* vessel that contains the immaterial portion; i.e.; maintaining the physical part of that dual condition of "life."

As previously stated, the VLF is capable of being interfered with immaterially, *before* reception by the material target; and interfered with materially, *after* reception by the target.

Areas of the nervous system are currently believed to be the intended material recipient of this VLF. Much like a radio receiver receiving *material* electromagnetic waves, and converting the same into that which can be understood; parts of the nervous system represent that junction between the *immaterial* VLF, and the material. That intelligence which is needed to maintain the physical body is received from the *immaterial*, and converted into the *material*, by parts of the nervous system.

As an aside; that which is referred to as *spirit*, although often used synonymously for "anything immaterial," is similar to the VLF; but solely with respect to *inanimate* matter.

"Spirit" is technically that *immaterial* phenomenon which either gives or gave the material existence; and/or that which *maintains* the existence of the material. When the immaterial kinetic energy that created the universe manifested, was this energy flow a "one time" event; or does this energy continue to flow? This is difficult to comprehend; much less answer; as it also emanates from this realm with no time.

Before there was the material realm, there was not a material realm. As previously stated, the *cause* of the material realm therefore could not have been contained in the yet to be created material realm.

The same can be said of *natural* law, or the laws of the *material* realm. Natural law or the laws of the material realm therefore also had to first exist in the immaterial; else whence did they originate?

Hence one meaning of: "As above so below."

Perhaps a hackneyed expression, but nevertheless one which essentially contains as much revelation as one is willing to seek. It really could not be any other way. Perhaps another phrasing of this concept would be: "Thy will be done, on earth, as it is in heaven;" here with heaven meaning the immaterial realm, and not "the heavens," or the "space" between the celestial bodies. This is usually approached from a bit of a different angle though, because it is phrased in a manner suggesting that it is hoped or desired that God's will be done here on earth, in the same way and manner as it is done in heaven.

All that was *originally* brought into physical existence; was brought into existence because of, and completely consistent with; the will of God. Thus from the other viewpoint, when examining the known physical realm as the accomplished *result* of God's will, this physical realm necessarily was already done on earth as it is or was in heaven, according to His will—at least through the end of Genesis 1:1.

Therefore, the physical laws we know to exist on earth, necessarily have their origins in the will of God. For each physical law, then there must be a corresponding law in the non-physical or immaterial; which some might choose to use the term supernatural, realm.

> *"Any action which is preceded by conscious*
> *thought, is a two-fold phenomenon;*
> *having both material and immaterial components."*[8]
> —Emma B. Quadrakoff

In Malachi 3:10 (NAS) God tells us:

> *"Bring the whole tithe into the storehouse,*
> *so that there may be food in My house,*
> *and test Me now in this,"*
> *says the* LORD *of hosts,*
> *"if I will not open for you the*
> *windows of heaven*
> *and pour out for you a*
> *blessing until it overflows."*[9]

The most striking words or phrase in this passage is the phrase "test Me." God does not state that we are to examine or quiz Him, but rather to "test" (*bachan*)[10] Him. This is not an invitation to inquire as to the nature of God. Neither is it an invitation to quiz Him to see how much he knows; but rather is an invitation to actually test Him.

This "test," is in the sense of finding out not if He actually is what *we* say He is; but rather if He is actually what *He* says He is. This is similar to the acid tests for testing precious metals such as gold. In those tests, one is generally trying to determine if the metal is actually what the metal is being proffered to be.

The nature of this "test" involves the very same physical principles or laws we encounter in our everyday existence:

The following may at first appear very complicated, but is not. For some reason, many people seem to become intimidated when confronted with symbols.

Nevertheless, the following is really quite simple:

"Newton's Second Law of Motion" states:

*"The acceleration of an object
as produced by a net force
is directly proportional to the
magnitude of the net force,
in the same direction as the net force,
and inversely proportional
to the mass of the object."*[11]

All this really means; is that if you push on something with enough force, it will move in the direction in which you pushed it. It is expressed as F = MA, where F = force, M = mass, and A = acceleration.

It really is that simple. Push on a mass, (M), with a force, (F); and it will move (A). And the greater the mass, the slower it will move given the same force.

When something is moving, it has either velocity or speed. This is a change in the distance it travels in a certain amount of time. A car traveling 60 MPH will travel sixty miles in one hour. *(v=Δd/Δt velocity or speed equals change in distance or displacement divided by the change in time; for speed and velocity respectively.)*

In order to make an object such as a car, (or a blessing), change its speed or velocity; this requires some type of acceleration. This acceleration, or A, is considered to be the change in the object's speed or velocity. This happens when one pushes down on either the gas pedal, (accelerator), in a car; or the brakes. The gas pedal provides *positive* acceleration, and the car increases its speed or velocity. The brakes provide *negative* acceleration, (deceleration); and will slow the car down. *(A=Δv/Δt acceleration equals change in speed or velocity divided by the change in time)*

F = MA simply tells us that force equals mass multiplied by acceleration. All this really means, is that if the object is a large mass; then it takes more force to accelerate it, (change its velocity or speed), a given amount; as compared to a smaller mass. If the mass is small, and it is subject to the same force, its acceleration will be greater.

When the car is carrying a heavy load, the gas pedal has to

be pushed farther down in order to get more force from the engine to cause the car to increase its speed, (accelerate), as compared to an empty vehicle. Although not technically exactly correct, if we consider the weight of the car to be M, this is all that F = MA means. *(Technically mass and weight are different, but this matters little here.)*

The "test" in the passage from Malachi previously cited, refers to 4 things:

1) the *window*
2) the *tithe*
3) the *blessing*
4) the *pouring*

The *window* is a binary, in that it must be either open or closed. It is essentially *allegorical*, as it is far from certain that literal windows, at least as we know them to be; actually exist in heaven. This "window," essentially means merely a route for something to travel from the immaterial to the material.

Assuming this route exists, meaning the window is open; this leaves the *tithe*, the *blessing* and the *pouring*. These can be expressed in the terms of Newton's second law, F = MA or more specifically here, F_T = MA where:

F_T = total value of faith
M = the quantity of the blessing (how much stuff)
A = the pouring or movement. (the increase in velocity of the blessing from zero, to some speed or velocity) This determines how fast the blessing will get to you.

The "test" referred to in this example from Malachi, refers to the *results* of tithing. F_T or total faith value in this context is essentially "putting your money where your mouth is." It is equal to the *amount* you tithe, multiplied by the *reasons* for which you tithe; or, more simply put; how much did you tithe, and why did you tithe it.

Here is the where the: "*Any action which is preceded by conscious thought, is a two-fold phenomenon; having both material and immaterial components,*" rule comes into play. In the case of tithing in Malachi; there is both the *tithe*, and the *reason* for the tithe.

The *tithe*, (amount), itself is essentially a *material* phenomenon. One donates the fruits of ones labor to that which they believe should be the recipient, according to God's instructions in Malachi. This action is essentially *material kinetic* energy, resulting in *material potential* energy in the earthly recipient. The recipient now has this new material potential energy, which can ultimately be converted into material kinetic energy, by utilization of the material value of this tithe to produce change.

The *reason* for the tithe is an *immaterial* quantity. Once the tithe is given, (becomes kinetic), as per the will of the giver; both the *amount* of the tithe and the *reasons* for the tithe; (F_T); become *immaterial* kinetic energy released into the immaterial realm.

This release initially produces an imbalance in the immaterial realm, and ultimately results in immaterial *potential* energy.

Since kinetic energy relates to *motion*; and motion requires both *distance* and *time*; it is unclear as to how this could possibly remain kinetic in a realm that has neither.

This immaterial *potential* energy balances the original immaterial imbalance caused by the F_T. And the same as a charged battery, this potential remains an *unbalanced* immaterial phenomenon, ready to be released.

Thus as stated, the giving of the tithe produces both material and immaterial *imbalances*:

In the *material* realm, the *material* amount of the tithe results in increased potential energy to the recipient of the tithe in the *material* realm; and this increase is commensurate with the amount of the tithe. Said recipient can now make material changes by converting this now material potential energy, into material kinetic energy; with this subsequent action, (spending or consuming), subject to his, (the recipient's), will.

At the same time in the immaterial realm, the *immaterial* amount of the tithe—which is the *amount* of the tithe and the *reasons* for the tithe; ultimately results in increased potential energy in the *immaterial* realm—essentially with the "tither's" name written upon it.

Two different *material* quantities or amounts, have two different *immaterial* quantities or contributions to the total. The subsequent conversion of this immaterial potential energy, into immaterial *kinetic* energy, is subject to His, (God's), will.

We generally can easily calculate the material *amount* we tithe; but this multiplier, here meaning the value of the actual *reasons* for tithing, which are also necessary for determining the total amount which F_T represents; can only be calculated by God.

Perhaps a better way to describe this, would be that the value of the faith total is calculated in this manner: $F_T = F_A \times F_R$ The faith subscript "A" represents the *amount* of a tithe or other "good works;" and subscript "R" represents the *reasons*. The value of this F_R, is the factor by which the thirty fold, sixty fold, and one hundred+ fold realms are calculated. Matthew 13:8 provides insight into these realms of increase.

This reason, or "why factor" is extremely important. This is not only because this factor largely determines the *quantity* of the blessing; but also because of our *material* limitations for the actual amount, (how much), of the giving.

One cannot reasonably give more than 100% of what one has. In the tithing example, even if one tithed all of their increase instead of the required 10%, this in itself would result in only a tenfold increase in the blessing. But the *reason* or why factor could easily result in a return in the "hundred fold realm."

This concept is further illustrated by Proverbs 16:2 (NAS), where it tells us:

> "All the ways of a man are clean in his own sight,
> But the LORD weighs the motives."[12]

Weight is actually a force. (Weight itself, is technically a function of mass, and the acceleration of gravity.) Proverbs is telling us here, that God determines, ("*weighs*"), the value of the motives or reasons. This *is* the F_R.

Inevitable Balance

"Weighing" something, is generally determining the resultant force of its mass, multiplied by the acceleration of gravity.

In the F = MA equation, M is being used here to represent the blessing; or precisely what it is that travels through this "window," from the immaterial to the material.

The use of the term "Blessing" here means: "increase *consistent* with natural law." This is to be distinguished from "increase *inconsistent* with natural law," which is better termed a "miracle."

This in no way means that miracles cannot be a result of tithing; but rather only that in Malachi, it is *blessings* which are under discussion.

"A" represents the actual acceleration, resulting in the movement or pouring out of this blessing. This acceleration is actually the direct result of God's intervention.

"Newton's First Law of Motion" states:

"An object at rest stays at rest
and an object in motion stays in motion
with the same speed
and in the same direction
unless acted upon by an unbalanced force."[13]

This essentially means that an object that is moving, will stay moving; unless acted upon by another force. Or an object that is not moving, will continue to not move; unless a sufficient force is applied to make it move.

This, (not moving), is the initial status of the M, or the blessings, (potential energy), which are in heaven. They are already there, but will not move or change their direction of movement unless a force is applied.

For those who might argue that these blessings might already be moving; it would seem that if this were so, then said movement is definitely not towards this window, or God would merely open the window, and would not have to pour them out. Thus, let's assume they are stationary.

In order to move, they must have a change in velocity from

zero to something. For any mass; any change in velocity with respect to time represents an *acceleration*, and this requires a *force*.

It is the conversion of the immaterial *potential* energy into immaterial *kinetic* energy, that provides this force, and determines the magnitude of the "blessing."

As previously stated:

> "Any action which is preceded by conscious thought, is a two-fold phenomenon; having both material and immaterial components."

Following is a representation of this "two-fold" phenomenon:

(Amount) → Material Kinetic → Material Potential → Eventual Material Kinetic

Tithing → ↕

(Amount and Reason) → Immaterial Kinetic → Immaterial Potential → Eventual Immaterial Kinetic

Here is where Newton's Third Law of Motion comes into play:

> "For every action, there is an equal and opposite reaction."[14]

Newton's Third Law of Motion probably represents the most fundamental law of compensation, or "karma."

When the value of F_T is established, this represents the force of faith, which we cause by tithing or giving; this being something which is always done for some type of reason. The amount or value of the gift (F_A) is one factor; the other being the reason (F_R) we are doing it.

It must be clearly stated here that the value of this reason is not necessarily the reason we may tell others; and it is not necessarily the reason we tell ourselves. Rather; it is based upon the true reasons, which God always knows no matter what we may say or do; and it is God alone who "weighs" these.

Thus here this F_T represents the first action as referenced in Newton's third law. When this action is consummated; when we tithe; an equal but opposite reaction is undertaken by God, being "paid for" with the immaterial potential/kinetic energy of the F_T. This results in another $F = MA$.

Again it is important to remember that it is not just how much we give alone; but the value of that gift *and* the "reason" multiplier, which determines the total value of this force.

This A, (change in velocity), of M, (the blessing); is the result of the equal and opposite action undertaken by God, as a direct result of our actions. It is equal to His calculation of F_T, but "opposite" in direction, as now; instead of going *from* us, it travels *to* us.

The rest of the *second*, ($F = MA$), equation also holds. The acceleration is inversely proportional to the mass of the object. In the physical world this means that given whatever the total force applied may be; the greater the mass, the less the acceleration, and the slower the resultant movement to you. Likewise: the lesser the mass; the greater the acceleration, and the faster the resultant movement toward you.

This same relationship holds in the immaterial realm. The mathematical product of this God induced MA, must remain constant; and is equal to, but is opposite in direction to, the original F_T, (original tithe and reasons), for this particular event.

Thus, the *greater* the blessing you are to receive, the *longer* it may take to get to you. If the blessing is received *quickly*, the *amount* or mass of the blessing is sacrificed or diminished in exchange for the rapidity with which it is received. This is necessary to keep the equation in balance.

How does God decide whether to provide a smaller blessing quickly, or a larger blessing more slowly?

Only He knows this for sure, but in the initial stages of faith, rapidity can be very important; as it is evidence to the "neophyte" that the system actually works. Once the system is known to work; even with a relatively small amount of increase, but an extremely rapid increase; the system becomes confirmed as functional by the believer. Thus he or she is much more likely to permit this to ascend to higher levels.

With subsequent tithing or giving, as the amount of one's faith, (God passed this test), increases; then God may choose to increase the magnitude of M at the expense of A; but again this must equal the new F_T.

This is a different result, (more quantity of blessing, or M), than the above ""rapid" process; but God's priorities may be different. With this increased *quantity* of blessing, the acceleration will be *less* in order to balance the F=MA equation. This means the velocity or speed of the blessing will be *less*, and subsequently this *greater* amount of blessing will take *longer* to arrive.

Whenever this results in a much greater, but slower to arrive, blessing being returned; of course the enemy knows this. He, (the enemy), has a way to sense when "due season" is near. During those dry periods, when it looks like God forgot all about you, and it appears that He isn't doing a thing; this is the dangerous period. That is when your faith is attacked, and it is not *examined* but actually "tested."

The enemy will remark with something like: "See, God aint gonna do nuthin. If God was gonna do sumthin, he (sic.) would have done it by now."

Is this because the devil does not know of this F = MA function? No, it is because he knows precisely of this function.

All the while this huge mass of blessing is heading toward you with a relatively slow acceleration having been applied; but with the magnitude of this mass or blessing being beyond your ability to think or imagine. The devil likely can sense this, and he is trying desperately to get you to do something; to get you to do *anything* that will cancel out your receipt of this blessing.

To be clear, all of this is not about storing up blessings in heaven; but rather in the here and now, in this *material* plane—most particularly, if the F_A is in any way material in nature.

This F = MA law is not unique to tithing. Rather, it applies to any action or inaction undertaken; and is sometimes referred to as *karma*.

Inevitable Balance

Anything we choose to do, or not do; has quantities that are calculable and the same rules apply. We should do unto others as we should do unto ourselves if for no other reason; because that is precisely what *will* be done unto us; and done according to the aforementioned rules.

If something is undertaken for this, (the *return* or "gimmee the money"), reason alone however; the value of F_T, and the subsequent value of the returning MA, is likely to be smaller; as the reason or motive value is diminished if it is largely a selfish act.

2 Corinthians 9:7 (NAS) tells us:

> *"Each one must do just as he*
> *has purposed in his heart,*
> *not grudgingly or under compulsion,*
> *for God loves a cheerful giver."*[15]

Why does God love a cheerful giver? Because it is His will that we prosper; and this gives Him license, arguably *requires* Him, to bless us not only based upon what we do; but more importantly why we do it.

This law cannot be changed; neither can it be avoided. It makes little difference what we say the weight of our motives are, as we are not *"in charge"* of weighing or calculating them; and thus our opinion of their value is essentially irrelevant.

One very reliable way to short circuit this process is to name your own blessing. If boasting about the amount of the tithe, (or whatever it may be), is undertaken; that is precisely what can easily happen.

Malachi 3:10 is about the *positive*. Meaning: that it is *blessings* that are the subject, as they relate to tithing. However the same rules apply with respect to so called "cursing."

Thus, if and when the F_T is "negative," the MA must also be "negative" in nature.

As previously stated, man has no choice but to act from the standpoint of *reality*. Man *by design*, is simply incapable of the perception of material actuality *in-toto*. Man's ability to hear is dwarfed by the hearing ability of canines or raccoons. Man's vision is arguably no more than an octave. Man's olfactory capabilities are dwarfed by those possessed by a deer. Taste is limited, and tactile discrimination leaves much to be desired. And all of man's senses are subject to error—the aforementioned mirage and a computer display being prime examples. Thus man is forced to act based upon what he *believes* is true.

The Solipsists have a valid point, when they state that the only thing one knows for *certain*, is that they; (the Solipsist); exist. Phrased another way; one's "I am," is all that is actually "known."

Why is it that one cannot obtain a positive F_T, simply by doing something negative, for terrible reasons?

For example: "I hated him, and wanted to really hurt him; so I stole money from him." Here it seems that the product of the *negative action*, and the *negative* reasons should be a *positive*. After all, a negative multiplied by a negative, does in fact yield a positive product. "It's not the case that I don't have any money," means one *has* money.

To understand this, another question must be asked. What number is it that is the most similar to the number 3? Most would answer that 2.99999... *ad infinitum* would be the answer.

But the truth; is that the number most similar to 3 is –3. The magnitude is exactly the same, but the direction is opposite; with each being exactly the same distance from zero on a number line—with the *absolute values* being equal. A $3.00 account receivable to one; represents a $3.00 payable to another. The quantitative actuality is exactly the same.

The amount of money "stolen from him," has an actuality independent of where it is or how it got there. If this money fell out of the thief's pocket, and was found by another; the "finder" would have no idea as to how it was obtained.

The fact that a car was stolen instead of purchased, has no effect whatsoever on the actuality of the car. There is no way to tell the difference between a stolen actuality; and the same actuality obtained legally, simply by examining the actuality.

If thieves believed that a $3.00 theft would ultimately become -$3.00, no one would ever steal. But it is worse, as the truth is that said $3.00 theft in actuality has a value of $\geq$ -$3.00; where here the "greater than" means increase in the "amount owed." How much more than $3.00 is "owed," depends upon the magnitude of the *reason* (F_R) for the theft.

If somehow one in actuality stole this same amount, but was genuinely unaware that they were stealing it; this does not mean they get to keep it. It merely means that only the amount that was equal to the amount stolen will be taken from them; hence the use of $\geq$ - $3.00, rather than merely greater than.

Being dual in nature, man is also designed with *immaterial* capabilities. Reception of the VLF, (Vital Life Force); is in certain senses autonomic, (as in autonomy), or automatic; but man is designed to receive much more than this from the immaterial realm.

However; unlike the VLF, these other capabilities are *not* necessarily automatic. Other than the VLF and some rudimentary capabilities; many of man's immaterial capabilities must be *developed*. There are some exceptions to this in those who either were born with these capabilities, or obtained them suddenly. But for most people most of the time, these capabilities must be developed.

It is the case with military secrets; that once an enemy knows that something *can* be done; said enemy will spend any and all necessary resources in order to find a way to also do it. This is precisely why the mere *existence* of various weapons is highly classified.

A similar condition exists with man's *immaterial* capabilities. The enemy knows that the very best way to stop any H. Sapien from developing their immaterial capabilities; is to make certain that no H. Sapien ever finds out that which is *possible*.

There is no political or religious bias required in order to state that there is, and has been, a "war on Christianity" in the United States for some time. Reasonable "objective observation" alone will prove that this is clearly a fact.

It must be asked *why* such a war exists? Is it merely a matter of ideology, or is there more than this involved. After all, the United States is largely a Christian country, founded on Judeo-Christian (and Masonic) principles.

The answer to this question has already been provided, but will be restated here.

Again, John 14:12 (KJV) tells us:

> "Verily, verily, I say unto you,
> He that believeth in me, the works that I do
> he shall do also; and greater works than these
> shall he do; because I go unto my father."[16]

Christians can and do debate "what this means," despite the unmistakable clarity. Christians can invent all sorts of explanations as to why this passage; again just as in the fact that Adam could *not* possibly be the first man; does not mean what it so clearly states. But nevertheless, the forces of darkness know precisely what it means.

Those same forces of darkness know very well what would happen to them; *if* Christians understood this passage, and began to do something about it. After all, "Christ" was not Jesus' last name; but rather refers to him as *The* "Anointed One." It is because of the anointing of the *third* part of the Trinity, upon the *second* part of Trinity that resulted in this "eponymous" quasi-surname.

Thus true *Christianity*, is largely about the *Christos*, or the anointing of the Holy Ghost. The source of the term *Christianity* itself refers to the *third* part of the Trinity. Were this not so;

"Jesusite" would likely have been the term chosen. Although no human can ever be *The* Anointed One, every human being can be *an* anointed one; and we are told one way to do this in the above John 14:12.

This in no way represents any attempt to minimize the importance of Jesus. Salvation/redemption/justification is really a two-part process. With respect to the first part, or Jesus' contribution: "It is finished." And with respect to the second part, this requires nothing more than each "man's" acceptance of this fact.

But Jesus clearly was about a lot more than man's salvation/redemption/justification—as important as this is. And without Jesus, not only would man still be waiting for a "Redeemer;" but the power increase Jesus spoke of in John 14:12 would not be available to man.

Today most representations of Jesus are either as a baby, or on the cross. This is done deliberately in an attempt to minimize Him. But one only need read about Him to understand that there is much more to Him than this.

Jesus was also a teacher—hence the term *Rabbi* or *Rabboni*. He taught much about how the "system" works, and how we should behave—with the former explaining why the latter. He provides the perfect role model for each of us.

Jesus also worked miracles, and assured us that each of us, that not only could we perform equal works, but *greater* works than He; *if* one merely met the criteria, *and* He went to the Father.

In certain ways, Jesus existed at a time similar to today. Many believe that outside of the practical concerns of those He helped, that the main reason for His performing of miracles was the fulfillment of prophesy—so that all would know who He is or was.

This is an interesting position, and worthy of some analysis:

If it is believed that the miracles Jesus performed, were alone to uniquely prove Him to be the Messiah; this is simply *not true*.

The truth is that many of the miracles He performed, had already been performed by others, and performed long before His birth. If the ability to perform miracles were the only criteria for being the Messiah; then Elijah, "double dose" Elisha, as well as others, could also qualify. Heck; a dead man jumped back to life after his body merely touched the bones of a long deceased Elisha.

The position should not be that of believing that Jesus performed these miracles primarily or simply to fulfill prophesy, even though that did in fact happen. The position should be based upon the answer to a question. The same being: "Why was this or were these prophesied?"

In other words: Outside of helping some individuals; why was it necessary for Jesus to perform these miracles, many of which had already been performed by others long before his birth?

The answer is a mere two words: "*They forgot!*"

The Father *knew beforehand*, that by the time of the birth of Jesus, His chosen people would have forgotten much regarding that which had been written. If it is stipulated that Malachi represents the end of the Old Testament, then the end of the Old Testament was written roughly five hundred years prior to Jesus' birth.

This represents a substantial period of time for the enemy to "work" His, (God's), people; utilizing the old "literal to allegory" trick—a particularly effective tool when dealing with miracles performed a very long time ago.

Knowing this, and always economizing; He, (God), instructed His prophets to include these miracles as parts of those prophesies written prior to Jesus' birth. Thus although Jesus had to perform these miracles to fulfill the prophesy; the true reason for their inclusion in the prophesy was education, or perhaps *re-education*—used here in its original benign meaning.

Thus it seems fair to say, that Jesus did not have the unique capability to perform most of the miracles He performed prior to His "death" because He was Jesus. Rather that because He was Jesus, He was to perform miracles primarily to educate or *re-educate*, and to fulfill prophesy only as a secondary matter. [One exception to this; is or was Jesus' "resurrection without recourse"—perhaps a unique event in the history of man.]

It is obvious that so many today have fallen for the aforementioned "literal to allegory" trick. Here what is *literal* in the Bible; is over time believed to be *allegorical*. In actuality, this represents "cutting a deal."

Inevitable Balance

There are those who ascribe "facts" to the Bible that cannot possibly be true—the age of the earth, and "no such thing as evolution" being prime examples. [*It is true that original man was created (bârâ), and thus this (the creation of man) was not the result of any evolutionary process. However this in no way precludes any subsequent evolution of man. Neither does this preclude any subsequent evolution of any other created life forms.*]

Maintaining these impossible positions as "Bible facts;" as is also the legal case with a witness who has lied; impeaches the credibility of the entire Word. This is particularly heinous, because the Bible does not even remotely state any such things. No references for these positions exist outside of the minds of their proponents.

But there is an *emotional* need to believe that the Bible is true, so here comes the "deal." Just as Tom Sawyer did with respect to the pirates in the cave; we'll "let on" that the Bible is not to be taken too literally, and those things such as miracles are merely allegorical.

And since any "allegory" is useless without explanation, any said attempts at explanation can make little or no sense, as the foundation of this is falsehood.

It is fair to say that *the Bible as originally written*, represents God according to *God*.

It is also fair to say that *religion*, represents God according to *man*.

Thus when the Bible does not support a religious tenet; it is the meaning of the Bible that is changed to conform—with this; [Adam was the first created man, and the subsequent incorrect age of the earth]; being merely one example.

Freemasonry is currently guilty of the exact opposite. Freemasonry is often defined as: "A system of morality, veiled in *allegory*, and illustrated by symbols."

Here Freemasons are *told* that by definition, that much of what is contained in Freemasonry is by design *allegory*, in order to facilitate concealment—largely because of prosecutions over the centuries.

Yet most nevertheless teach it as *literal*, and thus having no additional significance beyond flowery words. The "working tools," as *symbols* utilized for illustration, remain somewhat intact; but even these "meanings," are also slowly being changed over time.

The truth; is that Biblical *stories* that contain actual names are actual stories. One is certainly free to believe that any given story is true, or that the story is false. But no license exists to change the *intention* of the writer from literal to allegorical. The writers of these *stories* meant their works to be taken literally—irrespective of whether *believed* or not.

The *parables* contained in the Bible are there to teach principles, but do not necessarily represent actual events that actually occurred. The "Talent Man" story is a parable, albeit generally misunderstood today. [See Monograph #603 *"Donald Trump Candidacy According to Matthew?"* for the true explanation of this parable.]

This "Talent Man" *parable*, is not a *recollection* of any actual persons; but rather a means by which a system is being taught. The truth is that most people at sometime in their lives have behaved exactly like the one talent man. This was also the case at the time Jesus told the parable; which is precisely why He told it, and why it was memorialized.

By the deliberate altering of that which is *literal*, to that which is considered as *allegorical*; the *realities* of the *actualities* recounted in the Bible are likewise changed. And as previously mentioned, humans must always act from their realities, as there is no other choice.

According to the Bible, there was an actuality known as Legion. The *story* of Legion is neither a *parable*, nor an *allegory*. And as Jesus *literally* stated, and since He already went to the Father; today those who believe in Him and the things that He did, are *literally* capable of even greater things than these.

There is a passage in Matthew that merits extremely serious consideration. Here in this similar but different *story* than Legion, (is not a *parable*); the disciples had attempted to cast a demon out of a boy, but were unsuccessful.

The boy's father then brought the boy to Jesus to cast out the demon, and He, (Jesus), was successful. The disciples then inquired of Jesus as to why it was that they had failed.

Following is Matthew 17:14-19 according to *The King James Version*:

Inevitable Balance

*"And when they were come to the multitude,
There came to him a certain man, kneeling down to him, and saying, Lord, have mercy on my son:
for he is lunatick, and sore vexed:
for oft times he falleth into the fire,
and oft into the water.*

*And I brought him to thy disciples,
and they could not cure him.*

*Then Jesus answered and said,
O faithless and perverse generation,
how long shall I be with you?
how long shall I suffer you?
bring him hither to me.
And Jesus rebuked the devil;
and he departed out of him:
and the child was cured from that very hour.*

*Then came the disciples to Jesus apart,
and said, Why could not we cast him out?"*[17]

Matthew 17 verses 20-22 (KJV), then tell us:

20 *"And Jesus said unto them,
Because of your unbelief;
for verily I say unto you,
If ye have faith as a grain of mustard seed,
ye shall say unto this mountain,
Remove hence to yonder place;
and it shall remove; and nothing
shall be impossible unto you."*[18]

→21 *"Howbeit this kind goeth
not out but by prayer and fasting."*[19]←

*"And while they abode in Galilee,
Jesus said unto them, 'The Son of man
shall be betrayed into the hands of men:'"*[20]

The word "howbeit," which appears in verse 21; is not equivalent to: "How be it?;" which would then represent a *question*.

Rather; "howbeit" generally means "however;" representing a *statement* such as "nevertheless." This "nevertheless" represents an attempt to modify what was just stated rule in verse 20, for this particular situation. Thus this is represented as Jesus *answering* a question, and not the disciples *asking* another question.

Verse 20 has to do with that which is immaterial; here unbelief, and as will be seen is sometimes also translated as insufficient "faith."

But the inclusion of verse 21 completely negates what Jesus just stated in the preceding verse regarding unbelief or insufficient faith being *causative*; by stating in 21: "(nevertheless) *this kind not goeth out but by prayer and fasting.*" The "but" here could also be reasonably translated as "except."

It seems peculiar that Jesus would answer the disciples' question as He did in verse 20; and then in the very next verse tell them that all He just said in the previous verse did not apply in this case.

And this is especially odd, because the original question He was asked was about this specific matter. So as it reads, Jesus must then have first answered a question about something else entirely different; and then went on to answer the question he was actually asked, negating what He had just said about other matters of which He was not asked.

In addition, there is the matter of lack of specificity. In verse 20, Jesus speaks of the relative *quantities* of a "*mustard seed*," (cause); and a moving mountain, (effect). Yet; there is no mention in verse 21 of how much praying, or how much fasting is required.

And it is clear that verse 22 begins an entirely different matter that is unrelated to that which precedes it.

Following is Matthew 17:20-22; but here according to the *New American Standard Bible*:

> 20 *"And He said unto them,*
> *"Because of the littleness of your faith;*
> *for truly I say to you,*
> *if you have faith the size of a mustard seed,*
> *you will say to this mountain,*
> *"Move from here to there," and it will move;*
> *and nothing will be impossible to you."*[21]
>
> →21 [*"But this kind does not go out*
> *except by prayer and fasting."*][22]←
>
> 22 *And while they were gathering together in Galilee*
> *Jesus said to them, 'The Son of Man*
> *is going to be delivered into the hands of men;'"*[23]

The most notable difference here in the NAS version, is the inclusion of *brackets*. According to NAS: "[] = In text, brackets indicate words probably not in the original writings."[24]

So although clearly this passage appears in the KJV; it is likewise included in the NAS, but with the caveat that it is "probably not in the original writings."

But given the presence of verse 21 in each of these two popular "versions," surely it must have come from somewhere. It seems that although it is not known whence verse 21 came, it is known whence it did not—the original writings, at least according to NAS.

This leaves only writings that are *not original* as any possible source. It must also be remembered that this is a *story*, and these passages represent an eyewitness account.

Following is Matthew 17:20-22; but here according to the *New International Version Bible*:

> 20 *"He replied, "Because you so little faith.*
> *I tell you the truth, if you have*
> *faith as small as a mustard seed,*
> *you can say to this mountain,*

*'Move from here to there' and it will move."
Nothing will be impossible for you."*[25]

→21 (*No verse is present—nothing.*)[26]←

22 *"When they came together Galilee,
he said to them, 'The Son of Man
is going to be betrayed into the hands of men.'"*[27]

Much like the "thirteenth floor" on many buildings; here in the NIV, there is no 21st verse present in Matthew 17. Matthew 17 simply goes from verse 20, to verse 22; with no verse 21.

The difference here is that many buildings in fact do actually have a thirteenth floor; it is just called something else—meaning that there is the actuality of a floor 13 stories up, it is just *called* something different.

But here in Matthew, it is *not* a matter of these words existing, and merely a difference of opinion as to where they appear, or what they are numbered. Rather, there is disagreement as to whether or not Jesus actually ever spoke these words. Thus the existence of this very actuality itself is in question.

It should be asked precisely who or what non-"original" source would have added verse 21; and for what specific reason(s)?

Although it is not possible to ascertain the particular *source* of this particular "verse;" nevertheless, (*howbeit*), some *reasons* for this "addition" can be logically derived.

In verse 20, it is clear that Jesus is speaking of *belief* or *faith* that provides the means by which this enemy is cast out. This means that the source of this power is *the individual* that is directly involved in the casting out.

It is the *will* of the individual, along with *faith* that provides the F; and the MA is the subsequent exit of the demon; with the M here being considered as the demon, and the A the movement out.

But if verse 21 were true, then this would mean that a tiny force that is capable of moving a mountain; would somehow nevertheless be insufficient for casting out a demon.

And more importantly; here in verse 21, the source of the power becomes *indirect*.

Meaning; that here it is no longer the will of the individual along with faith that *directly* provides the actuality of F, and the subsequent MA of the exit of the demon.

Instead; this "fasting" and "prayer" merely provide an immaterial imbalance, (*potential*); which is then, (hopefully), balanced by God; by *Him* providing the F and subsequent MA causing the exit, (*kinetic*), of the demon.

The hierarchy is God, man, and then all else. This "all else" includes angels and demons. Angels must obey man's will, unless man's will conflicts with God's will. When man's will and God's will conflict; God's will necessarily prevails.

Since a fair argument exists that demons are or were actually angels, the same rule applies. Whenever a human is possessed by a demon, this is not God's will. But unfortunately, this is much more complex than it seems.

Up to a certain point, just as was the case with the *attacks* on Job; demonic *possession* is also often possible, because of the previous actions of the "host."

This *possession*, is part of the balancing of the actuality of the host's free will from previous willful actions. Simply because this may not be a part of any given host's *reality* regarding any given willful action, this in no way means it is not so. In these cases, it is merely another part of the *actuality* of the totality of the action. [See Monograph #602 "*It's Not Just a Theory*" for a study of this process.]

It is not God's will that any man be in the condition of demonic possession. But demonic possession can be the *secondary* result of man willfully disobeying God's will.

Thus it is the violation of God's will *by* man; which then results in a condition that is not God's will *for* man. In the case of Job, this was permission for the enemy to *attack*, (but not possess or kill), Job. In the case of possession; although the magnitudes may be different; the balancing *process* is nevertheless quite similar.

So *if* there is a verse 21, or perhaps better stated if verse 21 is an actuality; it seems that there are then *two* ways presented to cast out a demon.

One is *direct* and based upon the force created both by the will and the faith or belief of man, consistent with that which Jesus spoke in verse 20.

The other, is the creation of an immaterial imbalance by praying and fasting. This would represent an *indirect* action; as this force is not "directly directed" at the demon, which is the purported reason for verse 21.

What the question here *is not*; is whether the creation of a sufficient immaterial imbalance can sometimes provide God with sufficient "license" to cast out a demon, as this can happen.

Why license? Because if license were not required, and possession is against God's will; why then does He not just do it Himself without any "prayer and fasting?"

The answer is that He cannot do this without simultaneously *violating* His own laws. Man had previously been given this authority in Genesis 1:28. Thus for God to do this directly *Himself*, an immaterial imbalance created by man's will in prayer and fasting is required, in order to "pay" for;" i.e.; *balance*; this action on the part of God.

What the question here actually *is*; is whether or not Jesus made this statement in response to the inquiry as to why the disciples failed. The clear and convincing evidence is that He did not.

Thus with verse 21 removed, it was not the absence of prayer and fasting that caused, or even had anything to do with this failure of the disciples attempts. But rather, it was insufficient *faith*—just as Jesus stated in the verse, (verse 20), immediately preceding verse 21.

In order to maintain intellectual honesty, it must be noted that when what appears to be this same story appears in Mark, words similar to the "phantom" verse of Mathew 17:21 are included.

Mark 9:18-22 (KJV) tells us:

> *"And wheresoever he taketh him,*
> *he teareth him: and he foameth,*
> *and gnasheth with his teeth,*
> *and pineth away: and I spake to*

thy disciples that they should cast him out;
and they could not.
He answereth him, and saith,
O faithless generation,
how long shall I be with you?
how long shall I suffer you?
bring him unto me.

And they brought him unto him:
and when he saw him,
straightway the spirit tare him;
and he fell on the ground,
and wallowed foaming.

And he asked his father,
How long is it ago since this came unto him?
And he said, Of a child.
And ofttimes it hath cast him into the fire,
and into the waters, to destroy him:
but if thou canst do any thing,
have compassion on us, and help us."[28]

Here in Mark, is a description of the condition of the boy. It is interesting that in the beginning of these passages, the demon is referred to as "he" and "him;" but in the last passage is referred to as "it."

The father is telling Jesus, that Jesus' disciples could not cast "him" out. Here he is not asking Jesus *why* the disciples failed, but rather is asking Jesus for help: "*if thou canst do any thing, have compassion on us, and help us.*"

Mark 9:23-29 continues the *story*:

"Jesus said unto him, If thou canst believe,
all things are possible to him that believeth.

*And straightway the father of the
child cried out, and said with tears,*

*Lord, I believe; help thou mine unbelief.
When Jesus saw that the people
came running together,
he rebuked the foul spirit, saying unto him,
Thou dumb and deaf spirit, I charge thee,
come out of him, and enter no more into him.*

*And the spirit cried, and rent him sore,
and came out of him: and he was as one dead;
insomuch that many said, He is dead.
But Jesus took him by the hand,
and lifted him up; and he arose.*

*And when he was come into the house,
his disciples asked him privately,
Why could not we cast him out?
And he said unto them,
This kind can come forth by nothing,
but by prayer and fasting."*[29]

At the end, is the verse similar to the "phantom" verse Matthew 17:21, but appears here in Mark 9:29: *"And he said unto them, This kind can come forth by nothing, but by prayer and fasting."*

The actual Greek word translated as "nothing" is:

"3762 ŏuděis,; include. fem. ŏuděmia,; and neut. ŏuděn,; from 3761 and 1520; *not even one* (man woman or thing), i.e. *none, nobody, nothing...*"[30]

The use of *ŏuděis* here by Mark is quite inclusive or exclusive depending upon ones perspective: "Not even one man woman or thing."

So here it seems like: "This kind can come forth by *not even one man woman or thing*, but (only) by prayer and fasting." There seems to be disagreement as to whether the word "fasting" is actually present, but this matters little.

Thus according to *Mark*, while in *public*, Jesus seems to be telling the *father* of the boy, ("Jesus said unto *him*"); that all things are possible to those who believe or have faith: *"If thou canst believe, all things are possible to him that believeth."*

The question is whether Jesus was answering here the *yet unasked* question as to why it was that the disciples failed, (as later asked Him by the *disciples* in Matthew); or if Jesus was explaining to the boy's' father why he, (the father), himself was unable to do it?

One could argue that Jesus' statement had nothing to do with either; but rather was linking *Jesus'* own ability to cast it out to level of the man's' belief or faith. But if thought through, contextually the latter would seem to make little or no sense.

We do know how this message was received by the father, because he immediately, (straightway or straightaway). responded: *"And straightway the father of the child cried out, and said with tears, Lord, I believe; help thou mine unbelief."*

Thus the father is led to believe that this was referring to the father's unbelief, and not that of the disciples.

But then here when in *private*, Jesus; unlike in Matthew; says nothing about the level of His disciples' or anyone else's *belief* or *faith*.

Instead, He only tells his disciples that what He had just told the father in public does not in any way apply here, as *oudĕis*, or "not even one man woman or thing" is sufficient; but only by prayer, and possibly also fasting, this *"kind can come forth,"* or out.

According to *Matthew*, when in *public*, Jesus seems to "answer" the man—at least about *something*, stating: *"O faithless and perverse generation, how long shall I be with you? how long shall I suffer you? bring him hither to me."*

There is no *public* mention in Matthew of belief or faith—no mustard seeds or mountains when in *public*. And obviously, in no way do the disciples consider this as any answer as to why they failed prior to the appearance of the word *"apart."*

And also according to Matthew, then when in *private* ("apart"), Jesus tells his *disciples* "*Why could not we cast him out?*" is "*Because of your unbelief; for verily I say unto you, If ye have faith as a grain of mustard seed, ye shall say unto this mountain, Remove hence to yonder place; and it shall remove; and nothing shall be impossible unto you,*" just prior to the appearance of the "phantom" verse 21.

Thus if Mark 9 verse 29 is to be considered as genuine; it must be asked why Jesus would state that "*all;*" again a rather inclusive term; things are possible: "*If thou canst believe, all things are possible to him that believeth.*" when in public? And then subsequently when in private, with respect to the very same matter; state with equal inclusivity or exclusivity that ŏuděis or "*Not even one man woman or thing;*" could do this?

The likely answer, is that He could not and did not. In addition, if Jesus as a *man* is included in ŏuděis, He would arguably be stating that He alone could not do what He did. Thus verse 29 seems to be merely a recapitulation of this "phantom" verse contained in Matthew.

What is insufficient faith? Is this in actuality the *absence* of a sufficient quantity of faith; or can this better be understood as the *presence* of some degree of doubt?

Jesus also told us that faith in the quantity of a mustard seed had the power to move a mountain; so how much faith would then be required to cast out a demon; that is *required* to obey the will of man?

If it is stipulated that verse 21 in Matthew, and verse 29 in Mark, (hereafter collectively referred to as verse 21), were added; it then must be asked why?

The true answer, is that verse 21 was added to cause *reasonable doubt*. (*Present* tense is used here deliberately, as it still can and does.) If verse 20 is understood, and verse 21 were unknown; then any doubt in man's ability to cast out demons; either because he ate lunch that day, or forgot to pray that day, would be *unreasonable*. This would also be the case regarding any reasonable doubt because of the *length* of any fast, or the *amount* of any prayer. In fact, this would not even be considered.

Inevitable Balance

But by adding verse 21, things become unclear, and thus would cause reasonable doubt and questioning: "Is this one of those demons to which verse 20 refers; or is it one of those demons to which verse 21 refers?"

In the end, because of this *doubt*, (insufficient faith), all demons then by *design* will ultimately become those that verse 21 falsely refers to; as demons will exploit this doubt, just as was done here in Matthew. "Did I pray long enough?" "Did I fast long enough?"

It is the intention of verse 21 to change a binary to an analog. This easily can create more than enough "reasonable doubt" to cause failure.

In the sixty-six books that comprise the standard Bible, it is staggering as to how few actual *informative* references there are to the enemy. The reason for this is simple. Utilizing those whom he could control, the enemy simply had these references removed long long ago. This was phase *one*.

Phase *two*, was the mistranslations, today known colloquially as Bible "versions."

And phase *three* was the addition of verses such as Matthew 17:21 and Mark 9:29. With regard to Matthew 17:21, KJV "bought it," NAS straddled the issue, and NIV simply discarded it.

The enemy has, and has always had two serious problems:

The *first* is the matter of the previously referenced *hierarchy*. As a matter of *authority*, the enemy must in the general sense obey the will of man.

And more specifically; to the extent that the enemy is acting *against* the will of God, the enemy must obey man's will when man's will is consistent with God's will; e.g.; removal of demonic *possession*.

This hierarchy or authority matter, has essentially been a constant since early Genesis. And because of Calvary, the "power equation" shifted substantially in man's favor.

This is a *binary* with regard to casting out a demon.

The enemy is in a constant war with man in order to affect said (man's) *will*. In this usage, "will" is not merely wishing or hoping. "Where there is a will, there is a way;" is often heard. Another version is: "Where there is a will, there are relatives." Although the latter is provided as humor; nevertheless; whenever man wishes to act in a manner consistent with God's will, in certain senses, each is are true.

Will in furtherance of God's will often provide a "way," including *dunamis* or supernatural power—just as Jesus tells us.

And this "will" also attracts those who want to at a minimum to dissipate this will. These particular "relatives," are the "one third" we are *not* told went with him. Like moths drawn to a light source, they come to provide interference. Although it is beyond the scope of this Monograph, when it is the case that this light source is actually a *flame*; the results can become a bit interesting.

When *expressed*, as previously stated; *will* represents a force in the immaterial realm. When there is "doubt in will," this then arguably represents an oxymoronic expression.

As long as there is doubt, or perhaps better stated to the extent there is doubt; there is not will. Casting out a demon while *hoping* he will leave, is not an expression of will, but merely expressing desire. It is in furtherance of this conversion of *will* to mere *desire*, that is the main purpose for the creation and inclusion of these, as well as other, "phantom verses."

The *second* problem the enemy has; is one that has become substantially worse for him since Calvary. This second problem is that which Jesus referenced back in John 14:12—most particularly the *"greater works than these shall he do"* part.

And the enemy also knows very well the qualification, or the *"believeth"* part. Only Jesus is *The* Anointed One, and the enemy did not fare very well with Him. But anyone can be *An* Anointed one, with powers *greater* than those of The Anointed One—at least according to He Who was The Anointed One.

Thus in keeping with KJV style, it *"behooveth"* the enemy to attack said *"believeth."* This gives the enemy two distinct advantages:

The *first*, is to prevent man from having the *knowledge* of man's true capabilities.

And the *second*, is to see to it that man does not *qualify* for any *greater* capabilities.

Today's war on *Christianity* is therefore actually an attack on Jesus; or the *second* part of the Trinity, largely in an *indirect* manner. The enemy fears Jesus for certain; but what he is *terrified* of, is the utilization of the *Christos*, or anointing of the *third* part of the Trinity upon man.

Jesus provision of *justification* or *salvation* for the immaterial portion of man, was a part of a larger redemptive process at; and just prior to; Calvary. [See Monograph: "*Calvary's Hidden Truths*"]

Whether or not one chooses to *believe* that this is true, in no way changes that which is *purported* to be. Salvation/justification is an important part of, but only a part of, what we are told Jesus provided; and non-believers cannot in any way alter this. One is free to not believe it; however unbelief in this, is an insufficient means or justification for any changes in what is or is not stated.

But as stated in John 14:12, Jesus also ultimately provided additional miraculous capabilities, (dunamis), which are even greater than His had been. The enemy's knowledge and fear of man's increase in available *dunamis*, or supernatural power; whether *consciously* known by the anti-Christians or not; represents the main reason behind today's war on Christianity.

Tacit knowledge is knowledge that one "knows;" but one does not know he knows. This is "not knowing, (not being consciously aware of), what one *knows*;" as opposed to: "not knowing what one *does not know*."

"Christians" are of course free to espouse *realities* that make little or no sense, and thus these cannot possibly be true.

Proselytizing that a man that we are told was *formed* from *something*; not only *could* be, but in fact *is* the very same man that we are previously told was brought into existence from *nothing*; simply makes no degree of sense. And there is a price tag for this; "including but not limited to;" the ultimate result of prospective "believers" who must then discard science in order to become a believer—and many will simply discard these erroneous representations of the Bible and Christianity instead.

Likewise; it must be asked how is it that three days and three nights "like Jonah;" can somehow be "squeezed in" from Friday 3:00 PM until before early dawn on Sunday?

"This one" is the result of simply misunderstanding, through ignorance or otherwise; as to which particular "Sabbath" it is to which the Bible refers.

Willful proffering realities such as these; i.e.; at best "misinformation;" not only affects those who currently believe in Christianity, but also as stated: *prospective* Christians. This pleases the enemy greatly; but has nothing to do with what the Bible tells us—if the same is merely read without prejudice. Thus none of this has any effects whatsoever on the *actualities* involved.

The enemy was there, and he knows what exists; and thus he acts from a *reality* in accordance with these *actualities*—at least to the extent that he is able. It is true that "the truth is not in him." But this does not necessarily mean that he would touch a red-hot stove repeatedly.

It is extremely important to recognize that there is no such thing as a stimulus without a response. Neither is there any such thing as a response without a stimulus. The only known exception to this rule is God. It is God, and God alone that has or had no cause. He is the *primum movens*, or prime mover.

It is also important to recognize that there are two realms. One by definition contains matter and is referred to as the *material* realm. The other contains no matter and is referred to as the *immaterial* realm. This distinction is a binary.

The cause for the effect known as the material realm could not have existed in a yet to be created material realm. Thus the cause for this effect had to have been in the *immaterial* realm prior to the creation of this material realm. Science refers to the creation of the material realm as the "Big Bang;" with the very same event being described in Genesis 1:1.

Things that reside solely in the material realm, only affect the material realm. But anything that is dual in nature; i.e.; contains the "breath of life;" is a dual being. The actions of any dual being affect both realms.

In a sense it is like two "closed" systems with a portal between the two. In an absolute sense, one cannot light a match and not create an imbalance by increasing the temperature of the earth—however miniscule this change might be. And this very same action

Inevitable Balance

produces an imbalance in the immaterial realm depending on the *reasons* for the action.

All dual fold actions, (*action* and *reason*), are subject to similar laws; with balancing mechanisms for each.

Again assuming that any "key to the universe" actually exists, it could be argued from a very broad perspective that understanding *will* and *balance* represents this key.

When H. Sapiens exercise free will in the performance of any action or inaction; (Yup, that one sometimes counts too.); the results are not limited to the *reality* of the actions, but rather are determined by the *actuality* of the action.

From the standpoint of universal law, whatever one chooses to do to another; it is simultaneously chosen by him or her that the very same be done to them. It *is* one in the same—an indivisible package. Human realities can try to separate this actuality into a reality that suits them at the time, but this merely represents delusion.

When one gives, an actuality is created that requires giving back to the giver. But the calculations include the *reasons*. This is what Jesus was trying to teach people. And when one steals, an actuality is created that requires taking from the thief. Thus the "do unto others" admonition represents solid advice—for these very reasons.

Choose actions carefully, and choose *motives* even more carefully; as they will be balanced—*always*. It may look good or bad for a while, depending on the nature of the action; but the balance is inevitable.

Glossary

'âhab: (H) "157 'âhab or 'âhêb; a prim. root: to *have affection* for (sexually or otherwise): - (be-) love (-ed, -ly, -r), like, friend."[5-STS]

actuality: "A*ctuality*" is what currently exists or what "is;" what a thing objectively is, as opposed to a *reality* based upon *perception*. An "un-acted upon" actuality, remains an actuality; and that which is not an actuality remains not an actuality—irrespective of any *reality* of the same. The *reality* of a mirage is water, but the *actuality* of a mirage can be anything *except* water—if it is a mirage. No actuality can ever be 100% accurately perceived, thus reality always falls short.

actualization: To bring something from the thought process; (via imagination, quasi-reality); to a current actuality. One can ultimately produce an actuality through a reality (actualization), but not just by the existence of the reality alone—at least when confined to the material realm. Some level of energy or effort (ĕrgŏn) must be also utilized in the actualization process.

afterlife: That "state" of the immaterial part of man (soul), *after* leaving the previously alive or connected (incarnated) body or soma.

alive: In the *general* sense, refers to a *connection*, or connected.

argŏs: (G) "692 argŏs; from *1* (as a neg. particle) [*1* is A as used in negation whatever follows and *2041*; *inactive*, i.e. *unemployed*; (by impl.) *lazy, useless*: - barren, idle, slow."[32]-DT

arguriŏn: (G) "694 arguriŏn; neut. Of a presumed der. of *696*; *silvery*, i.e. (by impl.) *cash*; spec. a *silverling* (i.e. *drachma* or *shekel*): - money, (piece of) silver (piece)."[30]-DT

argurŏs: (G) "696 argurŏs; from argŏs (*shining*); *silver* (the metal, in the articles or coin): - silver."[31]-DT

'âven: (H) "205 'âven; from an unused root perh. mean. prop. to *pant* (hence to *exert* oneself, usually in vain; to *come* to *naught*) strictly *nothingness*; also *trouble, vanity, wickedness*; spec. an *idol*. . ."[15]-T

balance: If it can be so stipulated that balance is derived from the Latin *bi*, meaning two; and the Latin *lanx*, meaning "dish or plate;" then an image of the "scales" such as those representing the "scales of justice" comes to mind.

bârâ': (H) "1254 bârâ', a prim. root; (absol.) to create; (qualified) to cut down (a wood), select, feed (as formative processes): - choose, create (creator), cut down, dispatch, do, make (fat)."[G1]-H This verb requires creation out of nothing.

bâchan: (H) 974 bâchan, a prim. root; to *test*..."[G2]

beforelife: That "state" of the immaterial part of man (soul), *before* entering into that alive or connected (incarnated) condition with a body or soma. Whether souls are always "new," or sometimes "recycled," is irrelevant to this definition.

basilĕia: (G) "932 basilĕia; from *935*; prop. *royalty*, i.e. (abstr.) *rule*, or (concr.) a *realm* (lit. or fig.): - kingdom + reign."[6]-DT

Glossary

châbar: (H) "2266 châbar, a prim. root; to *join* (lit. or fig.); spec. (by means of spells) to *fascinate*: - charm (-er), be compact, couple (together), have fellowship with, heap up, join (self, together), league."[11-C]

chabbûwrâh: (H) "2250 chabbûwrâh, or chabbûrâh, or chăbûrâh, from 2266; prop. *bound* (with stripes), i.e. a *weal* (or black - and - blue mark itself): - blueness, bruise, hurt, stripe, wound."[10-C]

châcad: (H) "2616 châcad; a prim. root; prop. perh. to *bow* (the neck only [comp. 2603] courtesy to an equal), i.e. to *be kind*;..."[3-STS]

chânan: (H) "2603 chânan; a prim. root [comp. 2583]; prop. to *bend* or stoop in kindness to an inferior; to *favor bestow*..."[4-STS]

chay: (H) "2416 chay; from 2421; *alive*; hence raw (flesh); fresh (plant, water, year), strong; also (as noun, espec. in the fem. sing. and masc. plur.) life (or living thing), whether lit. or fig..." [The very next word in Strong's (2417), is likewise: "chay (Chald.)" also means "*alive*" or "*life*," but here the original *Chaldean*.][7-T]

checed (H) "2617 checed; from 2616; *kindness*;..."[2-STS]

dead: In the *general* sense refers to a *disconnection*, or disconnected.

death: Is roughly synonymous with "dead," but refers to the *event* of disconnection, rather than that *general state* where there is no connection. "Death" is when this disconnection occurs; and "dead" is the state after this occurrence.

dŏulŏs: (G) "*1401* dŏulŏs; from *1210*; a slave (lit. or fig., invol or vol.; frequently therefore in a qualified sense of subjection or subserviency): - bond (-man), servant."[9-DT]

duna: A unit of *relative* measure for the quantity or amount of *dunamis*;, or miraculous or supernatural power. This is utilized only for *relative,* and never for *absolute* quantities of *dunamis.*

dunamis: (G) "*1411* dunamis; from *1410; force* (lit. or fig.); spec. miraculous *power* (usually by impl. a *miracle* itself): - ability, abundance, meaning, might (-ily, -y, -y deed), worker of) miracle (-s), power, strength, violence, mighty (wonderful) work."[17-DT]

ĕgĕirō: (G) "1453 ĕgĕirō, prob. Akin to the base of 58 (through the idea of *collecting* one's faculties); to *waken* (trans. or intrans.), i.e. *rouse* (lit. from sleep, from sitting or lying, from disease, from death; or fig. from obscurity, inactivity, ruins, nonexistence): - awake, lift (up), raise (again, up), rear up, (a -) rise (again, up), stand, take up."[52-C]

ectoparisitosis: Oppression; through the idea of an abnormal condition of a parasite causing *oppression* from the *external.*

endoparisitosis: Possession; through the idea of an abnormal condition of a parasite causing changes from the *internal.*

ĕlĕuthĕrŏō: (G) "*1659* ĕlĕuthĕrŏō; from *1658;* to *liberate,* i.e. (fig.) to *exempt* (from mor., cer. or mortal liability): - deliver, make free."[17-T]

'ĕlôhîym: (H) "430 'ĕlôhîym; plur. of 433; *gods* in the ordinary sense; but spec. used (in the plur. thus, esp. with the art.) of the supreme *God;* occasionally applied by way of deference to *magistrates;* and sometimes as a superlative: - angels, x exceeding, God (gods) (-dess, -ly), x (very) great, judges, x mighty."[17-DT]

ĕrgazŏmai: (G) "2038 ĕrgazŏmai; mid. from *2041;* to *toil* (as a task, occupation, etc.)..."[26-DT]

ĕrgŏn: (G) "2041 ĕrgŏn; from a prim. (but obsol.) ĕrgō (to work); *toil* (as an effort or occupation); by impl. and act: - deed, doing, labour, work."[27-DT] *first hour*: Began at sunrise or about 6:00 AM, and lasted until 8:59 AM; but unlike the night watches, was actually followed by the *third*, (not second), hour beginning at 9:00 AM.[23-C]

first watch: Began at sunset or about 6:00 PM, and lasted until about 8:59PM, followed by the *second* watch.

gē: (G) "1093 gē, contr. From a prim. word; *soil*; by extens. a *region*, or the solid part or the whole of the *terrene* globe (includ. the occupants in each application): - country, earth (-ly), ground, land, world."[44-C]

g{e}bûwrâh: (H) "1369 g{e}bûwrâh; fem. pass. part. from the same as 1368; *force* (lit. or fig.);. . ."[13-T]

ghost: An immaterial breath-like (spiritus) entity specifically designed to "live in" or be connected with a physical vessel.

hagiŏs: (G) "40 hagiŏs, from hagos (an *awful* thing) [comp. 53, 2282]; *sacred* (phys. *pure*, mor. *blameless* or *religious*, cer. *consecrated*): - (most) holy (one, thing), saint."[50-C]

hamartanō: (G) "264 hamartanō, perh. from *1* (as a neg. particle) and the base of *3313*; prop. to *miss* the mark (and *so not share* in the prize), i.e. (fig.) to *err*, esp. (mor.) to *sin*; - for your faults, offend, sin, trespass."[3-C]

heaven (singular): "in the *singular*; generally refers to the *immaterial* realm where God resides; e.g.; the "heaven" in "Who art in heaven," refers to the *immaterial* realm."

heavens (plural): The *plural* of heaven: "heavens," generally refers to the space between the celestial bodies, and thus is contained (as "space") in the *material* realm.

hĕōs: (G) "2193 hĕōs, of uncert. affin.; a conj., prep. and adv. of continuance, until (of time and place): - even (until, unto), (as) far (as), how long, (un-) til (-l), (hither-, un-, up) to, while (-s)."[40-C]

imagination: *Imagination* is similar to a reality, but with the subjective knowledge or belief that the thing does not yet exist.

immaterial potential energy: Stored energy that is not contained in the material realm. The energy that created the universe just prior to its creation necessarily was not in the yet to be created realm.

immaterial kinetic energy: That energy which emanates from the *immaterial* realm, and causes manifestation in the *material* realm.

impetigo: (from Latin *impetere* to attack)[41-T]

kábac: (H) "3526 kábac, a prim. root; to *trample*; hence to *wash* (prop. by stamping with the feet), whether lit. (including the *fulling* process) or fig.: - fuller, wash (-ing).'"[8-C]

kâbash: (H) "3533 kâbash; a prim. root; to *tread* down; hence neg. to *disregard*; pos. to *conquer, subjugate, violate*: - bring into bondage, force, keep under, subdue, bring into subjection."[12-STS]

Kabbalah: In any of its various spellings, is generally considered as some evil religion that should be avoided. The fact is that Kabbalah is actually not a "religion;" has nothing to do with "voodoo;" and simply means "*to receive.*"

katapĕtasma: (G) "2665 katapĕtasma, from a comp. of *2596* and a congener of *4072*; something *spread thoroughly*, i.e. (spec.) the door screen (to the Most Holy Place) in the Jewish Temple: - vail."[37-C]

kathistēmi: (G) "2525 kathistēmi; from *2596* and *2476*; to *place down* (permanently), i.e. (fig.) to *designate, constitute, convoy*: - appoint, be, conduct, make ordain, set."[29-DT]

Glossary

kinetic energy: The energy that "a thing" has because it is in *motion*.

kikkâr: (H) "3603 kikkâr; from 3769; a *circle*, i.e. (by impl.) a circumjacent *tract* or region, espec. the *Ghôr* or valley of the Jordan; also a (round) *loaf*; also a *talent* (or large [round] coin): - loaf, morsel, piece, plain, talent."[13-DT]

kikkêr: (H) "3604 kikkêr (Chald.); corresp. to 3603; a *talent*; - talent."[14-DT]

klipot: shells, rinds, husk's etc. According to Kabbalah, these Klipot block "the Light," or God.

kŏimaō: (G) "2837 kŏimaō, from 2749; to *put to sleep* i.e. (pass. or reflex.) to *slumber*; fig. to *decease*: - (be a -, fall a -, fall on) sleep, be dead."[51-C]

lŏgŏs: (G) "3056 lŏgŏs; from *3004*; something *said* (including the *thought*); by impl. a *topic* (subject of discourse), also *reasoning* (the mental faculty) or *motive*; by extens. a *computation*; spec. (with the art. In John) the Divine *Expression* (i.e. *Christ*)..."[29T]

machaira: (G) "3162 machaira; prob. fem. of a presumed der. of *3163*; a *knife*, i.e. *dirk*; fig. *war*, judicial *punishment*: - sword."[25-T]

mâlê': (H) "4390 mâlê'; or mâlâ' (Esth. 7:5),; a prim. root, to *fill* or (intrans.) *be full* of, in a wide application (lit. and fig.)..."[10-STS]

massâ': (H) "4853 massâ'; from 5375; a *burden*; spec. *tribute*, or (abstr.) *porterage*; fig. an *utterance*,..." chiefly a *doom*, espec. *singing*; mental, *desire*: - burden, carry away, prophesy, x they set, song, tribute."[23-DT]

měizōn: (G) "3187 měizōn; irreg. compar. of *3173*; *larger*..."[5-IB]

miracle: Something that occurs in the *material* realm, but is contrary to natural law. In fact in order to be considered a miracle, it *must* contradict natural law or laws; natural law here meaning the law or laws of the *material* realm.

mnēměiŏn: (G) "3419 mnēměiŏn, from 3420; a *remembrance*, i.e. *cenotaph (place of interment)*: - grave, sepulchre, tomb."[48-C]

nâphach: (H) "5301 nâphach; a prim. root; to *puff*, in various applications..."[G3]

nâsâ': (H) "5375 nâsâ' or nâcâh; a prim. root; to *lift* in a great variety of applications."[24-DT]

nephesh: (H) "5315 nephesh; from 5314; prop. a *breathing* creature..."[8-T]

nephiyl: (H) "5303 nephiyl, or nephil, from 5307; prop., a *feller*, i.e. a *bully* or *tyrant*: - giant. 5307 naphal, a prim. root; to *fall*, in a great variety of applications (intrans. or causat., lit. or fig.)..."[G6]

n^{e}shâmâh: (H) "5397; n^{e}shâmâh; fr. 5395; a *puff*, i.e. *wind*, angry or vital *breath*...;"[6-T]

ŏpsōniŏn: (G) "3800 ŏpsōniŏn; neut. of a presumed der. of the same as *3795*; *rations* for a soldier, i.e. (by extens.) his *stipend* or *pay*: - wages."[9-T] (It must be noted that no *reasonable* relationship between 3800 and 3795 could be found.)

ŏrŏs: (G) "3735 ŏrŏs; prob. from an obsol. ŏrō (to *rise* or "*rear*"; perh. akin to *142*; comp. *3733*); a *mountain* (as *lifting* itself above the plain): - hill, mount (-ain)."[4-DT]

ŏuděis: (G) "3762 ŏuděis,; include. fem. ŏuděmia,; and neut. ŏuděn,; from *3761* and *1520*; *not even one* (man woman or thing), i.e. none, nobody, nothing..."[30-IB]

Glossary

ŏuranŏs: (G) "3772 ŏuranŏs; perh.from the same as 3735 (through the idea of *elevation*); the *sky*; by extens. *heaven* (as the abode of God); by impl. *happiness, power, eternity*; spec. the *Gospel*, (*Christianity*): - air, heaven ([-ly]), sky."[3-DT]

phĕrō: (G) "5342 phĕrō; a prim. verb...to *"bear"* or *carry*"[6-DT]

physical death: Refers to that state where the immaterial part of man, (soul), is no longer connected to the material part of man (body).

physical life: That condition where the immaterial part of man, (soul), is connected to the material part (body).

pnĕuma: (G) "4151 pnĕuma; from 4154; a *current* of air, i.e. *breath* (*blast*) or a *breeze*; by anal. or fig. a *spirit*, i.e. (human) the rational *soul*, (by impl.) *vital principle*, mental *disposition* etc..."[26-T]

potential energy: Energy that is *stored*.

primum movens: Or prime mover, is God. God is the only entity that exists without a cause.

râdâh: (H) "7287 râdâh; to *tread* down, i.e. *subjugate*; spec. to *crumble* of: - (come to make to) have dominion, prevail against, reign, (bear, make to) rule, (-r, over), take."[13-STS]

râphâ': (H) "7495 râphâ', or râphâh, a prim. root; prop. to *mend* (by stitching), i.e. (fig.) to *cure*: - cure, (cause to) heal, physician, repair, x thoroughly, make whole."[12-C]

reality: The belief or "understanding" of "what a thing is or is not" based upon perception.

realization: The process by which the perception of a "thing or things" produces an awareness, belief or understanding (reality) of said actuality or actualities. *Realization* (process) and *reality* (result) are always less than the actuality, and often incomplete and/or erroneous.

recollection: The process of "remembering." Recollection is similar to a reality, but with the subjective knowledge or belief that the thing may no longer exist.

reincarnation: In a very general sense, the reintroduction of that immaterial part of man (soul) into a *new* and *different* physical body. (see text)

resurrection: The reintroduction of that immaterial part of man (soul) into the *same* physical body.

retrophesy: To obtain knowledge "unnaturally" about the *past*, in the same way and manner that *prophesy* is concerned with the *future*.

rhēma: (G) "4487 rhēma; from 4483; an *utterance* (individ., collect. or spec.); by impl. a *matter* or *topic* (espec. of narration, command or dispute); with a neg. *naught* whatever..."[27-T]

rôhab: (H) "7296 rôhab; from 7292; *pride*. . ."[14-T]

schizo: (G) "4977 schizo, appar. a prim. verb; to *split* or *sever* (lit. or fig.): - break, divide, open, rend, make a rent"[47-C]

sĕiō: (G) "4579 sĕiō, appar. a prim. verb; to *rock* (*vibrate*, prop. sideways or to and fro), i.e. (gen.) to *agitate* (in a any direction; cause to *tremble*); fig. to throw into a *tremor* (of fear or concern): - move, quake, shake."[45-C]

sĕismŏs: (G) "4578 sĕismŏs, from 4579; a *commotion*, i.e. (of the air) a *gale*, (of the ground) an *earthquake*: - earthquake, tempest."[43-C]

shâmar: (H) "8104: shâmar; A prim. root; prop. to *hedge* about (as with thorns), i.e. *guard*; gen. to *protect, attend to*, etc.: - beware, be circumspect, take heed (to self), keep (-er, self), mark, look narrowly, observe, preserve, regard, reserve, save (self), sure, (that lay) wait (for), watch (-man)."[23-T] [See MeekRaker Monograph #601 "*Shâmar to Sharia*"]

skŏtŏs: (G) "4655 skŏtŏs, from the base of 4639; *shadiness*, i.e. *obscurity* (lit. or fig.): - darkness." "4639 skia, appar. A prim. word; "*shade*" or a shadow (lit. or fig. [darkness of *error* or an *adumbration*]): - shadow."[22-C]

sōma: (G) "4983 sōma, from 4982; the *body* (as a *sound* whole), used in a very wide application, lit. or fig.: - bodily, body, slave.[49-C]

soul: Refers to that *immaterial* part of man, often inadequately described as "will, intellect and emotions."

spiritual: Can refer to a myriad of immaterial or "breath like" entities.

spiritual death: Refers to that state where the immaterial part of man, (soul), is disconnected from its original source.

spiritual life: Refers to that state where the immaterial part of man (soul) is connected to its original source.

sûwk: (H) "7753 sûwk a prim. root; to *entwine*, i.e. *shut* in (for formation, protection or restraint):- fence, (make an) hedge (up)."[22-C]

tala: A unit of *relative* measure for the quantity or amount of talantŏn, or a bearing or balancing weight. This is utilized only for *relative*, and never for *absolute* quantities of *talantŏn*.

talantŏn: (G) "5007 talantŏn; neut. Of a presumed der. of the orig. form of tiaō (to *bear*; equiv. to 5342); a *balance* (as *supporting* weights), i.e. (by impl.) a certain *weight* (and thence a *coin* or rather *sum* of money) or "*talent*": - talent."[15-DT]

tamrûwq: (H) "8562 tamrûwq, or tamrûq, or tamrîyq, from 4838; prop. a *scouring*, i.e. *soap* or *perfumery* for the bath; fig. a *detergent*: - x cleanse, (thing for) purification (- fying)."[16-C]

tērĕō: (G) "5083 tērĕō; from tĕrŏs (a *watch*; perh. akin to 2334); to *guard* (from *loss* or *injury*, prop. by keeping *the eye* upon..."[8-STS]

tetragrammaton: YHWH, the "ineffable" name of God in all of its various spellings, is referred to as the *tetragrammaton*.

thanatŏs: (G)"2288 thanatŏs; from 2348; (prop. an adj. used as a noun) *death* (lit. or fig.): - x deadly, (be...) death."[3-T]

thĕŏs: (G) "2316 thĕŏs; of uncert. affin.; a *deity*, espec. (with 3588) the supreme *Divinity*; fig. a *magistrate*; by Heb. *very*: - x exceeding, God, god [-ly, -ward]."[21-STS]

Tikkune: is essentially the process of correcting one's faults.

tsâbâ': (H) "6635 tsâbâ' or tsᵉbâ'âh from 6633; a *mass* of persons (or fig. things), espec. reg. organized for war (an *army*); by impl. a *campaign*, lit. or fig. (spec. *hardship, worship*): -appointed time, (+) army, (+) battle, company, host, service, soldiers, waiting upon..."[1-C]

tuptō: (G) "5180 tuptō, a prim. verb (in a strength. form); to "*thump*", i.e. *cudgel* or *pummel* (prop. with a stick or *bastinado*), but in any case by *repeated* blows; thus differing from 3817 and 3960, which denote a [usually single] blow with the hand or any instrument, or 4141 with the *fist* [or a *hammer*], or 4474 with the *palm*; as well as from 5177, an *accidental* collision); by impl. to *punish*; fig. to *offend* (the conscience): - beat, smite, strike, wound."[55-C]

yâd: (H) "3027 yâd; a prim. word; a *hand* (the *open* one [indicating *power, means, direction*, etc.]. in distinction from 3079, the *closed* one)..."[34-T]

Glossary

yâtsar: (H) "3335 yâtsar; prob. identical with 3334 (through the *squeezing* into shape); ([comp. 3331]); to *mould* into a form; espec. as a *potter*;..."[G2]

yom or yôwm (H) "3117 yôwm, from an unused root mean. *To be hot*; a *day* (as the *warm* hours), whether lit. (from sunrise to sunset, or from one sunset to the next), or fig. (a space of time defined by an associated term), [often used adv.]: - age, ... season..."[G3]

YHWH: The *tetragrammaton*, in all of its various spellings is generally considered to be the usually unspoken or ineffable name of God.

yir'âh: (H) "3374 yir'âh; fem. of 3373; *fear* (also used as infin.); mor. *reverence*: - x dreadful, x exceedingly, fear (-fulness)."[19-T]

zōē: (G) "2222: zōē; from *2198*; *life* (lit or fig.): - life (time). Comp. *5590*."[2-T]

(H) = Hebrew   (G) = Greek
Footnote Legend: STS = *"Shâmar to Sharia"*
DT= *"Donald Trump Candidacy According to Matthew?"*
T = *"Its Not Just A Theory"*   C = *"Calvary's Hidden Truths"*
IB = *"Inevitable Balance"*   G = Glossary

Bibliographies

Donald Trump Candidacy According to Matthew?

1) *New American Standard Bible:* 1995 update. 1995 (Matthew 25:14-30) The Lockman Foundation: Lahabra, CA
2) *New American Standard Bible*: 1995 update. 1995 (Matthew 25:1) The Lockman Foundation: Lahabra, CA
3) Strong, James. *Strong's Exhaustive Concordance of the Bible.* © 1890 James Strong, Madison, NJ p. 53 (Greek)
4) Strong, James. *Strong's Exhaustive Concordance of the Bible.* © 1890 James Strong, Madison, NJ p. 53 (Greek)
5) Strong, James. *Strong's Exhaustive Concordance of the Bible.* © 1890 James Strong, Madison, NJ p. 474

6) Strong, James. *Strong's Exhaustive Concordance of the Bible.* © 1890 James Strong, Madison, NJ p. 18 (Greek)
7) Strong, James. *Strong's Exhaustive Concordance of the Bible.* © 1890 James Strong, Madison, NJ p. 936
8) Strong, James. *Strong's Exhaustive Concordance of the Bible.* © 1890 James Strong, Madison, NJ p. 937
9) Strong, James. *Strong's Exhaustive Concordance of the Bible.* © 1890 James Strong, Madison, NJ p. 24 (Greek)
10) Strong, James. *Strong's Exhaustive Concordance of the Bible.* © 1890 James Strong, Madison, NJ p. 937
11) Strong, James. *Strongest Strong's Exhaustive Concordance of the Bible.* © 2001, Zondervan, Grand Rapids MI p. 1068
12) *New Open Bible,* © 1990, 1985, 1983, Thomas Nelson Inc. p. 31
13) Strong, James. *Strong's Exhaustive Concordance of the Bible.* © 1890 James Strong, Madison, NJ p. 55 (Hebrew)
14) Strong, James. *Strong's Exhaustive Concordance of the Bible.* © 1890 James Strong, Madison, NJ p. 55 (Hebrew)
15) Strong, James. *Strong's Exhaustive Concordance of the Bible.* © 1890 James Strong, Madison, NJ p. 71 (Greek)
16) Strong, James. *Strong's Exhaustive Concordance of the Bible.* © 1890 James Strong, Madison, NJ p. 75 (Greek)

"5342 phĕrō; a prim. verb (for which other and appar. not cognate ones are used in certain tenses only); namely,... ĕnĕgkō; to "bear" or carry (in a very wide application, lit. and fig., as follows): - be, bear, bring (forth), carry, come, + let her drive, be driven, endure, go on, lay, lead, move, reach, rushing, uphold."

17) Strong, James. *Strong's Exhaustive Concordance of the Bible.* © 1890 James Strong, Madison, NJ p. 24 (Greek)

"1411 dunamis; from 1410; force (lit. or fig.); spec. miraculous power (usually by impl. a miracle itself); - ability, abundance, meaning, might (-ily, -y, - y deed), (worker of) miracle (-s), power, strength, violence, mighty (wonderful) work." "1410 dunamai; of uncert. affin.; to be able or possible: - be able, can (do, + - not), could, may, might, be possible, be of power."

18) *Chambers Dictionary of Etymology.* © 1988 The H. W. Wilson Company, New York, NY p. 308

Bibliographies

19) *New American Standard Bible:* 1995 update. 1995 (Proverbs 30:1)
    The Lockman Foundation: Lahabra, CA
20) *King James Bible,* Proverbs 30:1
21) *New American Standard Bible*: 1995 update. 1995 (Malachi 1:1)
    The Lockman Foundation: Lahabra, CA
22) *King James Bible* Malachi 1:1
23) Strong, James. *Strong's Exhaustive Concordance of the Bible.* ©
    1890 James Strong, Madison, NJ p. 73 (Hebrew)
    "4853 massâ'; from 5375; a burden; spec. tribute, or (abstr.) porterage; fig. an utterance, chiefly a doom, espec. singing; mental, desire: - burden, carry away, prophesy, x they set, song, tribute."
24) Strong, James. *Strong's Exhaustive Concordance of the Bible.* ©
    1890 James Strong, Madison, NJ p. 80 (Hebrew)
    "5375 nâsâ' or nâcâh; a prim. root; to lift in a great variety of applications, lit. and fig. absol. and rel. (as follows): - accept, advance arise, (able to, [armour], suffer to) bear (-er, up) bring (forth), ..."
25) *New American Standard Bible:* 1995 update. 1995 (Luke 12:48)
    The Lockman Foundation: Lahabra, CA
26) Strong, James. *Strong's Exhaustive Concordance of the Bible.* ©
    1890 James Strong, Madison, NJ p. 32 (Greek)
    2038 ĕrgazŏmai; mid. from 2041; to toil (as a task, occupation, etc.), (by impl.) effect, be engaged in or with, etc.: - commit, do, labor for, minister about, trade (by) work." "2041 ĕrgŏn; from a prim. (but obsol.) ĕrgō (to work); toil (as an effort or occupation); by impl. and act: - deed, doing, labour, work."
27) Strong, James. *Strong's Exhaustive Concordance of the Bible.* ©
    1890 James Strong, Madison, NJ p. 32 (Greek)
28) *New American Standard Bible:* 1995 update. 1995 (Proverbs 14:23)
    The Lockman Foundation: Lahabra, CA
29) Strong, James. *Strong's Exhaustive Concordance of the Bible.* ©
    1890 James Strong, Madison, NJ p. 38 (Greek)
30) Strong, James. *Strong's Exhaustive Concordance of the Bible.* ©
    1890 James Strong, Madison, NJ p. 15 (Greek)

31) Strong, James. *Strong's Exhaustive Concordance of the Bible.* © 1890 James Strong, Madison, NJ p. 15 (Greek)
32) Strong, James. *Strong's Exhaustive Concordance of the Bible.* © 1890 James Strong, Madison, NJ p. 15 (Greek)
33) Strong, James. *Strong's Exhaustive Concordance of the Bible.* © 1890 James Strong, Madison, NJ p. 32 (Greek)

Bibliographies

SHÂMAR TO SHARIA

1. *The Holy Bible, KJV* Exodus 20:6, *kingjamesbibleonline.org*, retrieved 7 March 2016
2. Strong, James. *Strong's Exhaustive Concordance of the Bible.* © 1890 James Strong, Madison, NJ p. 41(Hebrew)
3. Strong, James. *Strong's Exhaustive Concordance of the Bible.* © 1890 James Strong, Madison, NJ p. 41(Hebrew)
4. Strong, James. *Strong's Exhaustive Concordance of the Bible.* © 1890 James Strong, Madison, NJ p. 41(Hebrew)
5. Strong, James. *Strong's Exhaustive Concordance of the Bible.* © 1890 James Strong, Madison, NJ p. 9(Hebrew)
6. Strong, James. *Strong's Exhaustive Concordance of the Bible.* © 1890 James Strong, Madison, NJ p. 118(Hebrew)
7. *The Holy Bible, KJV* John 14:15, *kingjamesbibleonline.org*, retrieved 7 March 2016
8. Strong, James. *Strong's Exhaustive Concordance of the Bible.* © 1890 James Strong, Madison, NJ p. 71(Greek)
9. *The Holy Bible, KJV* Genesis 1:28, *kingjamesbibleonline.org*, retrieved 7 March 2016
10. Strong, James. *Strong's   Exhaustive Concordance of the*

Bible. ©   1890 James Strong, Madison, NJ p. 66(Hebrew)
11. *The Holy Bible, KJV* Esther 7:5, *kingjamesbibleonline.org*, retrieved 7 March 2016
12. Strong, James. *Strong's Exhaustive Concordance of the Bible.* © 1890 James Strong, Madison, NJ p. 54(Hebrew)
13. Strong, James. *Strong's Exhaustive Concordance of the Bible.* © 1890 James Strong, Madison, NJ p. 107(Hebrew)
14. *The Holy Bible, KJV* Revelation 7:14, *kingjamesbibleonline.org*, retrieved 7 March 2016
15. *The Holy Bible, KJV* Revelation 19:16, *kingjamesbibleonline.org*, retrieved 7 March 2016
16. *The Holy Bible, KJV* Psalm 82:6-7, *kingjamesbibleonline.org*, retrieved 7 March 2016
17. Strong, James. *Strong's Exhaustive Concordance of the Bible.* © 1890 James Strong, Madison, NJ p. 12(Hebrew)
18. *The Holy Bible, KJV* Exodus 20:2, *kingjamesbibleonline.org*, retrieved 7 March 2016
19. *The Holy Bible, KJV* Psalm 82:7, *kingjamesbibleonline.org*, retrieved 7 March 2016
20. *The Holy Bible, KJV* John 10:34-35, *kingjamesbibleonline.org*, retrieved 7 March 2016
21. Strong, James. *Strong's Exhaustive Concordance of the Bible.* © 1890 James Strong, Madison, NJ p. 36(Greek)
22. Strong, James. *Strong's Exhaustive Concordance of the Bible.* © 1890 James Strong, Madison, NJ p. 407
23. *Interlinear Bible Hebrew Greek English, 1 Volume Edition.* © 1976, 1977, 1978, 1979, 1980, 1981, 1984. Second Edition, © 1986 Jay P. Green, Sr., Hendrickson Publishers (Genesis 1:2)
24. *The Holy Bible, KJV* 1st Corinthians 8:9, *kingjamesbibleonline.org*, retrieved 7 March 2016
25. *The Holy Bible, KJV* 1st Samuel 15:18, *kingjamesbibleonline.org*, retrieved 7 March 2016

Bibliographies

Its Not Just A Theory

1) *King James Bible* Romans 6:21-23
2) Strong, James. *Strong's Exhaustive Concordance of the Bible.* © 1890 James Strong, Madison, NJ p. 35 (Greek)
3) Strong, James. *Strong's Exhaustive Concordance of the Bible.* © 1890 James Strong, Madison, NJ p. 35 (Greek)
4) *King James Bible* Genesis 2:7
5) Strong, James. *Strong's Exhaustive Concordance of the Bible.* © 1890 James Strong, Madison, NJ p. 81 (Hebrew)
6) Strong, James. *Strong's Exhaustive Concordance of the Bible.* © 1890 James Strong, Madison, NJ p. 81 (Hebrew)
7) Strong, James. *Strong's Exhaustive Concordance of the Bible.* © 1890 James Strong, Madison, NJ p. 38 (Hebrew)
8) Strong, James. *Strong's Exhaustive Concordance of the Bible.* © 1890 James Strong, Madison, NJ p. 80 (Hebrew)
9) Strong, James. *Strong's Exhaustive Concordance of the Bible.* © 1890 James Strong, Madison, NJ p. 53 (Greek)
10) Strong, James. *Strong's Exhaustive Concordance of the Bible.* © 1890 James Strong, Madison, NJ p. 98 (Hebrew)
11) *King James Bible* Genesis 5:27
12) *King James Bible* Psalms 90:8-10
13) Strong, James. *Strong's Exhaustive Concordance of the Bible.* © 1890 James Strong, Madison, NJ p. 25 (Hebrew)
14) Strong, James. *Strong's Exhaustive Concordance of the Bible.* © 1890 James Strong, Madison, NJ p. 107 (Hebrew)

15) Strong, James. *Strong's Exhaustive Concordance of the Bible.* © 1890 James Strong, Madison, NJ p. 9 (Hebrew)
16) *King James Bible* Genesis 5:27 Deut. 34:7
17) Strong, James. *Strong's Exhaustive Concordance of the Bible.* © 1890 James Strong, Madison, NJ p. 27 (Greek)
18) *King James Bible* Proverbs 9:10-11
19) Strong, James. *Strong's Exhaustive Concordance of the Bible.* © 1890 James Strong, Madison, NJ p. 52 (Hebrew)
20) *King James Bible,* Exodus 20:12
21) *King James Bible,* Job 1:10
22) Strong, James. *Strong's Exhaustive Concordance of the Bible.* © 1890 James Strong, Madison, NJ p. 113 (Hebrew)
23) Strong, James. *Strong's Exhaustive Concordance of the Bible.* © 1890 James Strong, Madison, NJ p. 118 (Hebrew)
24) *King James Bible,* Ephesians 6:17
25) Strong, James. *Strong's Exhaustive Concordance of the Bible.* © 1890 James Strong, Madison, NJ p. 46 (Greek)
26) Strong, James. *Strong's Exhaustive Concordance of the Bible.* © 1890 James Strong, Madison, NJ p. 58 (Greek)
27) Strong, James. *Strong's Exhaustive Concordance of the Bible.* © 1890 James Strong, Madison, NJ p. 63 (Greek)
28) *King James Bible,* Ephesians 6:17 John 1:1
29) Strong, James. *Strong's Exhaustive Concordance of the Bible.* © 1890 James Strong, Madison, NJ p. 45 (Greek)
30) *King James Bible,* Ephesians 6:17 Matthew 4:11
31) Strong, James. *Strong's Exhaustive Concordance of the Bible.* © 1890 James Strong, Madison, NJ p. 10 (Greek)
32) *New American Standard Bible*: 1995 update. 1995 (Job 1:8) The Lockman Foundation: Lahabra, CA
33) *Interlinear Bible Hebrew Greek English, 1 Volume Edition.* © 1976, 1977, 1978, 1979, 1980, 1981, 1984. Second Edition, © 1986 Jay P. Green, Sr., Hendrickson Publishers (Job 1:8) p. 443
34) *New American Standard Bible*: 1995 update. 1995 (Job 2:3) The Lockman Foundation: Lahabra, CA
35) *New American Standard Bible*: 1995 update. 1995 (Job 1:9-12) The Lockman Foundation: Lahabra, CA

Bibliographies

36) *MeekRaker Beginnings...*, © 2011 Quadrakoff Publications Group, LLC, Wilmington DE, p. 155-156
37) *Interlinear Bible Hebrew Greek English, 1 Volume Edition.* © 1976, 1977, 1978, 1979, 1980, 1981, 1984. Second Edition, © 1986 Jay P. Green, Sr., Hendrickson Publishers (Job 1:12) p. 443
38) Strong, James. *Strong's Exhaustive Concordance of the Bible.* © 1890 James Strong, Madison, NJ p. 47 (Hebrew)
39) *King James Bible*, Gen. 6:3
40) *King James Bible*, Gen. 6:1
41) *King James Bible*, Gen. 6:2
42) *New American Standard Bible*: 1995 update. 1995 (Gen. 6:4) The Lockman Foundation: Lahabra, CA
43) Strong, James. *Strong's Exhaustive Concordance of the Bible.* © 1890 James Strong, Madison, NJ p. 79 (Hebrew)
44) *MeekRaker Beginnings...*, © 2011 Quadrakoff Publications Group, LLC, Wilmington DE, p. 199-200
45) *King James Bible*, Gen. 1:2
46) *Chambers Dictionary of Etymology.* Copyright © 1988 The H. W. Wilson Company, New York, NY p. 512

Embedded from MeekRaker Beginnings...

MR1) *New American Standard Bible*: 1995 update. 1995 (Job 1:8) The Lockman Foundation: Lahabra, CA
MR2) *Interlinear Bible Hebrew Greek English, 1 Volume Edition.* © 1976, 1977, 1978, 1979, 1980, 1981, 1984. Second Edition, © 1986 Jay P. Green, Sr., Hendrickson Publishers (Job 1:8) p. 443
MR3) *New American Standard Bible*: 1995 update. 1995 (Job 2:3) The Lockman Foundation: Lahabra, CA
MR4) *New American Standard Bible*: 1995 update. 1995 (Job 1:9-12) The Lockman Foundation: Lahabra, CA

Bibliographies

Calvary's Hidden Truths

1. Strong, James. *Strong's Exhaustive Concordance of the Bible*. © 1890 James Strong, Madison, NJ p.98 (Hebrew)
2. *King James Bible* Genesis 1:27
3. Strong, James. *Strong's Exhaustive Concordance of the Bible*. © 1890 James Strong, Madison, NJ p.10 (Greek)
4. *New American Standard Bible*: 1995 update. 1995 (Luke 22:39-46) The Lockman Foundation: Lahabra, CA
5. *New American Standard Bible*: 1995 update. 1995 (John 13:25-27) The Lockman Foundation: Lahabra, CA
6. *New American Standard Bible*: 1995 update. 1995 (John 18:4-6) The Lockman Foundation: Lahabra, CA
7. *New American Standard Bible*: 1995 update. 1995 (Lev. 16:20-27) The Lockman Foundation: Lahabra, CA
8. *New American Standard Bible*: 1995 update. 1995 (Is. 53:5) The Lockman Foundation: Lahabra, CA
9. *Interlinear Bible Hebrew Greek English, 1 Volume edition.* © 1976, 1977, 1978, 1979, 1980, 1981, 1984. Second Edition, © 1986 Jay P. Green, Sr., Hendrickson Publishers (Is. 53:5) p.572
10. Strong, James. *Strong's Exhaustive Concordance of the Bible*. © 1890 James Strong, Madison, NJ p.36 (Hebrew)
11. Strong, James. *Strong's Exhaustive Concordance of the Bible*. © 1890 James Strong, Madison,   NJ p.36 (Hebrew)
12. Strong, James. *Strong's   Exhaustive Concordance of the*

Bible. © 1890 James Strong, Madison, NJ p.110 (Hebrew)
13. *New American Standard Bible*: 1995 update. 1995 (Prov. 20:30) The Lockman Foundation: Lahabra, CA
14. *Interlinear Bible Hebrew Greek English, 1 Volume edition.* © 1976, 1977, 1978, 1979, 1980, 1981, 1984. Second Edition, © 1986 Jay P. Green, Sr., Hendrickson Publishers (Prov. 20:30) p.522
15. *Interlinear Bible Hebrew Greek English, 1 Volume edition.* © 1976, 1977, 1978, 1979, 1980, 1981, 1984. Second Edition, © 1986 Jay P. Green, Sr., Hendrickson Publishers p. 522
16. Strong, James. *Strong's Exhaustive Concordance of the Bible.* © 1890 James Strong, Madison, NJ p.125 (Hebrew)
17. *New American Standard Bible*: 1995 update. 1995 (Mal. 3:2) The Lockman Foundation: Lahabra, CA
18. Strong, James. *Strong's Exhaustive Concordance of the Bible.* © 1890 James Strong, Madison, NJ p.54 (Hebrew)
19. *New American Standard Bible*: 1995 update. 1995 (Matt 27:45) The Lockman Foundation: Lahabra, CA
20. *Wikipedia.com*
21. *Mreclipse.com*
22. Strong, James. *Strong's Exhaustive Concordance of the Bible.* © 1890 James Strong, Madison, NJ p. 65 (Greek)
23. *Holy Bible, The New Open Bible™ Study Edition NASB.* copyright © 1990 Thomas Nelson, Inc. Nashville, TN p.1545
24. *New American Standard Bible*: 1995 update. 1995 (Mark 15:25) The Lockman Foundation: Lahabra, CA
25. *New American Standard Bible*: 1995 update. 1995 (John 19:14-15) The Lockman Foundation: Lahabra, CA
26. *New American Standard Bible*: 1995 update. 1995 (John 19:26) The Lockman Foundation: Lahabra, CA
27. *New American Standard Bible*: 1995 update. 1995 (John 19:31-34) The Lockman Foundation: Lahabra, CA
28. *New American Standard Bible*: 1995 update. 1995 (Deut 21:22-23) The Lockman Foundation: Lahabra, CA
29. *New American Standard Bible*: 1995 update. 1995 (Matt. 12:40) The Lockman Foundation: Lahabra, CA

Bibliographies

30. *New American Standard Bible*: 1995 update. 1995 (John 20:1) The Lockman Foundation: Lahabra, CA
31. *New American Standard Bible*: 1995 update. 1995 (Mark 15:42-44) The Lockman Foundation: Lahabra, CA
32. *Comparative Study Bible, Revised Edition.* Copyright © 1999 The Zondervan Corporation, Grand Rapids, MI (KJV) (Mark 15:42-44)
33. *New American Standard Bible*: 1995 update. 1995 (Luke 23:42-43) The Lockman Foundation: Lahabra, CA
34. *New American Standard Bible*: 1995 update. 1995 (John 20:17) The Lockman Foundation: Lahabra, CA
35. *New American Standard Bible*: 1995 update. 1995 (Acts 1:3) The Lockman Foundation: Lahabra, CA
36. *New American Standard Bible*: 1995 update. 1995 (Matt. 27:50-54) The Lockman Foundation: Lahabra, CA
37. Strong, James. *Strong's Exhaustive Concordance of the Bible.* © 1890 James Strong, Madison, NJ p.40 (Greek)
38. *New American Standard Bible*: 1995 update. 1995 (Ex. 26:31-33) The Lockman Foundation: Lahabra, CA
39. *Interlinear Bible Hebrew Greek English, 1 Volume edition.* © 1976, 1977, 1978, 1979, 1980, 1981, 1984. Second Edition, © 1986 Jay P. Green, Sr., Hendrickson Publishers (Matt. 27:51) p.765
40. Strong, James. *Strong's Exhaustive Concordance of the Bible.* © 1890 James Strong, Madison, NJ p. 34 (Greek)
41. *Holy Bible, The New Open Bible™ Study Edition NASB.* copyright © 1990 Thomas Nelson, Inc., Nashville, TN p. 114
42. *New American Standard Bible*: 1995 update. 1995 (Luke 4:5-7) The Lockman Foundation: Lahabra, CA
43. Strong, James. *Strong's Exhaustive Concordance of the Bible.* © 1890 James Strong, Madison, NJ p. 64 (Greek)
44. Strong, James. *Strong's Exhaustive Concordance of the Bible.* © 1890 James Strong, Madison, NJ p. 20 (Greek)
45. Strong, James. *Strong's Exhaustive Concordance of the Bible.* © 1890 James Strong, Madison, NJ p. 64 (Greek)
46. *New American Standard Bible*: 1995 update. 1995 (Eph. 4:9-10) The Lockman Foundation: Lahabra, CA

47. Strong, James. *Strong's Exhaustive Concordance of the Bible.* © 1890 James Strong, Madison, NJ p. 70 (Greek)
48. Strong, James. *Strong's Exhaustive Concordance of the Bible.* © 1890 James Strong, Madison, NJ p. 48 (Greek)
49. Strong, James. *Strong's Exhaustive Concordance of the Bible.* © 1890 James Strong, Madison, NJ p. 70 (Greek)
50. Strong, James. *Strong's Exhaustive Concordance of the Bible.* © 1890 James Strong, Madison, NJ p. 7 (Greek)
51. Strong, James. *Strong's Exhaustive Concordance of the Bible.* © 1890 James Strong, Madison, NJ p. 42 (Greek)
52. Strong, James. *Strong's Exhaustive Concordance of the Bible.* © 1890 James Strong, Madison, NJ p. 25 (Greek)
53. *Illustrated Dictionary of the Bible.* Herbert Lockyer, SR., Editor, with F. F. Bruce and R. K. Harrison, Copyright © 1986 Thomas Nelson Publishers, Nashville TN, p. 267
54. *New American Standard Bible*: 1995 update. 1995 (Luke 23:48) The Lockman Foundation: Lahabra, CA
55. Strong, James. *Strong's Exhaustive Concordance of the Bible.* © 1890 James Strong, Madison, NJ p. 73 (Greek)
56. *Illustrated Dictionary of the Bible.* Herbert Lockyer, SR., Editor, with F. F. Bruce and R. K. Harrison, Copyright © 1986 by Thomas Nelson Publishers, Nashville TN, p. 191
57. *New American Standard Bible*: 1995 update. 1995 (Luke 18:13) The Lockman Foundation: Lahabra, CA
58. *King James Bible* Ephesians 2:8-9

Bibliographies

INEVITABLE BALANCE

1. *Chambers Dictionary of Etymology*. Copyright © 1988 The H. W. Wilson Company, New York, NY p. 72
2. *New American Standard Bible*: 1995 update. 1995 (Genesis 1:1) The Lockman Foundation: Lahabra, CA
3. *King James Bible* Matthew 19:26
4. *King James Bible* John 14:12
5. Strong, James. *Strong's Exhaustive Concordance of the Bible.* © 1890 James Strong, Madison, NJ p. 49 (Greek)
6. Quadrakoff, Emma, *The Emmanic Principles* © 2017 Quadrakoff Publications Group, LLC Wilmington Delaware
7. *King James Bible* Genesis 2:7
8. Quadrakoff, Emma, *The Emmanic Principles* © 2017 Quadrakoff Publications Group, LLC Wilmington Delaware
9. *New American Standard Bible*: 1995 update. 1995 (Malachi 3:10) The Lockman Foundation: Lahabra, CA
10. Strong, James. *Strong's Exhaustive Concordance of the Bible.* © 1890 James Strong, Madison, NJ p. 817 (Hebrew)
11. *Physicsclassroom.com*
12. *New American Standard Bible*: 1995 update. 1995 (Proverbs 16:2) The Lockman Foundation: Lahabra, CA
13. *Physicsclassroom.com*
14. *Physicsclassroom.com*

15. *New American Standard Bible*: 1995 update. 1995 (2 Corinthians 9:7) The Lockman Foundation: Lahabra, CA
16. *King James Bible* John 14:12
17. *King James Bible* Matthew 17:14-19
18. *King James Bible* Matthew 17:20
19. *King James Bible* Matthew 17:21
20. *King James Bible* Matthew 17:22
21. *New American Standard Bible*: 1995 update. 1995 (Matthew 17:20) The Lockman Foundation: Lahabra, CA
22. *New American Standard Bible*: 1995 update. 1995 (2 Matthew 17:21) The Lockman Foundation: Lahabra, CA
23. *New American Standard Bible*: 1995 update. 1995 (Matthew 17:22) The Lockman Foundation: Lahabra, CA
24. *New American Standard Bible*: 1995 update. 1995 The Lockman Foundation: Lahabra, CA introductory pages, not numbered
25. *The Holy Bible New International Version* © 1973, 1978, 1984 International Bible Society (Matthew 17: 20)
26. *The Holy Bible New International Version* © 1973, 1978, 1984 International Bible Society (Matthew 17: 21)
27. *The Holy Bible New International Version* © 1973, 1978, 1984 International Bible Society (Matthew 17: 22)
28. *King James Bible* Mark 9:18-22
29. *King James Bible* Mark 9:23-29
30. Strong, James. *Strong's Exhaustive Concordance of the Bible.* © 1890 James Strong, Madison, NJ p. 53 (Greek)

Glossary

G1. Strong, James. *Strong's Exhaustive Concordance of the Bible.* © 1890 James Strong, Madison, NJ p. 23 (Hebrew)
G2. Strong, James. *Strong's Exhaustive Concordance of the Bible.* © 1890 James Strong, Madison, NJ p. 19 (Hebrew)
G3. Strong, James. *Strong's Exhaustive Concordance of the Bible.* © 1890 James Strong, Madison, NJ p. 79 (Hebrew)
G4. Strong, James. *Strong's Exhaustive Concordance of the Bible.* © 1890 James Strong, Madison, NJ p. 51 (Hebrew)
G5. Strong, James. *Strong's Exhaustive Concordance of the Bible.* © 1890 James Strong, Madison, NJ p. 48 (Hebrew)
G6. Strong, James. *Strong's Exhaustive Concordance of the Bible.* © 1890 James Strong, Madison, NJ p. 79 (Hebrew)

Wisdom Essentials

Wisdom Essentials

ABOUT THE MEEKRAKER SERIES

What on earth is a MeekRaker? This word can be broken down into two parts "Meek" and "Raker." Capital letters were used in order to minimize any mispronunciations such as Mee-kraker; but the "etymology" is actually the fusion of these two words.

What is meek? And who in their right mind would ever want to be meek? Courage, strength, and bravery are characteristics that are generally considered desirable; but meek? No thanks. Unfortunately, the meaning of this word has been distorted over time to include things such as timidity, or shyness; weakness, or cowardice, but this is not; or rather should not be so.

Chambers states:

> "meek adj. Probably before 1200 meok gentle, humble, in Ancrene Riwle; later mec (probably about 1200, in the *The Ormlum*); borrowed from a Scandanavian source (Compare Old Icelandic mjukr soft pliant gentle...."[AT-1]

These origins seem to be adjectival in nature, and describe a condition of humility or softness. Thus a meek person, by these definitions would indicate a humble or soft person. The opposite of this would then be a person who is prideful or hard.

Humble vs. prideful is an easy one. Who would want to be prideful? The Bible is replete with warnings about pride; and it was pride that started all of the messes to begin with. Pride may make one "feel good" for a short period of time, but as previously referenced; the Bible is quite clear that on that path there lies destruction.

But what does the Bible actually have to say about being a meek person?

- It tells us that the meek shall (*not will or might*) inherit the earth.[AT-2]
- It further tells us that the meek will be guided in judgment will be taught His way.[AT-3]
- The meek will be lifted up by the Lord, and He will cast the wicked down to the ground.[AT-4]
- He will save all the meek of the earth.[AT-5]

And what about the Bible's statements regarding being "hard?"

- "For their heart was hardened."[AT-6] "Have ye your heart yet hardened?"[AT-7]
- "... their eyes and hardened their heart."[AT-8]
- "But they and our fathers dealt proudly, and hardened their necks, and hearkened not to thy commandments, and refused to obey, neither were mindful of thy wonders that thou didst among them; but hardened their necks, and in their rebellion..."[AT-9]
- "Happy is the man that feareth always: But he that hardeneth his heart shall fall into mischief."[AT-10]
- "He that being often reproved hardeneth his neck, shall suddenly be destroyed, and that without remedy."[AT-11]

The actual word in all of these citations which is translated as hard is:

"4456 poroo (a kind of stone); to *petrify*, i.e. (fig.) to *indurate* (*render stupid* or *callous*): - blind, harden."[AT-12]

With respect to hard, there is a clear Scriptural relationship between the same and disobedience; not being "mindful" of God performing wonders in one's life, rebellious, falling into "mischief," and being "destroyed," "without remedy."

In addition, by the very definition of the original word, one who is "hard" is also stupid callous and blind. (If a physical heart were actually to turn into stone, you are just dead; so surely that definition does not apply in this context or usage.)

Thus, meek or soft; that being the opposite of hard; would tend to be obedient, be mindful of God performing wonders, not rebellious, not falling into mischief, and not destroyed. Furthermore, one would not be "stupid," "callous" or "blind."

The use of the term meek as "soft," also implies *teachable*.

Hardhead: will not change mind. Hardhearted: will not change heart. Hard necked: junction between head and heart is hard, and will not permit mental change to be transmitted to change the heart.

If it is firmly established that the term "revelation" has the prerequisite of being *the* truth; when confronted with potential revelation; it has been the authors' experiences that hard persons; specifically those of the head, neck, and heart variety; will generally behave according to the "Three A's:"

> A_1 is *anger*. This is the first response. This anger is not so much because there is a remote chance that they may be wrong, but rather when it is somewhat clear that they *are* wrong. This would be best illustrated as a line on a graph rising from left to right; with the level of anger represented by the vertical axis, and time represented by the horizontal axis.
>
> A_2 is *argument*. This generally begins with emotionally (anger) driven arguments. As the arguments begin to fail, the level and usually the slope of A_1 will

increase. When all possible arguments, logical, relevant or otherwise have been proffered, the original arguments will then return. This would be best illustrated as a circle under the rising anger line referenced above. Often, what is just under the skin, (which is generally the reason for the pride and subsequent anger) will pop its "head" out; revealing things previously unknown about this individual.

A_3 is *absconding*. When all of the arguments and the repetition thereof have unquestionably failed, the hard person will generally abscond; or run away. This may be represented by actual physical separation, changing the subject or in some other manner. This could be perceived as the disappearance of the anger line, but is only subjective; as the true level of anger then becomes somewhat hidden.

Contrarily, the *meek* will weigh the value of any purported revelation; and then decide precisely what it is that merits their belief. Sincere questioning and even some arguments will be presented; but here not with the primary purpose of proving that they, the inquirer, is correct; but rather to understand precisely what it is that this revelation represents; knowing that if it in fact does represent revelation, then this will be to their benefit. A logical decision will then be made with respect to what constitutes the truth.

The primary basis for the actions of a "hard-head," is *emotional*. The primary basis for the actions of the meek; although perhaps including some emotional factors; (i.e. passion); is largely *intellectual*.

In a sense, the purpose of a rake is to separate the soft from the hard. The Bible refers to separating the wheat from the chaff, the silver from the dross; hence the origin of "*MeekRaker*". Meek or hard is not so much determined by what one believes; but rather by the *process* involved in making these determinations.

About the MeekRaker Series Bibliography

AT1 *Chambers Dictionary of Etymology.* Copyright © 1988 The H. W. Wilson Company, New York, NY p.648

AT2 *www.kingjamesbibleonline.org* (KJV) (Matt.5:5) retrieved June 2011

AT3 *www.kingjamesbibleonline.org* (KJV) (Ps. 25:9) retrieved June 2011

AT4 *www.kingjamesbibleonline.org* (KJV) (Ps. 147:6) retrieved June 2011

AT5 *www.kingjamesbibleonline.org* (KJV) (Ps. 76:9) retrieved June 2011

AT6 *www.kingjamesbibleonline.org* (KJV) (Mark 6:52) retrieved June 2011

AT7 *www.kingjamesbibleonline.org* (KJV) (Mark 8:17) retrieved June 2011

AT8 *www.kingjamesbibleonline.org* (KJV) (John 12:40) retrieved June 2011

AT9 *www.kingjamesbibleonline.org* (KJV) (Neh. 9:16) retrieved June 2011

AT10 *www.kingjamesbibleonline.org* (KJV) (Prov. 28:14) retrieved June 2011

AT11 *www.kingjamesbibleonline.org* (KJV) (Prov. 29:1) retrieved June 2011

AT12 Strong, James. *Strong's Exhaustive Concordance of the Bible.* © 1890 James Strong, Madison, NJ p. 63 (Greek)

You May Also Like These Other Fine QPG Publications:

MeekRaker Beginnings...

From inside the dust jacket of *"MeekRaker Beginnings..."*

"The primary purpose of this tome, is the reconciliation of the word of God with science; and to do so in such a manner as to be rendered inarguable by any rational mind. As stated in the Preface: "One must choose between being a "man of science" or a believer," because they are generally considered to be mutually exclusive. If one agrees that words mean things, then an unbiased fair read of God's Word presents no such paradox. But one must read what God actually said, not merely what one thinks He said, what one was told He said, what one wished He said, or would rather He had said."

STATISTS SAVING ONE

The Malignant Sophistry of Rights Removal by the Far Left

"...under the umbrella of "liberals" or "liberalism;" (as used today); there are actually two separate and distinct groups:
"True *liberals* believe very much in what they promulgate. They are truly concerned with the welfare of citizens, and they believe in policies that will benefit the same—at least in their view. There are neither nefarious purposes, nor any intellectual dishonesty.

Their objective is to improve the quality of life (and longevity), for as many people as possible.

"...Conservatives and liberals can often agree on the *ends*; but vastly disagree on the *means*. Giving a hungry person a fish is kind; but to conservatives, teaching him how to fish seems to be a better long term solution. It is not that conservatives object to the temporary giving of the fish; but rather they object to *not* teaching him how to fish.

"True liberals believe in the dignity of man; and promulgate policies in furtherance of this belief.

"Statists; the other group usually and often erroneously grouped under the "liberal" umbrella; are another matter. It is because of agreements with liberal *policy* that they are usually grouped under this liberal umbrella; but their *motivations*, *purposes* and *beliefs* are entirely different—arguably antithetical—to true liberalism."

Why should *liberals* read "*Statists Saving One*?"

>To understand that many who may appear to agree with your *means*, have entirely different *ends* in sight; and that these ends are antithetical to liberalism. True liberalism and statism are entirely incompatible. And all along you thought they were your friends.

Why should *conservatives* read "*Statists Saving One*?"

>To understand the difference between liberals and statists; and end the confusion. Many liberals agree with many conservative *ends*, merely proffering a different *means* to achieve them. But statists have entirely different ends in sight—no matter whom they may appear to agree with at any given time.

Why should *statists* read "*Statists Saving One*?"

>To understand the true motivations behind statism; and decide if continued actions are wise. The masquerade

is now over. Either change now; or "pack up and go home" while you can, as it will never become any easier in any current statist's lifetime.

OSTIUM AB INFERNO
[*The Opening From Hell*]

"The Original Monograph - According to the Father, The Christ Son and The Holy Ghost"

- What is hell? Why is there a hell?
  What openings from "hell" exist?
  What is the truth about "Abraham's Bosom?"
  And how does this or do these affect man?

- What are angels? Are angels named such because of structure or function?
  Precisely why were some angels sent to hell?
  Is it true that one third were banished to hell?
  And when did this all happen?

Much of that which is fanciful has been written about these questions. But the answers should not be sought from that which is the product of men's imaginations—albeit these may provide interesting reading. Rather; the answers should be sought from, and always remain: "according to The Father, The Christ Son, and The Holy Ghost." (Written in English.)

REINCARNATION — A REASONABLE INQUIRY

"Often times it is emotion(s) and not facts that determine what it is that is believed to be 'in fact so.'" —p.6

"When truth and perceived practicality conflict; unfortunately it is truth that often becomes the sacrificial lamb." —p.91

"He that answereth a matter before he heareth it, it is folly and shame unto him."
—Proverbs 18:13 (KJV)

   Some say reincarnation is a fact, and cite the Bible as the unimpeachable source regarding this matter.
   Others say reincarnation is fiction, and cite the Bible as the unimpeachable source regarding this very same matter.
   One of these groups is about to be shocked.

QPG Publications are available
wherever you buy fine books.

For a full list of QPG publications,
visit us at MeekRaker.com

www.ingramcontent.com/pod-product-compliance
Lightning Source LLC
Chambersburg PA
CBHW021141080526
44588CB00008B/160